Interpreting the Countertransference

Interpreting the Countertransference

Lawrence E. Hedges, Ph.D.

JASON ARONSON INC.
Northvale, New Jersey
London

Production Editor: Judith D. Cohen
Editorial Director: Muriel Jorgensen

This book was set in 12/14 Goudy
by Books of Deatsville, Alabama, and
printed and bound by Haddon Craftsmen of Scranton, Pennsylvania.

Library of Congress Cataloging-in-Publication Data

Hedges, Lawrence E.
    Interpreting the countertransference / Lawrence E. Hedges.
        p.   cm.
    Includes bibliographical references and index.
    ISBN 0-87668-532-7
    1. Countertransference (Psychology)   2. Countertransference (Psychology)—Case studies.   I. Title.
    RC489.C68H43   1991
    616.89′14—dc20   91-15933

Manufactured in the United States of America. Jason Aronson Inc. offers books and cassettes. For information and catalog write to Jason Aronson Inc., 230 Livingston Street, Northvale, New Jersey 07647.

This book is dedicated to
Ray Michael Calabrese,
whose loyalty, trust,
hard work, and unconditional love
have made this work possible

Contents

Acknowledgments

The ideas put forth in this book are the result of many people collaborating in classes, case conferences, and supervision over a number of years. I owe a debt of gratitude to the following colleagues for their courage in candidly making available their most difficult work for scrutiny in order to learn about the subtleties of countertransference: Fred Bailey, Kathryn Bailey, Marilyn Boettiger, Tony Brailow, Doug Citro, Paula Clark, Suzanne Clawson, Susan Cohn, Bill Cone, Charles Coverdale, Carolyn Crawford, Jolyn Davidson, Kim Dhanes, Cecile Dillon, Arlene Dorius, Leslie Drozd, Michael Elterman, Marguerite Fairweather, Paul Fairweather, Tim Gergen, Jacquelyn Gillespie, Flora Golden, Lyda Hill, Virginia Wink Hilton, Ron Hirz, Joyce Hulgus, Virginia Hunter, Cathearine Jenkins-Hall, Sandra Jorgensen, Marc Kern, Michael Kogutek, Wallace Kohl, Alitta Kullman, Marlene Laping, Jim Long, David Lynn-Hill, Diana Marder, Sally Miller, Pamela Drennan Moline, Priscilla Nauman, Bonnie Nelson, Ron Offenstein, Byron Perkins, Dolly

Platt, Ira Poll, Karen K. Redding, Linda Reed, Steve Rockman, Howard Rogers, Michael Russell, Sandra Russell, Amy Ruth, Laurie Ryavec, Sabrina Salayz, Karyn Sandburg, Amy Scher, Diane Schreader, Andrew Schwartz, Rene Sorrentino, Sean Stewart, Mariana Thomas, Nancy Toder, Gayle Trenberth, John Van Dixhorn, Judy Van Dixhorn, Robert Van Sweden, Steve Venanzi, Alice Vieira, Patti Wallace, David Wayne, William White, Ruth Wimsatt, Charlotte Winters, and Marina Young.

This manuscript has been painstakingly created and assembled by my daughter, Breta Hedges. Gary Conway has been an inspirational force throughout. Jason and Joyce Aronson have been most encouraging and helpful in moving this work toward publication. Joan L. Carlson has provided much of the transcription, Jacquelyn Gillespie and Karen Redding the careful constructive scrutiny, and Judith D. Cohen the editorial expertise.

Special Contributors

The following colleagues are special contributors who have made major theoretical and clinical contributions to this book, but for reasons of discretion, their names are not associated directly with their contributions: Tony Brailow, Karen K. Redding, and Howard Rogers.

PART I

THE COUNTER-TRANSFERENCE OPENING

A Countertransference Failure: The Case of Dora

THE ARRIVAL OF THE MUSE

Like so many of my colleagues in recent years, I have turned my attention to the problem of countertransference—to the many experiences that I, as analyst, undergo while listening to and interacting with the people who come to my consulting room. Aware that many new ideas about therapists' feelings were being discussed in the professional community, I committed myself some time ago to teaching several classes on countertransference in order to force myself to do the work required to catch up with what was happening.

In my own training programs, like in most others, the expectable feelings of the therapist in response to the interpersonal encounter of psychotherapy were generally neglected. This meant that we all squirmed in silence, trying our best not to notice the deep emotional reactions our work was stirring up and making sure not to mention them to our supervisors. Those troubling feelings were to be all worked out later in our training analysis. But for now, we must try to be objective and not to become overinvolved with our clients.

The more I read about countertransference and the more conferences I attended, the more interested and the more confused I became. Prominent clinicians held very divergent views on the subject. The traditionalists insisted that counter-transference feelings were always an indicator of a personal overinvolvement on the part of the therapist. Others held that feelings should be taken into account, but only very judiciously, and perhaps never shared with clients.

The most daring and dynamic clinicians were taking positions that seemed much more truthful and down to earth. They held that it was crucial for us to find ways of utilizing our subjective emotional lives actively and directly in the therapeutic relationship. Certainly honesty and directness are qualities we strive for in all of our relationships. But an analytic relationship by its very nature is very complex. There are so many things to be attuned to at every moment. By what criteria are we to judge the relative importance of feelings we may be experiencing at the time? How do we weigh the importance of countertransference expressiveness against other aspects of the relationship that are also of crucial importance? Are there certain kinds of analytic encounters or certain moments in which open acknowledgment of our emotional reactions is paramount? Likewise, are there other times and circumstances when, regardless of how impelling our affective responses may seem, they are of relatively lesser importance in the immediate situation? And most importantly, if there is a special skill involved in tuning into our feelings and making optimal expressive use of them for analytic effectiveness, how do we go about cultivating such a skill?

These were the kinds of questions I set about to investigate for myself, both in theory and in everyday practice. Finally, I committed myself to pull together an all-day seminar on "Countertransference and Its Relation to Empathy and Interpretation."

With a deadline approaching, I lay outside in my hammock one sunny afternoon, clipboard in hand, staring blankly off into the national forest, waiting for a muse. I began thinking of Dora, of how painful it was when she had stopped coming to see me several years before. How often I had ruminated over what went wrong, with no sense of resolution. At times I blamed myself. At times I blamed her. But the bottom line was that I didn't know what went wrong in our relationship and I felt badly about it. I began to jot ideas down on my clipboard. Page after page was ripped off, wadded up, and tossed at my favorite cactus. But suddenly my pen began to flow. In what seemed no time at all, with clarity and conviction, I wrote the account that follows. The moment was an inspired one. At last I had found an understanding that provided a sense of relief. This was the moment when countertransference issues began coming alive for me.

The woman I will speak of, Dora, saw me two to three times a week for the better part of two years in the late 1970s. After nearly twenty years of positive professional experiences, my work with her came to be and remains what I consider the only clear-cut treatment failure I have ever suffered. Since I have not asked permission of this woman to discuss her work, I will limit my remarks to countertransference issues that now seem to me to be the cause of the disruption that ended our work together, leaving me with a very painful and defeated sense of failure.

I always saw her as a very gifted woman whose intelligence, creativity, and physical beauty had somehow not been put to good use for her own enjoyment, or harnessed for purposes of self-enrichment and personal growth. To her, everyday existence in most of its particulars had come to be remarkably drab, commonplace, and deeply discouraging.

In our relationship she vacillated between elation, that I could see and appreciate the wonderful person that she hoped she was, to an almost delusional suspicion that I viewed her as sick, depressed, ugly, and basically the disgusting person she believed she really was. As bright and articulate people, we both were able to discuss these concerns in great detail and to relate them to current life circumstances, as well as to many growing-up experiences. I used the developmental metaphor *borderline* to describe for myself her chronic and, to her, depressing ways of relating to people around her.

The particular thread of our relationship that I wish to follow here was what we both came to see as her sexualized attraction toward me. Held in silence for more than a year, she confessed with trepidation one day that she had always had a weakness for blue eyes—especially in the exact combination with brown hair that I have. Several of her significant men friends have been of similar coloring and build. I handled her anxious confession with a series of inquiries meant to elucidate associations about why it had taken so long to share this with me. What problems was this attraction posing for her? If I was her type, as she said, why couldn't we simply enjoy that together? I wasn't sure what made her so uneasy over this issue. Was there anything I was doing that made things difficult? Was there anything I could do to make things easier? Our discussions brought her relief and in subsequent months, a series of expressions emerged. She was concerned that she wasn't supposed to be attracted to me, but she couldn't help it. Yes, at times her attraction had made it difficult to speak with me about certain issues, but if there ever were anything really important, she believed that she had been able to overcome it. She believed me to be a very accepting person. At the end of good hours she would often sit up a few moments before leaving and let me know what a pleasure it was simply to look at me and to feel that I was okay with her looking. She would sink into the couch in deep and pleasurable relaxation, feeling deeply reassured.

One day, while telling me about a friend of hers who had just been diagnosed with Kaposi's sarcoma, and explaining to me AIDS, the then new disease among gays, she confessed her concern that I might be gay. She was afraid I would be offended by her saying so and had carefully avoided any mention of the topic. Over the years she had been close to a number of gay men and had wondered about the implications of that closeness for herself and her sexuality. She had recognized several attractions to women friends in the past but had never wished to develop the sexual side of these relationships. Perhaps she was projecting her latent homosexuality onto me, she thought. I asked if the idea that I might be gay was reassuring to her. She immediately saw the potentially protective side of her fantasies, saying, "Then I wouldn't have to be concerned about my attraction toward you." But she hoped that I wasn't gay because her recently diagnosed friend had been miserable for years, searching bath houses and bars every night with one disastrous relationship after another. She hoped that whatever my personal circum-stances were, that I wasn't miserable and that I was safe from agony, disease, and death. She spoke of potential abandonment and her fear of being left alone. She concluded by reassuring either herself or me or both of us that there was really no need to worry since she was sure I wasn't gay. I must be a "good fuck," she said, the kind she had always imagined having for herself.

Now many will feel critical of my technique upon learning how, throughout this time, I handled numerous and frequent demands for reassurance. Did I think highly of her? I did. Could I see her artistic creativity in the productions she brought me? I could. Did I find her an attractive person? I did. And so on. I had attempted early on the usual set of inquiries about what brought these concerns up at this particular time. Was her question possibly related to other things she had been talking or thinking about? My inquiries not only failed to elicit associa-tions, but regularly increased her agitation. When I followed it up, the result was either deep feelings of worthlessness because I probably really didn't like her, or feelings of rage toward me for playing a cat-and-mouse game with her. After all, she believed she had a reasonable right to know what I thought of her. Even if she granted me the privacy of specifics, couldn't I at least acknowledge feelings and thoughts we both knew about anyway? In response to my suggestions that answers would reassure her and that then the anxiety, depression, and anger that she felt might be overlooked by both of us, she responded, "Bullshit— bullshit, bullshit, and more bullshit! There is no reason why we can't be honest here; after all, you are supposed to be completely analyzed, aren't you?" In some profound sense, she seemed to be right, and when I felt freer in my expressions toward her, our work went much more smoothly. But for some reason I was not happy having to serve a reassuring function for her so frequently. On several occasions she stared at my arms and chest with delighted squeals. She declared she had always been a "chest woman" and that my general build, and specifically my chest and the little black hairs that occasionally "peeped out" of my open shirt just drove her crazy.

In reviewing my feelings on the matter, it is clear that in many ways I enjoyed her sexual attraction to me. However, I came to be aware of feelings of self-consciousness, and in the morning I occasionally found myself sorting through which shirt or pants to wear on a day I would be seeing her. But all my attempts to make any analytic headway on these developments in our relationship resulted in a bland response. However, she gradually replaced most of her wardrobe and began paying attention to small details in makeup and hair. Her current sexual relationship improved considerably. She discussed this jubilantly as her progress at getting out of her "drab, weepy, homely self." She was enjoying making the best of what she had. She attributed the changes to new freedoms she was developing as a result of her therapy—something I believe in many ways was true. She was further able to say that seeing herself through my eyes made her alive to the fine person she was and to the ways she might come to enjoy herself, others, and the world in general. There was similar evidence of increased self-esteem in a variety of social and occupational shifts. Her improvement in fact was dramatic—in retrospect, perhaps, a sign to me of the developing problem. Looking back, I see that what was perhaps never made fully explicit was how much the improvements in self-esteem and related activities remained dependent upon my real or fantasized estimate of her. At this point in writing up my work, I found myself developing a severe headache—a frequent complaint of hers.

In general, however, we both felt good about the analysis and others close to her experienced a considerable easing of tension. A temper tantrum or terrible-twos quality that she called "bitchiness" would occasionally appear that we could relate to her relationship to her mother. Later, in grasping at straws to understand what was going wrong, I was able to formulate for consultation with colleagues a detailed set of interactions or scenarios I had been considering. I still believe these dyadic interaction patterns to be accurate descriptions derived from her early relationship with her mother. But no amount of work on the symbiotic and separating replications was able to avert the impasse that developed. We both saw and could talk about her behaving toward me as she had toward her mother. We could even discuss her behaving as her mother had behaved toward her in her final actions toward me.

The usual "regressions" and "resurgences of symptoms" occurred prior to weekend and holiday breaks. I might add that Kohut-styled interpretations of empathic failure were seldom useful. On the other hand, she took readily to developmental metaphors. Once she saw a copy of Kaplan's *Oneness and Separateness* (1978) lying on my desk and she asked to borrow it. She derived much mileage from the book in terms of understanding her own ambitendent relationship with her mother and the pronounced but erratic mood swings to which she was prone. Another time, just before a holiday, she brought a lovely black pebble that she had found on the beach and had taken to have polished for me. It sits to this day in an antique inkwell—my grandfather's—in my office. I occasionally pick it up and think fondly of her.

The seeds of the trauma that eventually resulted in her breaking off our relationship were sown one day about midway through the two-year period of analysis. She had begun enjoying her newfound capacity to tell me about her attraction toward me and to just sit quietly for periods, taking pleasure in listening to me or looking at me. I felt squirmy when she did this, but at some level I also enjoyed being looked at and being enjoyed in the deep and satisfying way she took me in. I was pleased that she derived a great deal of pleasure from our interaction, because there were so few pleasures for her at that time. One day, however, in what way I don't know, she caught my discomfort. I was trying hard to be there for her in the way I was sure she wanted me to be, and was cautious about letting my uneasiness show. But my guard must have been down and she caught me flinching or averting my gaze in some way or other. Nothing was said at the time. I had been painfully aware for a while of my growing dislike of her parading her erotic attachment in front of me and my wish to escape her gaze, her intensity, and the sense of intrusion that stimulation by this very attractive woman was provoking in me.

The following session she came in bedraggled, wearing old clothes and no makeup. She lay down on the couch wordlessly. I waited a long while until quiet sobs began. She had frequently cried bitterly, but this seemed somehow different—much deeper and worse. Not until she began talking was I aware that she had detected my discomfort in the previous hour. She had concluded that our whole relationship had been a giant fraud, just as she had vaguely suspected all along. I didn't really like her—it was a "therapeutic trick—make the patient feel better so they keep coming." She had been wasting her time. She had hoped after all the years of never being recognized or responded to, that at last she had found someone who could like her and be her friend. There was more withdrawal and hurt, and then anger. I sensed no qualities of manipulation or even of hope—rather there was a total collapse of all that had been experienced as good, and a very deep sense of despair and rage.

I have often wished I could recall my exact responses during that hour, but it passed too quickly. I was struggling so hard to stay afloat that I am not even sure I could have recalled the details sufficiently to make notes. I was basically able to empathize with how perfectly terrible she must feel and was even able to add specifics from my understanding of her that portrayed her devastation even more vividly and related it to past devastations and losses. But while she acknowledged and appreciated my empathy, it could not, as she said, "put Humpty Dumpty together again." It seemed clear to me that I must try somehow to acknowledge the truth of what she saw. So often in the past her correct perceptions had been invalidated by adult opinion. Somewhat reluctantly, I confirmed that in fact I had become uncomfortable with her admiration of me and my body and I was not completely sure exactly what I was feeling yet. However, I told her that as nearly as I could tell, she was wrong in her interpretation that I hated her, that I was perpetrating an analytic hoax, and that it was all an act, presumably for her own good.

Hoping to save the scene and to ease her out of her dreadfully painful state, I told her that she should not hold herself responsible for my reactions to her admiration. I disclosed that my emerging feelings of discomfort more likely related to interfering features from my own past than to her way of relating to me in the sessions. In fact, while I did not mention it to her, I had been occupied for some time in attempting, as a result of my uneasiness, to dredge out some experiences from my own preadolescent stage, when for a protracted period of time I had felt subjected to similar erotic-intrusive staring and the parading of an erotic attachment that had produced similar feelings of overstimulation and uneasiness in me. When she registered astonishment and disbelief at my taking responsibility for "flinching," as we came later to refer to the incident, I partially revealed some of my previous experience and apologized for its intrusion into her processes in this very painful manner. The disclosure and the apology were authentic and did serve to pull her out of her disastrous state.

Summarizing the aftereffects of the incident, I will say that our work resumed its regular pace after a few halting sessions. She did, however, carefully refrain from "overwhelming" me again by staring or making a point of enjoying me. My inquiries into why she felt she had to alter her spontaneity to protect me were met with responses somewhere between, on the one hand, an understanding and respect for an area that was sensitive to me personally, and on the other hand, a mild sarcasm that meant she must not express to me her true self and risk offending or upsetting me or my abandoning her. When I challenged this, she acknowledged that she didn't really think I was so fragile, but she liked me a lot and part of what she had been working on everywhere as a result of her therapy was becoming a better person to people—a trend she was having some good integrating experiences with. I remained unconvinced of this explanation of the alteration in our relationship and from time to time told her so. The "flinching" incident came up in a variety of ways over the next year and was put to good use on a number of occasions by both of us.

The final blow took me entirely by surprise. For a full year she had been preparing for an advanced examination relating to her career—taking classes, studying, and working through trial exams and review seminars. Her preparations were loaded with anxiety, but also full of forward-looking hope and creative prospects. She was doing much better than people who had far more experience than she. The exam came and she felt pleased that she had maintained well, budgeted her time efficiently, and completed the test with a reasonable sense of security.

The day of triumph came several weeks later with an on-top-of-the-world sense of glee, a tenth of champagne, and two champagne glasses for us to celebrate her having attained the highest possible percentile score. It was eleven o'clock in the morning so I managed to beg off the champagne with a few celebration sips. She was in her glory. We celebrated all of her successes over the last two years and the immense prospects for her future career in the new placement that the exam had made possible. As in most such champagne reviews, we were discussing the before-and-after picture, jointly taking credit for the big step forward into a new, never-before-dreamed-of sense of success and independence.

During our review she asked me to tell her how I viewed our work together. Trying as much as possible, as is my custom, to stay with the metaphors provided by the person in analysis, I said, "When we began, you were so invested in thinking of yourself as 'weepy, drab, and homely.' Now we've proved that all wrong." At first she seemed pleased with my assessment. But after a few moments, her whole affect suddenly changed to enraged grief and our celebration came to a screeching halt. The truth had finally come out. All along I had seen her as a weepy, drab, homely person and now she had heard it with her own ears. She knew it was true. I had even tried to lie my way out of it, saying my flinch was personal and unrelated to my feelings about her. She would never be able to trust me again. She screamed at me with huge tears running down her face and at last stormed out. To say I was speechless wouldn't be entirely correct, but nothing I could say seemed to help. She was adamant that she had not misunderstood me; I simply had finally confirmed what she had known all along. She called and left a message canceling all future appointments. However, after a few weeks, she consented to come in and see me several times again. It was very clear that our therapy was over and no effort on my part to turn the tide was of any use. She did, at my request, consult with a woman therapist I suggested. During the three sessions, the consultant reported back to me, there was a constant desperate plea by the woman to be able to see me and restore our relationship, but a firm refusal to do so because her trust had been so entirely shaken. No other possibilities could be entertained. I telephoned her several times. She always seemed pleased to hear from me, but saw no point in our trying to get together again. I was a good person who had helped her greatly and she very much appreciated that, but there was no way to continue. Her new career work was exciting and going extremely well. She felt better than ever about most aspects of her life and relationships, except the loss of her analysis. Her comments seemed free of accusation, manipulation, or guilt induction. By the second call, she had read *August* (Rossner 1983) and had started seeing a woman who could relate to her warmly, the way she felt the analyst in *August* had. I found myself soundly defeated. I had taken a number of opportunities to consult on my work with colleagues, but was ultimately dismayed and, I must say, mildly disenchanted and disgusted when she told me the kind of warm, accepting therapist she had found. I was not personally acquainted with her new therapist, but I had given her several names of people I knew to be good. Somehow I doubted now that she would get what she needed.

There are many points at which discussion of such an unhappy story might begin. Those versed in separation-individuation themes in therapy with borderlines will be quick to point out the loss of symbiotic at-oneness that the jubilant ascension into independent selfhood may have precipitated. Her sudden affect change might be considered as heralding an abandonment depression with its accompanying helplessness, rage, and disenchantment. Or the enraged grief might be considered an attempt to restore the stormy symbiotic mode of relatedness she was losing as a result of her analytic work. I can assure such observers that these themes had been present all along in the therapy and that I believe for the most part they were attended to by both of us rather well, though at the climax,

I'm sure these must have been some of the active components. However, she refused adamantly all attempts to interpret along these lines at the time. And, I might add, this refusal came from a bright and perceptive woman who did not want her analysis destroyed.

The content of the opposition scenarios, which I have mentioned but omitted in this write-up because they are her private material, might also be looked to for explanatory themes that were no doubt also active in the climactic break. But all attempts at interpretation of various interaction patterns or scenarios in this area were rejected also.

Potentially questionable issues regarding my technique, such as reassurances, gratifications, mutual expressions of interest, breaking the frame with sexual looking and champagne, would all have a definite but, I believe, minor place in any systematic attempt to reconsider this work. I would, however, reject out of hand any old-guard hypotheses about untreatable pathology, insurmountable ego weaknesses, or charges of my attempting inappropriately to do analytic work when I should have been doing supportive work. As in any depth analysis, there are many places where issues of technique might be fruitfully raised, but what critical element, theme, or activity might be isolated in order to gain a meaningful perspective on this precipitous break?

I now believe that the self-disclosure is related to the problem. Yet we all know that self-disclosures per se frequently do have their place when analyzing preoedipal issues. Kohut (1977) even speaks of a brief oedipal period that regularly follows the long analysis of a self disorder. He speaks of how important it is for the person to feel the analyst's personality in concrete utterances and to have emerging oedipal curiosity valued and responded to warmly and humanly. Any notion of negative effects from a break in the frame per se caused by the disclosure would also be too simplistic an explanation for a piece of work in which two people were so attached and were working so well. So to what, then, would I attribute the disastrous break, now that I have five years of hindsight and considerably more experience with countertransference responsiveness under my belt?

I can now see ever so clearly that she was right. That in essence I had been living a lie with her all along and that she knew it while I did not! Furthermore, I now believe she did the right thing in stopping the therapy. She could sense that I had not, and could not at that time, have spotted the problem—as sincere as she knew I was in trying to understand her.

And what was the lie I was living? The lie was that I told her I did not dislike her for intruding, that I did not loathe the way she stared at me and spoke of my sexual appeal for her, that I did not hate her for the way she made me be on my guard every moment, to not let her see how uneasy, how vulnerable, and frightened she was making me feel. Instead, I felt forced to reassure her of what a fine person she was, how much I liked her, and how her intrusions were no bother to me. True, my disclosure hit the mark in telling her the genetic history of why *I* was uneasy, but it carelessly sidestepped what *she* needed me to see—*that we had succeeded in our relationship in replicating the traumatic circumstances of her childhood.* I had fallen into the position she always occupied in relation to her fragile, vulnerable, and demanding mother who watched her every move like a vulture, measuring her own self-esteem and fullness by the child's good false-self conformity. She had always portrayed her mother as a horrible person. But we can now ask, "Was her mother as intrusive and vicious as she maintained?" From one standpoint, yes. Her mother fostered the development of this dreadful way of responding and relating. From another standpoint, no. Her mother's own frightened, fragile personality always stood in danger of collapsing in despair and rage if her daughter's responsiveness was not approving, apologetic, self-effacing and, in many ways, on guard and conforming to the mother's relatedness demands. This sensitive child, out of a deep sense of attachment to her mother and a thorough knowledge of her mother's vulnerabilities, systematically warped her own personality to support her mother's perpetually fragmenting self states and precarious confusions. This woman was doing to me what had been done to her, and at some level she knew it. I had not yet understood her communication through the interactions, and when confronted, I basically lied, as she had always done. I was not fully aware of the nature of the lie I was perpetuating until much later.

This process is not new to psychoanalytic writing. In a similar vein, Freud spoke of the tendency in human development to turn passive trauma into active mastery. Anna Freud formulated this kind of phenomenon in terms of identification with the aggressor. Klein spoke of projective identification. Kernberg speaks of alternating self- and object-representations projected into the analyst. All of these ideas point toward a general set of events in analytic work in which the analyst comes to experience the relationship in much the same way as the person once experienced basic attachment and separation relatedness in early childhood.

At a paraverbal or nonverbal level, this woman knew all of these things and tried her very best in a most creative way to show me her life story—to show me by doing, by engaging and involving me in her relatedness patterns. Her creativity had found a way of replicating her truth in our relationship. She was relying on me to find some way of reverberating, of resonating, and ultimately of reflecting her truth to her at a higher level of representation—one that would have the power to transform her adult life.

I failed her. I flinched, which wasn't so bad in itself. In fact, flinching was very much to the point, indicating my personality's response to her lifelong position with her mother and later with everyone else. My attempts to acknowledge responsibility for my personal contribution to our interaction, that is, my disclosure per se, wasn't necessarily faulty either. She had found an ingenious way to use my personality sensitivities, to replicate the flinch, and thereby to register accurately the central problem for which she sought analysis. She had found a way of stimulating my hatred for her for what she was doing to me. I had found no way to experience or to show her my hatred and then to show her how I could now understand the treacherous nightmare she had lived in relation to her mother for her entire life. I was not successful in articulating how my position toward her was stunting me, strangling out whole areas of my spontaneous creative personality functioning, and forcing me into unnatural and guarded responsiveness. When I failed to find a way to acknowledge that in certain ways I had indeed experienced her as the weepy, drab person she projected that she was, and when I failed to understand and admit just how she had succeeded in stunting my personality, in alienating me, and in arousing my hatred toward her, she realized that I could not help her further. I had let her down with no indications whatsoever that I would be able to do better in the future.

DISCUSSION

One interesting feature of this vignette common to a number of replication/counterreplication engagements is the sexualization of the analytic exchange. While the sexualization may take various forms and be attributed to many different causes, a few common themes often emerge. One frequent determinant for the sexualization of the replication of early dyadic experience is the fusion or confusion between affection and sexuality. This confusion results from the prolonged period required for human development. That is, certain kinds of affectionate attachments from early childhood are retained in the personality through puberty, when they become enmeshed in an individual's sexuality. The sexualized affection is then transferred to all or to certain subsequent relationships, including the analytic one. Another cause for sexualization of replicated interactions arises from the ways in which mind–body boundaries form imperfectly or fail to form in early childhood relationships. In various ways, mind–body boundaries may remain defined idiosyncratically and, to a greater or lesser extent, be imbued with erotic or incestuous overtones. Early ego functions surrounding issues of interpersonal boundary definition may have been limited or peculiar for a variety of reasons. The result is that later sexual development does not become integrated smoothly into conventional definitions of interpersonal boundaries and certain merger experiences may remain erotized.

In the present vignette a third possibility, different from those ordinarily encountered, arises to account for the sexualization of the replication. Here, the sexualized replicated transference shows up as a function of the therapist's personal vulnerabilities or sensitivities, which would not need to be at all sexual in nature. When a symbiotic or separating dyadic exchange is replicated in the analytic relationship, it is the affective mode of relatedness that is reestablished on a pre- or nonverbal basis. The creative ingenuity of people in analysis to establish, on a nonverbal or preverbal basis, emotional qualities in a relationship, is uncanny. The content of the interaction is often not of particular interest in itself, but what is of crucial importance is the affective nature of the emotional interchange to be replicated.

What had to be replicated here, in order to be communicated, was a particular style, pattern, or mode of early mother–child relatedness in which the child felt that whole sectors of her spontaneous and creative potentials had to be suppressed in order to support mother's vulnerable personality functioning.

Mother's dependency hung heavily on this child as she de-
manded incessant reassurances, leaving the girl feeling elated
that her mother loved her and simultaneously helpless and
stifled by her mother's attention, so totally fixed on her in order
to maintain mother's cohesiveness and functioning in the world.
This woman had derived remarkable enjoyment and satisfaction
from my permission to let her gaze at me and to feel consolidated
as a result of her erotically tinged scrutiny. So far as I could
determine, there was no history of overt incest in her family,
although her brother was obnoxious with double entendres with
off-color implications. I would have to surmise that she was very
skillful in ferreting out an aspect of my personality that was
vulnerable to a similar quality of emotional threat that her early
relationship with her mother, and possibly also with an insinu-
ating brother, contained. In teaching therapists about this
particular symbiotic skill, I have often said that people have an
uncanny capacity to sense the unconscious reactions of the
analyst in such a way as to use the personality qualities of the
therapist to recreate the emotional or affective constellation to
represent their own replication. The analyst is incorrect to
assume that it is the personal countertransference in the narrow
sense that is the important aspect of such interactions. That is,
the person in analysis who wishes to represent the preverbal
emotional exchange with his or her caretakers must do so
paraverbally since the exact experience to be transferred into the
analysis relates to an emotional way of being with someone.
Mother and child develop an idiom of being and interacting that
is peculiar to that dyad. The emotional exchange or interaction
then becomes the person's way of representing in the analysis the
emotionality of early childhood that must be analyzed. My
assumption that the problem was created by a series of episodes
in my preadolescence or a vulnerability in my personality dating
to my own symbiosis ignored the possibility that she was actively
employing this vulnerability at a level not conscious to either of
us for the purposes of recreating a certain stylized and highly

charged emotional atmosphere. In considering the countertransference material in the narrow sense and acknowledging a specific vulnerability in my historical past, I failed to appreciate the replication involved. I thereby lost the opportunity to move the consideration of the replication of uneasiness, fear, hatred, confinement, and strangulated creativity onto the plane of the analysis.

I realize that the foregoing countertransference study is presented without benefit of the usual validating analytic processes that would add specificity to my working hypotheses and confirm in collaborative narrational activity this way of considering the replication of early childhood interactions. To critics I can reply in two ways. First, I can say that as I wrote this study, I had the sense for the first time in five years that I understood in large part what had happened. I even experienced a lifting of the sense of guilt and pain that I have carried. I did the best I knew how at the time. And I now see, at least in broad outline, where I had gone wrong. But perhaps more validating is that this way of understanding the replication and the countertransference did not emerge suddenly from a reconsideration of this work. In concurrent and subsequent studies on the subject of borderline personality organization, I had begun to grasp the notion of replication introduced by Gertrude and Rubin Blanck in 1979. I had learned from Searles and Giovacchini, in their 1979 papers, the importance of scrutinizing the countertransference for embedded material. In my own book on listening perspectives (Hedges 1983), I evolved the concept of scenarios to capture the interactional aspects of attachment and separating activities. I had even come to speak of active and passive replications for noting the reversal of roles long familiar to me from child analytic training. But more significant than any other was the clarifying influence of Bollas (1983). Bollas's work stems from a rich tradition begun by Winnicott (1947). Through personal contacts with Bollas and his way of working and my study of a series of his very important papers (Bollas 1987), I have learned to identify quickly countertransference responsiveness that arises from a reversal of roles or from the therapist's identification with the projected child self that has been subjected to emotional demands from older people. As a supervisor, I learned to apply what I came to call the "Bollas Twist," with the general result that symbiotic issues became more understandable and workable through detailed analysis of the countertransference.

But exactly how does one come to work with or to interpret countertransference reactions? Bollas's first response is, "Very carefully!" But after that it becomes clear that countertransference interpretation takes months of collaborative work to accomplish. It is subject to considerable creative interaction between two people. In replication, the unique personality features of the analyst are utilized for expressive purposes. The relevant dimensions can be expected to become embedded in or entangled with the personal images and idioms peculiar to the analyst's personality. Thus, the analyst is never in a favorable position to make a clear or clean-cut interpretation of the countertransference, which is independent of his or her personality or personally biased ways of experiencing the world.

Stressing that he is *not* referring to the analyst's thoughtless discharge of affect that might be relieving to the analyst but only serves his or her own self-cure, Bollas (1983) speaks of "countertransference readiness" as a cultivated state of "freely roused emotional sensibility" that is available to the analyst through hunches, feeling states, passing images, fantasies, and imagined interpretive interventions. Like many clinicians, Bollas entertains the possibility that for differing reasons and in varied ways analysands recreate their infantile life in the analytic relationship. Patients may enact fragments of a parent, thus inviting us to learn unconsciously, through experience, how it felt to be the child. Or they may hyperbolize the child to see if we become the "mad" parent. Bollas holds that preoedipal patients tend to create idiomatic environments in which the analyst is invited to fill differing and changing self and object roles. (My experience is that all people attempt to recreate their symbiosis in the analytic ambience in one way or another.)

Bollas emphasizes that we must sustain long periods of not knowing how we are meant to function while the person manipulates us through "transference usage" into "object identity." More often than not, he says, we are made use of through our affects, much as a baby "speaks" to mother by evoking a feeling-perception in her that inspires some action on the baby's behalf, or leads her to put the object use into language, thereby "engaging the infant in the journey toward verbal representation of internal psychic states" (p. 204).

Bollas's working technique follows Winnicott's (1974) attitude in regarding the analyst's thoughts as subjective objects to be put into the potential space between—objects with which two can play. As examples, Bollas might preface a feeling or subjective statement with "'what occurs to me,' 'I am thinking that,' 'I have an idea,' . . . [or] 'now I don't think you are going to like what occurs to me but' . . . [or] 'this may sound quite mad to you but'" and then proceed to say what he thinks or feels (p. 206). Bollas points out that, like the early situation with mother, the analyst seeks out and relates to the unconscious gestures of the patient. That is, the analyst is finding and supporting the infant speech in the analysand and doing so, ironically, by speaking up for his own nonverbal sensations. Bollas believes that responsible and comfortable rootedness in subjective experience, shared by two, leads toward a mutual "sense of appropriate conviction that the patient's true self has been found and registered" (p. 210).

I have developed several suggestions regarding interpretations of countertransference arising in response to symbiotic replications.

1. At this level the best interpretation is often action—
   simply being there in some important way (rather than
   the abandonment previously experienced).

2. A format for presenting countertransference interpretation is a tentative and slow head-scratching, yawning
   attitude, such as, "I've had some thoughts I can't
   account for. Perhaps they are relevant to *our* experience." The first person plural pronoun reflects the
   symbiotic sense. Comments such as, "*I* have some
   feelings about *you* . . ." or "Perhaps others react to you
   in similar ways . . ." are social commentary, but are
   not interpretations of intrapsychic experience. The
   sense of the symbiotic *we* always needs to be present.

3. It is often valuable to discuss the "two levels" of our
   relationship: (a) the real level ("All is going well
   between us as part of the analytic hours") and (b) the
   fantasy of transference and countertransference work
   level ("I am beginning to feel angry, bored, deprived,
   hungry, depressed" implies "You're causing me to feel
   that way" or "I'm picking up a certain message from
   you." The tone here would be: "You have fantasies and
   dreams about me or us that are helpful for us to examine
   and perhaps we can also learn by examining sensations,
   feelings, or dreams of mine—we are in this together)".

4. Here are two rules regarding interpretation that I find
   helpful when I am not certain of the developmental
   level involved: (a) content-wise—I try interpreting at
   the lowest level first, that is, at the level of symbiotic
   need and deficit rather than the level of conflict of
   thoughts, desires, and inhibitions. If I am wrong, the
   effect is harmless or, at worst, regarded as Pollyanna,
   whereas if I interpret at the highest (oedipal) level, I
   may create a major misunderstanding and therefore a
   break of empathy; (b) form-wise—I interpret or respond
   at the highest level of abstraction first, that is, at the

verbal-symbolic level rather than the selfobject or merger interaction levels. If I am wrong, I simply won't be heard, whereas if I interpret at the lower level I may not maximize the symbolic possibilities of the moment.

THREE COMMON ERRORS

In attempting to analyze merger or symbiotic scenarios, three technical errors commonly arise in handling the counter-transference. The first and perhaps most widely noted error is the therapist's simply ignoring disturbing feelings because he or she knows them to be related to recurring personal issues or sensitivities or simply does not know what to do with the feelings. The second technical error is the therapist's disregard of probable countertransference distortions or idiomatic biases in favor of getting some fix on what is really happening—perhaps in the form of a theoretical notion borrowed from or confirmed by a well-known authority. Armed with the truth, the therapist may then assail the person in analysis with an interpretive line in an effort to establish the validity or correctness of the analyst's view—an endeavor with which the person in analysis is altogether too likely to cooperate. Now two can agree that what is happening relates to themes of defensiveness, splitting, narcissistic rage, incestuous entanglements, empathic failure, emerging archetypes, or whatever.

This report of my countertransference entanglement illustrates yet a third variety of technical error, perhaps even more devious in its effects than the first two—a readiness on the analyst's part to assume personal responsibility for the emerging disruption of untoward feelings, thereby sidestepping completely the more important interactional component that contains the crucial processes and imagos of the analysis, whose emergence two people are resisting. The collaborative narrational work required is always long, difficult, and frequently touchy to one or both of the participants.

I have now learned how to identify broadly and to launch into collaborative work on specifics of this kind of countertransference entanglement. I have a confident sense of the right general direction this case might have taken and did not. In this book I will present what I have learned from my own countertransference studies as well as discuss ideas and experiences numerous other therapists have shared with me.

2

The Beginning Work: Relatedness

THE RELATEDNESS PARADIGM

Personal relatedness claims a central position in our lives today. All aspects of contemporary existence in one way or another have come to be based on our capacities for relatedness with others. We can no longer move comfortably through a day without encountering an array of people with whom we must interact in order to create and facilitate our personal purposes and objectives. Contemporary psychoanalytic studies reflect the pressing need for understanding and flexibility in developing and maintaining relationships in a society where the basic problems of distribution of goods and services have receded into the background.

Effective relating with another person demands a capacity to appreciate who that person is on his or her own terms. Clarity in relating necessitates the cultivation of ways of understanding how we experience each other from moment to moment. Rewarding interpersonal relatedness requires (1) mutually evolving appreciation of the kinds of shared responsiveness we might be able to develop together; (2) joint understanding of the forces in ourselves that oppose relatedness; (3) a fund of ideas about how mutually evolving responsiveness can be created and sustained; and (4) shared notions about what conditions may precipitate or constitute a breach in, a separation from, or a termination of relatedness.

Until quite recently most relating was accomplished within the frameworks of established role expectations inherent in the social institutions of marriage, family, work, religion, and politics. But now each of us is essentially "on our own," with the clarity of established role expectations in everyday life rapidly diminishing. As the culture of relationships expands, we find ourselves either disoriented and confused or reassured and comforted as we experience various forms of distress and harmony in our relationships. We are pleased with ourselves when we have successfully negotiated a difficult passage in a relationship. And we are filled with feelings of discontent, loneliness, or despair when we are up against a relationship problem that we cannot find the means to solve. Languishing in nostalgia for a time and place where life was or might yet be less demanding and complex is certainly one way of maintaining needless suffering while simultaneously avoiding the difficult work involved in various kinds of relating!

The purpose of this book is to report on an exciting new system of thought that has evolved within psychoanalysis over the last four decades and that promises to alter permanently the way we think about ourselves and our relatedness to others and the world around us. But, unlike previous psychoanalytic concepts that have often tended to be highly technical, if not tedious and esoteric, the new ideas are in a language accessible to any intelligent person with common sense and a willingness to think about and work on personal relationships.

The fundamental assumption guiding previous psychoanalytic thinking has been articulated most clearly by physicists, not psychoanalysts. The work on relativity theory, quantum mechanics, and chaos/turbulence theories has exposed this assumption as perhaps the fundamental myth of Western civilization, a myth first articulated by Archimedes, often acclaimed as the greatest of the ancient Greek scientists. Overjoyed with having discovered the mathematical principle of the lever, Archimedes reportedly said, "Give me a place to stand and I will move the earth." In its most devious form, this myth has promoted the spectator view of knowledge. The notion that we can stand apart in order to contemplate and control forces that influence our lives has been an integral part of the deterministic perspective central to the history of science.

> The idea that we can step outside our systems of interpretation, our language, and somehow talk sensibly about the world as it really is seems to be one of the most deep-seated beliefs we have. The concept reached its scientific zenith in the triumphs of classical physics. The English physicist and cleric J. C. Polkinghorne said, "Classical physics is played out before an all-seeing eye." The "all seeing eye" is a metaphor, so much that it never appears to us to be an assumption, but seems simply to be "the way things are." It is this metaphor, acting as an undisclosed assumption that allows us to talk about how our theories reflect the way the world really is. That is, it allows us to talk about comparing theories with the world. The metaphor of an all-seeing eye entrances us. As Wittgenstein said, "A *picture* held us captive. And we could not get outside of it, for it lay in our language, and language seemed to repeat it to us inexorably." [Gregory 1988, pp. 190–191]

Traditional views of relationships place us as consistent, knowing selves interacting before an all-seeing eye. In this view, we work to achieve a degree of certainty about who we are and who the people around us are. We then follow various relationship conventions, or at least establish and abide by a set of more or less personal standards and expectations in relating.

Traditional psychoanalytic concepts were developed to bring into focus personal conflicts as seen from the perspective of an all-seeing eye. According to this view, personal desire is at loggerheads with linguistic and cultural expectation such that private action and thought require a great many compromises and adaptations if life is to be lived satisfactorily before the all-seeing eye. Added to this cultural dilemma are the daily necessities of proximity to and interaction with a variety of different people forced upon us by the effects of technology, urbanization, media exposure, and corporate life. Suddenly the task of living decently or even sanely before an all-seeing eye becomes overwhelming, if not unbearable. Relationships run the risk of becoming some sort of fetish we passionately and relentlessly search after. Relationship dilemmas function like mythical beasts who chase us until we fall exhausted in our lair hoping for a reprieve that is nowhere to be found since, after all, the beasts of relatedness live within us. Someone in analysis recently said, "All I want is to be in a relationship and to be happy." The response: "Isn't that just a bit contradictory?"

As a culture we have not yet emerged sufficiently from guidance by role expectations to have developed effective tools for dealing with the kaleidoscope of changing relatedness patterns facing us daily or to have evolved realistic expectations regarding the amount and kinds of work required to sustain important relationships. The received wisdom about relationships first took the form of rules, as in the Ten Commandments. Later, principles of relating were spelled out, as in the Sermon on the Mount. A new ethical system, based on mutual appreciation of idiosyncratic and ever-changing relatedness patterns, is slowly emerging. We now realize that anyone who approaches creative relating based on rules or principles alone is in for trouble. In deciphering the difficulties and formulating viable approaches to developing and maintaining relationships, psychoanalysis has been able to achieve a jump on general culture rather than lagging behind, as it has been so often accused of doing in the past. This book is about spelling out that leading edge, which the people who have undergone psychoanalysis over the last century have created.

For purposes of speaking about the complexities involved in interpersonal relating, the many skills and capacities for relatedness that each of us actively cultivates for receiving information from another will here be collectively referred to as *listening*. The various positions from which we resonate with the many things that other people tell or show us about themselves will be considered *perspectives*, vantage points that we establish in order to understand more fully, on an ongoing and expanding basis, who the other is in relation to ourselves. Conceived as arbitrary and ever-changing points of view we establish in order to orient ourselves in relationships, the notion of listening perspectives will be shown to have special relevance for dealing with the problem of interpersonal relatedness, which has assumed such a central position in our lives. Cultivating an ongoing attitude of listening to relatedness possibilities in relationships contrasts sharply with studying the laws of psyche as lived out before the "all-seeing eye."

THE EMERGENCE OF A NEW WAY OF THINKING ABOUT OURSELVES

We have all been beaten, bruised, manipulated, cajoled, forced, and seduced in particular ways through language and cultural and familial systems. These have stimulated the creation of various modes of living and relating that we call our unique human selves. The emergence of our concept "self" as conceived in Western civilization might be likened to the castling move in the game of chess, a convention that adds interest, excitement, and intrigue to the game. In chess all pieces have ritualistic and set rules for play. But, if conditions are right, players agree to one decisive move called castling. The existence of this possibility for enhancing the safety of the king changes the complexion of the entire game. Our collective acknowledgment of the right to have an independent self manifests itself in many ways in our culture, not the least of which is the first person singular pronoun, "I."

Blind for centuries to the nature of the human psyche, psychoanalytic research at last lifts the veil. But alas, no sooner do we glimpse the beauty and mystery of psyche with our scientific research tools, than she once again eludes us, gliding away into the mists that have always prevented our seeing the nature of things clearly. Suddenly we find ourselves in the company of physicists, chemists, biologists, and astronomers who have long preceded us in realizing that the richness and vastness of the universe are not simply things to be understood as such. We are forced into realizing that the sensory impressions and logical thought systems that we have trusted to inform us of the nature of things have failed us miserably. The universe we thought was there is not. Contemporary thinkers have been forced into the realization that reality and psyche cannot be so easily caught in the nets constructed by human convention as we once imagined. But the pictures of reality we have drawn over the ages have so completely captivated us that we are shocked when we are told by modern studies that they can't possibly be so. Quantum research demonstrates that whatever realities there might be are, in principle, forever unknowable. Quantum leaps and chaotic happenings irreversibly challenge our fantasies about the nature of human knowledge. "I think, therefore I am" comforts us by providing us with a sense of certainty, which we now understand exists nowhere but in our own imaginations. Einstein's and Bohr's challenge to Descartes is echoed by Freud, who declares that it is by tolerating perennial uncertainty that the mysteries of our existence can be momentarily glimpsed. It is in our moments of greatest uncertainty—dreams, slips of the tongue, physical symptoms, and sexuality—that eternally elusive psyche allows herself to be apprehended ever so fleetingly.

But if reality cannot possibly be what we have made it out to be and if psyche cannot possibly be a formation of certainty, what ways of thinking can we muster to help us reorient more effectively to ourselves, to each other, and to the many and diverse worlds around us? These are the questions that haunt contemporary psychoanalysts who, out of the heap of a century of research, are raising a new phoenix, one completely unlike anything ever imagined before. The new vision of psyche currently emerging fits more comfortably within a relativistic, quantum, and chaotic universe. The "new think" about psyche stands squarely on the shoulders of all that has gone before in psychoanalysis and provides a breathtaking panorama of questions and considerations never before dreamed of. New think is about relationships and how whatever we speak of when we say "psyche" resides forever and inextricably in the way people experience and choose to relate to, communicate with, and represent themselves to each other. Psyche is no longer a thing to be hunted down and dissected in order to discover her natural laws. As Heisenberg has taught us through physics, the object of our new studies can only be what we can directly observe and speak about. Nor are we free any longer to assume what psyche is doing when we cannot observe her. We only know she makes her presence felt and available for scrutiny in moments of greatest uncertainty in human relationships. We no longer search to uncover her true nature but seek to live and question psyche as fully and actively as we possibly can.

We know that during human infancy and childhood psyche becomes encumbered with burdensome restrictions. Gradually, through time and experience, she loses her multitudinous and diverse potentials, her vitality and enthusiasm, her capacity for spontaneous creative gesture, her wide-eyed curiosity, and the incredible powers and naive understandings she was born with. Lowen (1990a) speaks of this loss of the natural gracefulness of our body-selves through childhood experiences as our spirits falling from grace. Yet we also know that our collective psyche has achieved a high level of cultivation, enlightenment, and dominion over the earth and the beyond. How can it possibly be, as Rousseau first suggested, that in all our wisdom and progress our very essences have become progressively constricted, inhibited, filled with doubts, worries, physical disease, sexual inhibition, nightmares, general joylessness, bodily constrictions, and a general lack of joy and fulfillment in our daily occupations?

A century ago psychoanalysts set out to study systematically these questions, according to the nineteenth-century model of science, using the best thought modes available at the time. Pathological instances of various aberrations of human life have been subjected to study until it has become painfully obvious that these so-called psychic aberrations are nothing but ourselves in extreme and visible forms. Psychoanalysts have had to face the fact that they are no different from the people who come to them for consultation. The pains, miseries, uncertainties, stylized interactions, crippling inhibitions, internal conflicts, perversions, affect storms, and bizarre thoughts that have motivated people to seek treatment are in essence no different from those that characterize all humanity. Psychoanalysts have discovered that these very afflictions comprise the human condition, but their influence remains largely hidden from view by early life conditioning that teaches people not to notice themselves, not to have or to display feelings or conflicts, not to cry, not to think or do bad or perverse things. In short, we are taught to hold our body-selves in certain ways and to turn away from appreciating the richness of our private lives, away from enjoying the flow of life energy in our bodies, and away from cultivation of the rich prospects for self-transformation that are offered by interpersonal relatedness. By the age of four or five, children are already marching in lines, controlling disruptive behavior, compulsively doing things according to demand, saying and thinking acceptable words and thoughts, and giving over the capacity for joyous living and the plenitude within to the influence of the dominant cultural ethic. Psychoanalytic research has now forced us to see the whole conditioning process, which is essential to human development, as simultaneously corrupting to the human soul. Earlier experiments in liberalizing the conditions of childrearing have demonstrated that many time-honored strict and prohibiting training procedures are not necessarily desirable. Studies in hospitalization, separations from parents in early childhood, and various forms of neglect and abusive intrusion have mandated that we provide increased support and protection for our children. But time and study have shown that even under optimal childrearing conditions, the human soul nonetheless progressively undergoes a series of constricting transformations that seem absolutely unavoidable. Depending on the individual, these constricting transformations produce different effects with differing long-term implications for their lives. The interesting question is no longer whether a person is developing or living normally. Normality in this context has lost its meaning altogether. Rather, how are the inevitable constricting influences from childhood operating in our lives and what hazards in daily living, relating, loving, and health do we face as a result? And, most importantly, how can we begin to consider our constrictions and blocks in such a way as to begin breathing, living, and loving more freely once again?

Perhaps not so surprisingly, psychoanalytic research has gradually focused its probing light on the way we live our personal relationships, designating interpersonal relatedness the mother lode for generating answers to the critical questions of human existence. Capturing the current spirit of awareness of the human condition, Lowen (1990b) boldly declared at a

conference, "For the millions out there who have no understanding of themselves, life is Hell!"

The emerging relatedness paradigm to be described in this
book is the result of a century of study by some of the most
brilliant minds to live in the newly created communication
conditions afforded by the twentieth century. Like other
scientific endeavors, the leading paradigm of psychoanalysis
originated with a single person, Sigmund Freud. The initial
psychoanalytic paradigm, that of the dynamic unconscious,
permitted Freud and other analysts to conceptualize previously
inexplicable phenomena such as dreams, slips, jokes, and
sexuality. That paradigm has guided research and spawned many
competing schools of thought and practice. Over time, the
diversity of thinking has raised new questions that have been
unanswerable within the parameters defined by the original
dynamic unconscious paradigm. Freud himself was the first to
introduce in 1923 a paradigm shift toward considering psyche as
an internal structure based on balances and ratios of instinctual
energy (Id), moderating influences (Ego), and sociocultural
influences (Superego). Not unlike the history of other sciences,
systematic research and diverse practices have produced a
demand for a new way of conceptualizing old problems and
observations. Paradigm shifts as described by Kuhn (1962)
historically have possessed the power to change the fundamental
concepts and methods of a field of study, if not the basic data
themselves. The task of this book is an examination of the
paradigm shift now taking place in psychoanalysis and radically
transforming its basic terms and practice.

LISTENER RESPONSIVENESS: THE COUNTERTRANSFERENCE

The pivot on which the entire shift revolves is the so-called
countertransference. Countertransference as a technical term in

psychoanalysis refers to the feelings and emotional states aroused in the analyst-listener as the psychic life of the patient-speaker progressively unfolds. In keeping with the spirit of the new paradigm, certain language alterations are mandated that necessarily sound awkward at first. Henceforth, for reasons that will become clear as we go along, the traditional doctor role will be referred to as "listener" and the patient role as "speaker." Over the last four decades, studies of countertransference responsiveness, that is, emotional responsiveness of the listener in a relationship, have created an opening for the emergence of a new thought paradigm to guide the entire psychoanalytic enterprise. But more importantly, the wave of countertransference studies that has pointed toward the paradigm shift has suddenly made possible the extension of psychoanalytic principles to an understanding of human relationships in general and invites widespread application of psychoanalytic understanding to all areas of human life where relationships are important.

OUR JOURNEY

We will begin by moving immediately to the center of the paradigm shift, listener responsiveness (countertransference), and see that its essence can be traced back to the earliest beginnings of psychoanalysis. After a glimpse at some of the countertransference studies that have opened the thought revolution in relatedness, the major parameters of the paradigm shift will be outlined. Part II will trace the origins of "self and other" psychology, culminating in a review of the listening perspective approach. Countertransference will be examined again and various kinds of listener responsiveness placed in the context of the four listening perspectives. Working and interpreting countertransference responsiveness will be illustrated. There will be opportunity to begin imagining how to apply the new countertransference findings to important relationships, personal as well as professional. Part III will present transcripts of actual case conferences of groups of professional therapists struggling to work the countertransference in order to see in real life situations how the new ways of thinking can work. It will focus on several detailed psychoanalytic case studies that reveal the processes of working the countertransference for the diverse kinds of information it contains. Part IV will conclude the study by re-contextualizing the countertransference as listener responsiveness within the broader frameworks of listening perspectives and human relationships.

3

The Road to the New Relatedness

THE ORIGINS OF LISTENER RESPONSIVENESS

More than a hundred years have passed since Bertha Pappenheim first invented psychoanalysis. It was she who coined the phrase *the talking cure* to describe the relief she experienced from her numerous physical complaints as she daily related the thoughts and fantasies that preoccupied her to her physician, Dr. Joseph Breuer. His curiosity and attentiveness led him to go considerably out of his way on occasion to accommodate her insistence. During one period she actually required him to make lengthy and frequent train rides to her country residence in order to be with her. At another time it was necessary for him to feed her daily when she refused to eat otherwise.

The relationship metaphor of her spending days in "dreamy clouds" until her doctor came in the evening to "penetrate" her unconsciousness with hypnosis, thus relieving her agonies like a "chimney sweep," would not be missed by modern analysts. Nor would the timing of the upsurge of her physical complaints, which coincided with her beginning to nurse her beloved father through a terminal illness, be overlooked today.

At the outset Bertha was, by all standards, a "basket case." She presented a wide variety of physical and mental symptoms. Today she might be seen as "borderline psychosis, severe," but in the early literature she was referred to as an hysteric. Devoted as he was to her care, Dr. Breuer simply did not understand what all of her symptoms and metaphors were about. His new wife, however, understood a few things quite clearly because she was apparently becoming increasingly jealous of the relationship. It is not difficult to imagine Mrs. Breuer's feelings when, just about the time dinner would be ready to go on the table, she would receive a message from her husband that he would be late. Bertha was requiring extra time again. Dr. Breuer felt the strain that Bertha's treatment was placing on him and on his marriage. After considering the matter from many angles, the good doctor must have recognized the need to press for some sort of relief as rapidly as possible so that he could terminate the burdensome relationship. Through suggestion and his influence as her physician, he induced Bertha in a variety of ways to give up her symptoms, a technique we today might call a "false self" cure.

We can imagine the day that Dr. Breuer was to declare Bertha cured. His wife no doubt arranged a special candle-lit dinner celebration with all of the expectable intimacies of a long overdue romantic evening together. Suddenly there came a knock at the door. Bertha's family had sent for the doctor. He must come at once. There was an emergency. The candles were snuffed and the dinner reluctantly placed back in the oven to keep warm. Dr. Breuer dutifully put on his coat and headed for Bertha's place. When he arrived Bertha frantically reported a dramatic resurgence of all of her troubling symptoms. But there was something new. Bertha announced that she was pregnant and that the baby she was carrying was his! With Dr. Breuer's reactions to Bertha culminating in his decision to leave her and her false pregnancy, we witness the birth of what we now call countertransference.

DEFINING TRANSFERENCE AND RESISTANCE

Dr. Breuer's (Breuer and Freud 1893–1895) early work with Bertha Pappenheim is known in the literature as the specimen case of psychoanalysis, "Anna O." Events had so upset Dr. Breuer and his wife that he transferred the case immediately to his friend and colleague, Sigmund Freud, and promptly fled on a second honeymoon. Freud later recalled that upon hearing about Breuer's work with Bertha, he first understood the power of the unconscious. *From manifestations in their relationship Freud intuited the important connection between unconscious fantasies and psychically determined physical manifestations. Moreover, he understood that highly personal unconscious influences in both doctor and patient could be mobilized and laid bare for observation under the influence of an intense personal relationship.* As a side note, it is interesting to learn that Bertha Pappenheim became a well-known social worker, noted both for her work with juveniles and her pioneering efforts in the women's movement, for which she was recently commemorated on a postage stamp.

After extensive psychoanalytic investigation of unconscious processes, Freud (1912) is able to articulate how psychoanalysis moves forward based on an understanding of the ways one person experiences and relates to another. He formulates that distressing ideas and affects from the past tend to become reactivated in the context of the intimacy of the present relationship. These intense relatedness possibilities deriving from prior experience with significant others make their appearance in the present relationship through emotional experiences that emerge in response to the setting of the relationship (analysis) and to the person of the other (the analyst). Freud defines the analyst's role as being like an opaque mirror whose relationship function is to elicit and then to reflect (through interpretation) these intense and recurring personal unconscious experiences, which he termed *the transference*.

Freud (Breuer and Freud 1893–1895) speaks of transference in a cursory way in *Studies on Hysteria*, conducted in collaboration with Joseph Breuer from 1893 to 1895. But he structures no explicit or comprehensive formulation of transference manifestations until 1912. In his paper, "The Dynamics of Transference," Freud (1912) discusses the nature of the transfer of unconscious relatedness patterns from one significant emotional relationship to another and how this tendency reappears in the intimacy and privacy of the analytic relationship. He concludes that transference is the greatest obstacle yet to be encountered in the search for relief of neurotic symptoms. Freud observes that as people begin to establish the kind of relationship with their analyst that would lead to the elucidation of the neurotic symptoms, specific and troubling contents from past relationships become automatically and unconsciously activated and transferred to the setting of the analysis and onto the person of the doctor. The memories of old fears, hatreds, neglects, abusive intrusions, loves, and seductions become reactivated not so much, as Freud had anticipated, in the progressive unfolding of the free associational content of the analytic work per se, but rather in the context of the evolving relationship with the analyst. Freud writes that these relatedness memories transferred to the analytic situation and onto the analyst regularly intervene to disrupt the treatment before the neurotic symptom can be analyzed. That is, thoughts and affects transferred from the past into the present relatedness situation interfere with and often prevent the full understanding or analysis of the various elements that have been symbolically linked together through past experience to form neurotic symptom complexes.

Freud begins to conceive of psychoanalysis as a process analogous to chemical analysis of his time. Analysis as a process of understanding seeks to break down complex compounds into their constituent elements. Following this metaphor, Freud repeatedly attempts to define the elements of human experience and to develop psychological techniques to foster the analysis (understanding) of psychological complexes. Transferred experiences, according to this way of thinking, serve as resistance to the analytic breakdown process.

Freud soon comes to realize that the apparently disruptive experiences transferred onto the analytic relationship paradoxically turn out to be manifestations of the very memories that the analysis could, and should, be seeking to understand. That is, the very thoughts and affects that serve as resistance to the free flow of discussion and relatedness between the person and his or her analyst-listener *are themselves transference!* Thus the second great obstacle Freud encounters after transference in the analysis of neurotic symptoms is the resistance to deepening the analytic relationship occasioned by relationship manifestations transferred from past relationships into the analytic setting or onto the person of the analyst.

FREUD'S PARADIGM OF THE DYNAMIC UNCONSCIOUS

Freud formulates the central ideas that have historically guided the development of psychoanalytic theory and technique in the investigation of neurosis:

1. Interpersonal manifestations that provide resistance to the flow of analytic relatedness and thus to analytic insight are considered transference from past significant relationships.

2. Thoughts and affects arising in response to the analytic relationship and to the person of the analyst that serve as resistances to the development of the analytic relationship and thus to analytic understanding of neurotic symptoms are also transferred from past emotional relationships.

3. Both transference and resistance relatedness manifestations are the bearers of crucial (unconscious) emotional memories into the analytic relationship that bear witness to the influences of various intense relatedness experiences in the past (see Freud 1912).

THE EMERGENCE OF COUNTERTRANSFERENCE

No sooner does Freud become able to define transference and resistance as attitudes brought by the psychoanalytic speaker-patient into the relationship, than he finds it necessary to begin considering the analogous attitudes in the analyst-listener.[1] These attitudes have come to be called countertransference and counterresistance (Freud 1915a).

The natural countertendency on the part of the listener to

---

[1]Throughout the text I will primarily use the term "speaker" to designate the person often referred to as analysand, patient, or subject of the analysis. For the most part, I will use the term "listener" to designate the person in the role of therapist, analyst, or doctor. On occasion I will employ similar terms to denote the relationship roles such as "expressor" and "receiver." Such terms reflect more accurately the role designations as understood in contemporary psychoanalysis and mark a move away from the traditional medical or healing paradigm based on conceptions of normality and pathology, health and illness. Current conceptions rest upon grasping the analytic situation as an interaction between the experiencing and speaking subject and the experiencing and listening other/object. Use of the terms "speaker" and "listener" maintains greater clarity in discussions of the psychoanalytic process.

transfer ideas and affects from his or her past into the analysis is considered, like transference at first, an unwelcome influence. Freud formulates countertransference as likely to act as an impediment to the psychoanalytic process—to detract or to distract from the analyst's mirroring capacities. The "impediment theory of countertransference," as I shall refer to this view, reflected Freud's earliest ideas, which have been exceedingly influential in subsequent thought about listener responsiveness. If the analyst's reactions emerge disruptively, Freud's basic prescriptions are consultation on the case with a colleague, followed by more personal analysis for the analyst if the troubling features do not subside after consultation.

These two time-honored recommendations, like many psychoanalytic concepts, are tinged with a hidden morality that has exerted a crippling influence on subsequent theoretical developments. If countertransference is, by definition, unconscious and dilatory because it is an impediment to the therapeutic relationship, then the analyst-listener "should" get help in order to stop "bad" things from happening as a result of listener bias. This moralistic attitude still represents the dominant way in which countertransference is considered.

COUNTERTRANSFERENCE AS A LISTENING TOOL

Historically, the definition of countertransference as a tool for psychoanalytic research has emerged more slowly than definitions of transference and resistance, perhaps because of its elusive nature. But there has also been a tendency in the field to guard the privacy of the analyst who reports his or her work to colleagues for scientific scrutiny. This need for privacy on the part of teaching and publishing analysts has meant that the most enmeshed aspects of analytic work have remained largely unscrutinized. It can be surmised that the great legal and ethical

issues facing psychotherapists of all disciplines regarding enmeshments of all kinds would be more clarified by now had
analytic reporters been more courageous in reporting complications, enmeshments, therapeutic abreactions, and other types of
countertransference dilemmas more freely in the past.

Another major obstacle in the systematic elaboration of
countertransference as a study tool has been the difficulty
encountered by the requirement that the analyst function
simultaneously (or alternatingly) both as objective observer of
another person's ideas and affects and as subjective receiver. The
information and interactions received in an intense analytic
situation are bound to stimulate personal reactions in the
listener that demand scrutiny by his or her own free associative
processes. As if studying another person's actions and activities
weren't enough, must the analyst also be required to study his or
her own reactions and their possible relevancy in understanding
the relationship? Perhaps the best answer in the traditional
attempts to study neurosis would be no. But for a variety of
reasons, the scope of psychoanalytic study has been increasingly
widening for the past three decades. With this expansion has
come the necessity to study psychological constellations other
than those called *neurosis*, and for that reason countertransference has become a crucial area of increasing focus.

Just as transference and the tendency to oppose or resist its
establishment have come to be understood as the awakening of
relatedness memories relevant to the current analytic work, so
too has countertransference provoked by the relationship
gradually come to be understood as a source of valuable and
relevant information in psychoanalytic relationships. Despite
the fact that countertransference reactions, by definition, reflect
the personal, unconscious relatedness patterns of the analyst-
listener's past emotional life, they are increasingly coming to be
viewed as worthy of careful scrutiny as listening tools in various
systematically specified circumstances.

Freud's impediment theory of countertransference responsiveness held a firm grip on the psychoanalytic community until the 1950s, in London. The publication of *The Clinical Diary of Sandor Ferenczi* in 1988 makes clear that Ferenczi, Freud's closest friend and colleague, had been studying listener responsiveness at least as early as 1932, although there is no significant mention of it in the literature. Ferenczi died before his ideas could be systematized and published. Freud remained skeptical of Ferenczi's work in this regard. Following the Second World War, Winnicott began treating psychotic patients and in 1947 wrote the kickoff paper, "Hate in the Countertransference." He expressed the view that psychotic states in people expectably elicit a sense of helplessness, frustration, and hatred in the analyst. The hatred is not to be ignored, but to be taken into the analyst's overall understanding of the patient.

Next in this remarkable series is Heimann's 1950 paper, "On Counter-transference." Reacting to a tendency among candidates in psychoanalytic training to develop a certain ideal of the detached analyst, she developed the thesis that "the analyst's emotional response to his patient within the analytic situation represents one of the most important tools for his work. The analyst's counter-transference is an instrument of research into the patient's unconscious" (p. 81). She held that in addition to freely hovering attention, the analyst-listener needs a freely roused emotional sensibility so as to allow understanding of the patient's unconscious through his own—"the most dynamic way in which his patient's voice reaches him." Heimann adds:

> The analyst's immediate emotional response to his patient is a significant pointer to the patient's unconscious processes and guides him towards fuller understanding. It helps the analyst to focus his attention on the most urgent elements in the patient's associations and serves as a useful criterion for the selection of interpretations from material which, as we know, is always overdetermined. . . . The analyst's counter-transference is not

only part and parcel of the analytic relationship, but it is the patient's *creation*, it is part of the patient's personality. [Heimann 1950, p. 82]

Heimann speaks of the patient dramatizing his conflicts in the analytic relationship. She interprets Freud's demand that the analyst recognize and master his countertransference to mean not that the analyst be emotionally detached, but rather that he or she use emotional responsiveness as a key to the patient's unconscious. "The emotions roused in the analyst will be of value to his patient, if used as one more source of insight into the patient's unconscious conflicts and defences" (p. 82).

Little (1981) followed with a series of courageous papers demonstrating how with preneurotic (so-called preoedipal) patients, the analyst's countertransference feelings provided necessary material for the analysis. Not only did she maintain that all countertransference feelings might be useful, but she held that the analysis cannot go forward adequately without the feelings of the analyst taking center stage at certain points. Little's work stimulates thinking about how, whether, and under what conditions the analyst might usefully communicate his or her feelings to the patient (the so-called disclosure issue that has been hotly debated in recent years). Little wrote about a case in which it appeared retrospectively that the analyst had been envious because his patient was going to be on a national radio broadcast. At the time, the analyst interpreted the envious feelings as a wish that the patient's recently deceased mother could hear him speak. It wasn't until the analysis was terminated and the analyst by chance came into contact with the patient at a social gathering that the patient provided material that made it clear that the feelings of the analyst upon which the interpretation was made were very much to the point, but because the analyst was defending against his own envy, the interpretation was wrong. Years later Little revealed that this case example was taken from her own training analysis with Ella Freeman Sharpe (Little 1985).

Work on understanding the countertransference continued more or less quietly in London, particularly in the Independent group—independent from the schools of psychoanalytic thought established by Melanie Klein and Anna Freud. But only in the last two decades have the findings of a long tradition of study paid off in a series of breakthroughs in clinical work that are bound to have a profound impact on all psychotherapy. Contemporary studies center on issues concerning when and how to make systematic use of the countertransference for developing and sustaining intense emotional relationships.

The key paper in the series is Bollas's (1983) "Expressive Uses of the Countertransference." Bollas's work has made the thinking in the present book possible. He has pointed the way toward actualizing the shift to the relatedness paradigm. In his brilliant paper, rich with clinical illustrations, Bollas demonstrates how countertransference thoughts and feelings freely roused in the course of listening can serve to represent various aspects of the infantile position of the patient-speaker that are otherwise unrepresentable. He further demonstrates how, in speaking the countertransference, feeling and bodily states of the analyst can be shown to contain crucial memories belonging to the patient and can be given interpretive value. This is the theme to be followed in this book—exactly how listener responsiveness evolving in a relationship serves to point toward the elucidation of representations of the speaker's infantile states that continue to be experienced and known about but have not yet been brought into the realm of symbolic thought—in Bollas's language, to begin discovering and putting into language "the unthought known."

4

The Paradigm Shift

PARADIGM SHIFTS IN HUMAN THOUGHT

The history of the development of human thought is marked by an occasional shift that, in retrospect, seems radically discontinuous with previous patterns of thought. Suddenly, as key ideas become articulated in fresh ways, the world under consideration appears very different. Human realities have continued to change through time under the impact of ever broadening concepts that have the power to reorient and reorganize our ways of thinking about things.

Our intellectual history is replete with examples of various kinds of changes in the fundamental patterning of thought systems—referred to as paradigm shifts (Kuhn 1962). Jaynes (1976) tells us that in ancient Greece the gods were known to speak to all humans through five regions of the body. But along with increasing cooperative work, psyche (soul) gradually became localized in the head. Furthermore, in order to minimize confusion and social conflict, only the group leader (later the god-king) was permitted direct communication with the divine regarding humankind's affairs. This radical shift in thought, spanning perhaps a thousand years, served to reorganize human social groups.

Likewise, we may well suppose that the shift in language structure from Phoenician and Egyptian to the complex but more flexible grammar of Latin represented a significant leap in thought potential.

In the more modern world we have the examples of Galileo, Copernicus, Newton, Descartes, Darwin, Pasteur, Luther, and many others who are credited with originating radical shifts in the way human realities are considered. In physics Newton set the pace with his laws of motion, which established a concept of a universe that ran like a clockwork. Following Newton, classical physics set about the task of systematically discovering the laws of the physical universe and their implications for human life. The problem of the conflicting particle and wave theories of light pushed Einstein into a formulation of relativity theory under which the previous findings of classical physics came to be considered special instances. Previous knowledge became subsumed in a special place within the new framework organized by the concept of relativity.[1] Einstein's relativity theory is now seen by many as a special case subsumed under the broader and more far reaching conceptual canopy of quantum mechanics. Others prefer the view that relativity theory ac-

---

[1]The fascinating saga of twentieth-century chemistry and physics viewed against a backdrop of the history of science and forming the basis for the current text is taken from several sources listed here in order of relevance to our topic: Gribbin (1984), Herbert (1985), Gregory (1988), Dyson (1988), Gribbin (1988), Capra (1983), Briggs and Peat (1984), Gribbin (1986), Dyson (1979), Gribbin (1983), Briggs and Peat (1989), Peat (1987), and Gleick (1987).

counts for the larger picture of the universe, whereas quantum theory accounts for the subatomic world. Exactly what the relation of the new multidisciplinary chaos and turbulence studies and the sciences of wholeness will be to relativity and quantum mechanics remains to be determined. Suddenly the world is becoming conceptualized in ways that defy common sense and have yet to be formulated into a comprehensive and unifying theory. Many theorists now even doubt the possibility or feasibility of there ever being a grand unification theory.

PARADIGM SHIFTS CONCERNING PSYCHE

Until modern times the human psyche (mind, soul) has been more or less taken for granted (or perhaps conceived of as a piece of the mind of God), with few questions raised about its exact nature. Whatever interest has arisen in the past regarding human mental functioning has either been of philosophical or theological import or has centered around coming to grips with the social problem of unusual minds that create problems and disruptions for other people. The failure to think and behave in ordinary and cooperative ways was for centuries attributed to the work of the devil and witchcraft. Only in the eighteenth and nineteenth centuries did the concept of mental illness become popularized. The growth of asylums for mentally ill people parallels the Industrial Revolution and urbanization of Europe and America. We might surmise that before group living had become lived so intensely and at such close quarters, people sporting a disruptive mental life could be tolerated quietly in their corner of the farm or village. Or if the disruptions they caused became too great they could be banished, exorcised, or burned at the stake. The rise of humanism and the diminishing belief in the influence of the devil in such matters led to a view that these unusual and intolerable people must be isolated, cared for, and contained in communal facilities. The nineteenth century saw the rise of neurological and psychiatric studies attempting to understand and treat various types of insanity.

It is out of this cultural context that the well-known story of Sigmund Freud arises. Finding it impractical in nineteenth-century Vienna to follow his natural inclinations as a philosopher, Freud trained in biology, medicine, neurology, and hypnosis, before publishing at the turn of the century his epoch-making book, *The Interpretation of Dreams* (1900). His psychological studies span from the late 1880s to 1938. His fifty years of labor have changed the face of twentieth-century thinking about the nature of humans and their psychic functioning. His psychoanalytic technique of free association—saying whatever comes to mind—was gradually and painstakingly distilled out of the more traditional physical therapies, hypnosis, and direct suggestion. Freud soon realized that while his concepts, originally developed to study neurosis, might be helpful in providing some understanding of the more severe disorders, his psychological technique had little to offer in the way of therapy for these individuals. For more than a century, psychoanalytic concepts as developed by Freud and his followers have fostered the notion of a biological or social-developmental basis for psychopathology. Freud's ideas chiefly centered around (1) the elaboration of a special free association setting for investigating the nature of psyche, (2) the definition of dynamic (repressed) unconscious mental activity (primary process thinking), which differs from ordinary cause-and-effect (secondary process) thinking, (3) the linking of psychic events to biological forces (instincts), (4) the division of mental functioning into various agencies with differing tasks (the id, the ego, and the superego), (5) the systematic elaboration of metapsychological principles, borrowed from other sciences, that are presumed to underlie psychological processes, and, (6) the systematic establishment of a set of contrasting points of view for considering psychic events. (For a survey of Freud's general theory of psychoanalysis, the metapsychological principles, and his specific theory of psychoanalysis, the points of view, refer to Hedges 1983, Chapter 5.) Clearly, Freud's notion of the working of a dynamic unconscious as a way of conceptualizing neurosis and the human psyche represents a paradigm shift from the neurological and psychiatric approaches of the nineteenth century, which employed chiefly physical therapies.

Psychotherapies of many varieties have been developed in an attempt to apply Freud's basic concepts to a wide range of unusual mental orientations. Most psychoanalysts have continued to employ Freud's basic approach for studying neurosis in order to elaborate highly refined theories of mental functioning and to account for why some individuals fall ill. A few psychoanalysts have worked to widen the scope of psychoanalytic research, theory, and treatment beyond the narrow bounds of neurosis that Freud originally established. But the important thing to be aware of is that for a century, a group of the world's finest minds quietly continued studying, in the privacy of the consulting room and in the arena of professional life, in order to elaborate and expand, to confirm and disconfirm Freud's theories of human mental life. This group of researchers has produced a formidable technical literature and a strong international movement dedicated to understanding the nature of human psyche.

This sizeable body of psychoanalytic researchers, working in cooperation and competition for a century, is slowly giving rise to a remarkably new way of considering psyche. Psychoanalysts now stand on the brink of realizing another major paradigm shift. The exact dimensions of this shift have but to be spelled out to make clear that psychoanalysis has made good the Freudian promise of continuing to provide fresh and fruitful ways of thinking about the human psyche. Humankind's self-understanding is now destined to undergo an irreversible transformation. The shift in thought has already been made; it remains for us to learn to live with it. To be sure, there is and will continue to be considerable resistance to the new and evolving psychoanalytic vision of human realities. But resistance to any shift in patterns of thinking has historically been the rule. Freud's ideas have certainly met with and continue to meet with great resistance. Something there is that refuses change, that strives to conserve what has become established as safe and familiar.

The task here is to delineate the paradigm shift that is currently underway. In order to do so some new vocabulary must be cultivated. I grasped the fundamental shift more than a decade ago, but when *Listening Perspectives in Psychotherapy* (Hedges 1983) was published, I chose to write about the history leading up to the shift within the framework and vocabulary of traditional psychoanalysis. Despite that choice, I was greatly disappointed when readers and reviewers generally failed to recognize the radical paradigm shift embedded in *Listening Perspectives*. Now, to avoid further misunderstanding, I must break from established conventions and create fresh frameworks to contain the paradigm that I am calling *relatedness*. Little or nothing of the old will be lost, but previous concepts and findings will be subsumed under a broader set of theoretical and technical considerations. I believe that Freud would not be at all surprised to find his discipline shifting in the direction that it is. But there was no way for him to foretell the changes in philosophical and epistemological doctrines of the twentieth century. He could not foresee the changes that would occur as a result of the impact of relativity, much less quantum physics and chaos/turbulence research. The innovative textual analytical procedures occasioned by linguistics and literary criticism point toward different issues of a constructionist, structuralist, decon-structionist, and narrational sort. Freud developed his concepts within the context of era-specific beliefs about science, biology, and medicine. His pioneering work opened for inspection the world of psyche.[2]

A paradigm shift is by nature extremely complex, and any attempt to outline its features is necessarily general, sweeping, and short-sighted in many regards. I choose here to discuss the relatedness paradigm as shifts in orientation from (1) healing to consciousness raising, (2) scientific objectivity to systematic subjectivity, (3) historical truth to narrative truth, (4) relativity to quantum realities, (5) mythical beasts to listening perspectives, and (6) frame technique to variable responsiveness.

The Shift from Healing to Consciousness Raising

To give lip service to the need for abandoning the medical model fails to grasp the magnitude of change required for the transition into a new way of thinking and being with others. Study of sexist language has made clear to all of us that we behave and think as we speak. If we wish to enter a different consciousness, we must be willing to alter the way we speak. The notion of disease and cure sets up a series of faulty ideas in terms of pathologies, syndromes, diagnoses, and treatment manipulations designed to promote cure. It is a simple fact that psycho-

---

[2]I will use *psyche*, the ancient Greek word, interchangeably with its anglicized equivalent, *soul*. Bettelheim makes clear how this humanistic accent was Freud's intent, but his English translators thwarted him by translating it into such terms as *mind*, *mental functioning*, and *the mental apparatus*. This translation bias was apparently due to a wish to put psychoanalysis on a firm "scientific" footing in the English-speaking world and to eliminate the modern spiritual and religious overtones that the word *soul* has accumulated (Bettelheim 1983).

Webster's Third New International Dictionary defines soul as, "the immaterial essence or substance, animating principle or actuating cause of life or of the individual. . . . a person's total self in its living unity and wholeness. . . . a seat of real life, vitality or action: PERSONALITY, PSYCHE."

analysis had and continues to have medical applications. But one of Freud's deepest worries was that psychoanalysis would be narrowed from its proper place at the head of social sciences to a place in medical technology (Freud 1926). The problem is not simply that even sophisticated medicine has given up the medical model, but rather that medically oriented thinking leads people to consider themselves sick, perverted, arrested, not normal, and so forth. It leads analysts to believe that their job is to cure the illness, alleviate the symptom, resolve the arrested development, and lead the patient toward so-called normal, symptom-free, mature human life. At best, healing modes of thought, which may be useful for many purposes, tend to detract from the possibility of noticing aspects of the human condition that are better thought of in different ways. True, patient and doctor can set up such a limiting collusion in words and actions. True, each may take comfort in the role assignments for his or her own private reasons. But the doctor–patient model immediately introduces a series of generally unwarranted assumptions, values, and connotations that are bound to exert a determining influence on the collaborative work. To believe otherwise is like the self-deception involved in believing that we are sexually liberated while still insisting that sexist language is more comfortable, more traditional, or more convenient to read and write! Uncomfortable with *doctor–patient*, writers and practitioners have tried using *analyst–analysand* and *therapist/counselor–client*. But despite advantages and disadvantages, these role designations continue to highlight the social structure in which the analytic process is conducted, rather than the functions performed in the relationship by the respective participants. The obvious designation of the one whose task it is to express him- or herself, through speech as much as possible, as *speaker*, and the designation of the other, whose task is to receive, to listen in all manner of ways, as *listener*, solves a multitude of problems. Medical overtone is banished at the outset by the functional rather than social role designations of speaker–listener. Every effort has been made throughout this text to eliminate all other assumptions of medical science in this essentially most human of all disciplines. I believe the results will be self-evidently pleasing as soon as the eye and ear become accustomed to the new look and sound. Furthermore, a greater freedom of thought and idea immediately becomes possible when it is no longer necessary to speak of symptoms, pathologies, and cures. The test will be in the increased freedom and latitude of the texts themselves— whether written, spoken, listened to, or analyzed.

Much has been said about consciousness raising in modern life. We are aware of how difficult it is to be mindful of newly emphasized aspects of human experience when we speak and think in long overconditioned patterns. Furthermore, we have become aware that speech creates consciousness. In order to elevate our awareness of many nuances of human life, we must begin thinking as well as speaking in new ways. As an example we might consider the global Beyond War movement. This grassroots movement of people everywhere has as its origin a global fear of annihilation by nuclear holocaust. The thinking is simple. The proliferation of nuclear armaments is shocking beyond the average person's wildest imagination. We are terrified of the many kinds of accidents that could occur that would result in the destruction of the earth and the human race. Beyond War holds that humans have always believed that disagreements can and should be solved through acts of threat and violence. Our history attests loudly and clearly to that belief. We must change our way of thinking, our consciousness, about how to handle conflicts. We must begin finding ways to alter our basic thought patterns so that resolution of conflict by violence is not only untenable but unthinkable. If we fail as a species to raise our consciousness to new ways of resolving differences, we surely face total destruction. The reasoning is clear. The goal is imperative. The path is not so easy to devise.

But putting the matter off is a luxury we cannot afford. Similarly, it should become increasingly evident in this book that the new level of thought currently being achieved in psychoanalysis is dependent on raising our consciousness from its original focus on healing to a higher, more abstract, and more encompassing goal of understanding the human soul through a study of relatedness representations and possibilities.

From Scientific Objectivity to Systematic Subjectivity

From time immemorial our general approach to gaining knowledge has been to define things and relationships between those things. As mentioned earlier, perhaps the greatest myth of Western civilization is the spectator view of knowledge—the notion that it is possible to stand aside from our perceptual and conceptual tools and see what is really out there. This objective view of the world pictures things as if from an all-seeing eye and has demonstrated its utility over the ages. Classical physics of the eighteenth and nineteenth centuries developed a language and conceptual system based on this view, and most other disciplines followed suit. Freud hoped to formulate psychoanalytic explanatory concepts after the Newtonian model of science and so couched its terms of study as things inside of human beings. Relationships between these things were conceptualized as dynamic processes to be defined and studied until the laws governing psyche could be formulated within a general science framework. The fact that no one had ever directly observed such things as the unconscious, the ego, the ego defenses, the instincts, and their fusions and defusions did not greatly bother anyone because no one had ever seen gravity or atoms either. But they were all believed to exist.

At the turn of this century there was great optimism that with the advent of technological advances, it would only be a matter of time before the great truths of the clockwork universe would be laid bare before our very eyes. But the history of chemistry and physics has not taken the anticipated course. Einstein's 1905 paper opening relativity theory was followed in 1925 with the shocking predictions of Heisenberg's mathematical matrices that led to the research confirming the unbelievable workings of quantum mechanics.[3] This decade we are confronted with the even more mind-blowing research in areas designated *chaos* and *turbulence*. All of these shifts in thought have entirely imploded previous thought modes. Psychoanalysis is the last of the structured scientific disciplines to begin assimilating the new world views and the research approaches that accompany them. Bridgman's 1927 invention of the operational definition and Heisenberg's declaration that we shall no longer make nonsense statements about things and relationships that we cannot directly observe (Heisenberg 1958), have set the pace for all responsible subsequent studies. It is clear by now that we do not know what is involved in a quantum leap. We can only state a probability that certain events will be observed, but we have no way of ever saying what happened. It is equally clear that determinism, conceived as simple cause-and-effect sequences, is not a viable way to consider the infinitely complex workings of the universe now revealing themselves to us. In a thousand ways, the philosophical, scientific, and epistemological foundations of psychoanalytic conceptualizing have been totally eroded in the course of time since Freud first devised them. Our painstakingly collected observations must now be reconceptualized wholesale—a paradigm shift of major proportions is imperative. But what sort of shift? If we are to keep our thinking in sync with contemporary epistemology and science, several directions are clear.

---

[3]Heisenberg's well-known visit to Helgoland to obtain relief from his hay fever in July 1925 gave him the opportunity in a day and a night to create the equations for quantum mechanics. The story is recounted in Pagels (1982).

1. Whatever theoretical definitions we do develop must be based on operations that produce results that can be observed and repeated.
2. All concepts and relations must concern directly observable events. That which is not observable must be clearly labeled as speculative, fanciful, or idiosyncratic.
3. Theoretical concepts must not only concern observables that can be tested, but they must also be falsifiable in order to be accepted.[4]
4. We must stop speaking about things happening that cannot be directly observed or disproved. This stipulation demands that our conceptual system in psychoanalysis be completely overhauled.
5. We shall no longer assume that there is any observer-free knowledge or reality that we are free to speak of. All human knowledge rests on perception and cognition so that, as has been demonstrated many times in science, we tend to see what we are looking for.

For any part of psychoanalysis that seeks to be scientific, these criteria are stringent but requisite. In the face of these requirements many analysts today are maintaining that psychoanalysis is not, nor was it ever, a science, because these standards are impossible to apply to our work. Furthermore, a scientific concept defines general features and universal relationships that can be averaged across individual variations. To the contrary, psychoanalysis by its very nature seeks to discover all that is unique and specific about each human being. We are left with the possibility that some general notions about psyche and her operation are likely to be made in such a way as to meet the stringent scientific criteria. But the bulk of our thinking and

---

[4]K. R. Popper, an Austrian-born philosopher, has taught us to insist that our notions be falsifiable. The story of the development of his ideas is recounted in Pagels (1982).

work is concerned with the unique event—with an individual human and the specific influences operating in his or her subjective life. This being the case, there are many who maintain that we need to conceive of our discipline along the lines of textual criticism, semiotics, or linguistics. There are also the general philosophical and epistemological concerns put forward by Ryle (1949) and Wittgenstein (1953) about the impossibility of considering mind as a thing and the impossibility of being able to see or know anything apart from the language games that comprise its definitions and operations. (For a detailed consideration of these general philosophical and epistemological issues refer to Hedges [1983, pp. 29–48]).

Numerous solutions have been put forth that point in the direction of considering our discipline as a systematic study of human subjectivity. But even so, in order to remain within the broader frameworks of human thought, we had best adhere to the basics of the contemporary scientific approach. Beyond that we have to make new rules, perhaps benefiting from other disciplines that have faced these difficulties before us.

Schafer, in his landmark book, *A New Language for Psychoanalysis* (1976), and in his follow-up writings, analyzes the central untenable complications we have gotten into as a result of uncritical usage of language. From time immemorial human-kind has been filled with angels and devils influencing us, and our language habits reflect that history. Furthermore, psychoanalytic language preserves the nostalgic flavor of nineteenth-century thought, when the world was a simpler and safer place to live, when the universe still ran like a giant clock set running by the hands of God. But our conceptual system leaves us currently in an untenable position, in danger of speaking erudite nonsense. Those who theorize about mind have grouped themselves almost into warring religious camps, each from its own dogmatic system arguing how many angels can dance on the head of a pin and how we can best help them do it. Schafer's solution is to move toward an action language in which all of our key concepts are embedded in a language of what we do (verbs) and how we do it (adverbs). This is certainly an approach fitting a postrelativistic universe and one that could exist within a framework of stringent contemporary scientific standards or one governed by textual analyses.

From a different standpoint Robert Stolorow, Bernard Brandchaft, and George Atwood (see Stolorow et al. 1987) review the existential and hermeneutic literature to find viable ways of speaking and thinking about clinical work that liberate us from thing language. Following the general tenets of existential philosophy and Kohut's (1971, 1985) self psychological approach, Stolorow and co-authors Brandchaft and Atwood address the relationship dyad in terms of the intersubjective field. Their approach studies the way each person's subjectivity is necessarily influenced at all times by the other's subjective internal world. This studied and systematic approach avoids the pitfalls of so-called individual psychology, which tends to fill the person with invisible features, creatures, and happenings. Instead, the observable and representable ebb and flow of the interpersonal exchange becomes the field for study. As an example of a carefully worked out system for studying interpersonal observables operationally and falsifiably, work on the intersubjective field represents a cutting edge of psychoanalytic thought.

From Historical Truth to Narrative Truth

Spence (1982) reminds us that the greatest truths of human life have always been embedded in stories rich with image, symbol, and myth. Physicists never tire of quoting the ancients and world folk wisdom as precedents for new lines of thought. In Spence's remarkable book, *Historical Truth and Narrative Truth* (1982), he asks why we ever believed that it was possible to unearth the historical truth of our early lives in the first place.

When we examine things carefully, we find that we are forever telling stories about ourselves that fit into new relationship contexts. Depending on what we are seeking to express in a certain relationship, we create a version of some aspect of our lives so as to be comprehended. We speak for and to our listener, and the way we weave the web of our narrative is determined by (1) our many and varied purposes, (2) the supposed effects of our expressions, and (3) the assumptions regarding the way the listener is likely to receive our utterances (including transference and countertransference). Both Schafer and Spence focus considerable attention on the ways in which we consciously and unconsciously construct narrations for a sensible, seamless fit. We do this even when we are quite uncertain, and even when we know that gaps in our version are being deliberately glossed over in the interest of some assumption or purpose in narrating or relating. They make a strong case for viewing analytic work as a series of narrations that arise in a specific relationship at a certain time. Our narrations may well be scrutinized from the standpoint of the many profound truths about human relatedness, and therefore psyche, that they contain. To merely look to uncover discrete aspects and events of the past without appreciating the narrational and relational aspects of the telling is at best naive.

Spence examines some of the functions of speech, especially metaphor. In *The Freudian Metaphor* (1987) he follows Lakoff and Johnson's (1980) penetrating study of how human life is governed by the metaphoric necessities of time, space, movement, culture, and language. Spence scrutinizes the psychoanalytic enterprise for its guiding metaphors with fascinating results. He sees psychoanalysis as a *journey* into the *under* world of the unconscious. Unacceptable thoughts are put *down* there, *deeply* repressed. Interpretation gives us *insight*, vision into the *inner* nature of our souls, as if they had an inside and an outside, and so forth. Parallel to Schafer's introducing an action language as a direction away from psychoanalytic naïveté, Spence suggests a case study approach similar to the way Llewellyn (1989) holds that case law is studied as a means of introducing a professional language with the properties of constancy of meaning across individual variations. That is, specimen cases could be used to introduce terms that would develop a certain clarity from the context. Subsequent cases and theory could then be discussed in the terminology developed in the specimen cases. Technical language could then be safeguarded against the introduction of meanings not explicit or implicit in a set of previous case instances without the additional presentation of definitions with clarifying case study observations. The case study method of language formation indeed has much to offer in terms of eliminating a priori assumptions and building a set of examples by which to judge and speak about our work.

The proposals of Schafer and Spence are major undertakings aimed toward raising our general consciousness by forcing us to clarify our meanings. Both of these brilliant approaches have been met with a barrage of conservative, nostalgic counterarguments, basically to the effect that developing a new language system is tedious, time consuming, and uninteresting next to our old, Victorian, and more fanciful way of thinking about cases. Many seem to prefer good fiction and disguised speculation to the development of precise and clarifying communication. Such counterarguments can only spring from intellectual laziness, a lack of wish to develop new consciousness, and a refusal to open one's eyes and ears to the march into the twenty-first century.

Carl Jung pointed to the crucial importance of the cultural and the archetypal in considering the formation of psychoanalytic narrations. Jacques Lacan and the Freudian school of psychoanalysis in France, since Lacan's Rome Report in 1953, have been studying intensely the role and function of speech and language in human discourse (Lacan 1977). The Lacanian emphasis is that language and a speaking horde precede our individual existences. When we accede to culturally formed human life as individuals, we are taken in by the determining power of language. Lacan defends the thesis that the human unconscious is structured like a language for these and other reasons. Lacanian-styled psychoanalysts spend considerable time studying received wisdom embedded in signifiers and signifying chains for an understanding of elusive psyche.[5]

All of these very different ways of thinking within psychoanalysis have in common the fact that they search the current narration and narrational interaction for an understanding of how psyche manifests herself in psychoanalytic discourse and what the relation of the human soul is to the structuring effects of language, relationships, and culture.

From Relativity to Quantum Realities

Einstein's specific and general theory of relativity were able to encompass the findings of classical physicists in a new network of thought. But Niels Bohr and the group of researchers in Copenhagen moved physics considerably beyond relativity. Heisenberg's mathematics, which pointed toward the experimentation confirming the unbelievable quantum world, no longer leave room for us to consider the makeup of the universe as certain or even as finally and completely knowable. Heisenberg's (1958) widely acclaimed uncertainty principle states, among other things, that we do not and cannot know what realities are doing when we are not observing them. All we can do is make probabilistic statements about how things are likely to appear when we do look. Stunning experiments demonstrate again and again that our naive reality view of the world simply isn't the way things are.

Pagels (1982) describes the frustration that he and other

---

[5]Perhaps the most reliable sources regarding the Lacanian way of viewing things have been written or edited by Schneiderman (1980, 1983, 1988).

quantum physicists experience when trying to picture what quantum realities might be like. A visual convention emerges as an attempt at understanding the implications of the mathematics or the experiments. But the minute a picture appears, the essence of the quantum finding itself is lost. Pagels calls to mind the famous Piaget experiment with young children in which different sized and shaped bottles are filled to the same level with water. When questioned if the bottles contain the same or different amounts the younger children reply, "The same." Only by ages 5 and 6 is the relation between size and volume understood. Do we, like the younger children, simply not have the requisite conceptual understanding to grasp the relations of the quantum world? Or, Pagels asks, like our dogs who live and participate in human realities but do not have the mental capacity to comprehend them, are we forever limited in how much of the universe we are equipped to understand?

As analysts, are we not in a more humbled but advantageous position when we acknowledge that the definitive search for psyche's laws is an ultimately uncertain endeavor? Can we not learn our lesson from the physicists and realize that ultimate certainty is, in principle, not possible, given the necessity of receiving sensory impressions from a universe that is infinitely weird and slippery to the touch, and the necessarily participatory quality of our observational stance?

Our course clearly must be (1) to set as our goals various forms of consciousness-raising endeavors, (2) to study human subjectivity in systematic ways, (3) to focus on narrational forms of truth that are observable, and (4) to make no assumptions about the nature of psychic reality that a physicist would not make about physical realities.

From Mythical Beasts to Listening Perspectives

All human cultures throughout time have sported their mythical beasts. Whether they soar high in the skies, haunt the dark underworld, or inhabit secret and hidden realms of the earth, beasts of all sizes and descriptions have filled the imagination of humankind. When we take a good look at these beasts and the myriad of myths that accompany them, their function in human culture becomes clear. The mythic images serve as abstractions onto which vaguely understood human concerns and issues are projected. A beast is likely to be the repository of a set of human issues, and the myths surrounding it serve to elaborate those concerns in the form of mental and physical characteristics, fascinating activities and adventures, and some sense of ultimate fate.

Think for a moment about our favorite Western mythical beast, the unicorn, who reigned in our collective imagination for centuries. Pictures typically show the unicorn in relation to the virgin and to masculine virility. The central and most common visual motif is the demure virgin, elegantly clad and peacefully seated inside a small white picket fence enclosure. Our hero, the gentle-spirited white unicorn, grazes nearby or is at rest just outside the enclosure, perhaps with his horn on the verge of crossing the barrier. He exists peacefully somewhere between protecting her space and penetrating into it. In the background are the lively and jovial mounted huntsmen with their trusty dogs held at bay by the unicorn's vigil over maidenhood. Other versions variously depict the deception of a virgin by the unicorn or the capture of the unicorn by a deceitful virgin. Can there be serious doubt that the unicorn mythologies have served to describe and structure the complex relations between men and women over the centuries? Or that unicorn motifs depict the conflict of interests between the will of God, the lust of men, and the desires of women? Like all mythical beasts, the unicorn allows for human truths to be considered and reconsidered. A real beast, only too well known in its actual habits, could not possibly illustrate these truths so well.

Likewise, in psychoanalysis it has seemed wise and relevant to create a series of mythical beasts to aid in the beginnings of a new area of study. At first we had the hysteric in all of her fluttering frigidity. Then the obsessional in all of his meticulous and emotionless perfection, his rituals and perpetual doubting, and his unending cleanliness in thought and deed. Then the asthenic, the phobic, the anal character, the masochistic body type, the schizophrenic, the narcissist, and now the borderline psychotic. *DSM-III* is a veritable Noah's Ark of mythical beasts. The heavy tome organizes mental pathologies under various descriptive rubrics not unlike those found in a botanical garden or zoo. The problem for the diagnostician is to determine if the person before him or her is an actual hysteric or really more of a borderline. Well, perhaps we see here the eyes of an eagle, the talons of a hawk, the scales of a dragon, and the small tufts around the ears that shoot poisonous quills to quiet enemies. This spoof is not meant to dishonor the many years of painstaking scholarship and observation that have helped our field grow in understanding human potentials. It is intended to show that the purpose of such classification is to further our thinking about the varieties of human living and relatedness possibilities. As a compendium, *DSM-III* organizes what is probably the best thinking on the subject of categorizing people ever put together. Its pages are also filled with the politics, legalities, and economics of American psychiatric practice that have steadily and almost imperceptibly permeated the beasts' descriptions. As a manual to catalog observations and practice it excels, but its truth value must be compared to the unicorn. It is another important cultural construction that has served to receive and organize projections of human issues and concerns. The power of mythical beast thinking is readily appreciated when we realize that no aspect of traditional psychoanalysis is far from its influence. Theory and practice are governed by first determining what kind of beast the person is, and then following a set of prescriptions for how the analysis should be conducted (hidden morality). Or perhaps more destructive, guideposts are used to determine whether a person is untreatable by psycho-

logical means or can only benefit from supportive psychotherapy.

In a clockwork universe made of God-given realities that it
is our duty to discover, ferreting out witches and rousting
mythical beasts out of hiding are honorable activities that are
supported by the cultural atmosphere. But in a postquantum
participatory universe, in which we dare not speak of that which
is unobservable, trying to say exactly what an electron is doing,
or concluding what it does when we are not watching it, is sheer
folly. But the cry goes up, "But there really are unicorns! We
have seen them with our own eyes! We have ten diagnostic
criteria that we apply to many who look more or less like
unicorns, but occasionally a true one appears and we all rejoice
at knowing that they really do exist!" This is all beside the point.
Any abstracting that aids thought consists of a series of compromises between individual instances. Of course there will be
instances that are fairly true to the stereotype. Neither the
abstracting process nor the potential use of abstractions is at
question. Rather, the consciousness raising advocated here
invites, nay demands, revising the ways in which we consider
and interact in human relationships. The traditional way was
based on a Newtonian motif of objectively defined entities
interacting before an all-seeing eye; it surely has its advantages.
But if we aspire to be alive to twenty-first-century thought, our
modes of considering human relatedness must shift to accommodate the emerging state of human awareness. Defining,
locating, and treating mythical beasts are not where it's at.

Contemporary study techniques demand that we begin with
an understanding that the particular ways we choose to look at
the universe determine what we see. If we believe in an
omniscient all-seeing eye and have faith in the finite certainties
of a divinely created clockwork universe, we will look for
mythical beasts, carefully categorize them according to characteristics and dangers, and then seek to develop ways of reforming
their activities. And, sure enough, we find them lurking

everywhere, just waiting to be cured! But if we acknowledge that we live in a participatory universe that is infinitely complex, we will begin our study by noting where we choose to stand and what tools for observation and thought we have at our disposal. In our systematic study we will not stray from the operational position because we realize that, the curves of space-time being what they are, we will surely lose our bearings. Our concepts will not be elaborated around mystical particles whose activities we cannot know so that we would only be creating "just-so stories." Rather, we will begin with sensible speech about what we can observe when we take certain defined positions. We will also be aware that where we choose to stand is arbitrary, and therefore we will attempt some rationale for why we choose to stand where we do.

As analysts we then begin our activity of listening—with more than our actual ears. We listen to how people speak and engage us. We listen to the utterances, activities, and actions they lay before us. We study how activities are performed and speeches are given. In raising our consciousness to new levels of awareness, we focus on what is actually present in the room between us, here and now. The stories people tell us, the affects they display, and the responsiveness we find in ourselves are all beginning ingredients to the ongoing engagement in which we participate, with no one sick and no one to cure, with no mythical beasts to bring out of hiding, with no angels or demons whose activities must be intuited, and no reliable clockwork dynamics to lend credibility to our work.

We will begin systematically organizing our subjective worlds in such a way that we can be as fully emotionally present as possible, so as to observe and consider exactly what is happening from moment to moment. For convenience in mapping and remembering our sensory impressions and thoughts, and then later for discussing our work with professional colleagues, we will begin defining a series of listening perspectives from which to observe and interact with the people who come to our consulting rooms. These same listening perspectives, by the very ways in which we define them, will guide us toward being as responsive as possible to the utterances and engagements offered us for understanding the varieties of human relatedness potential. We will make subjective use of all that we have learned about human life, from whatever sources, and we will be constantly aware of how much we ourselves bring to the situation.

Our basic assumption about the human condition is that in the course of growing up, through exposure to various relationships, psyche becomes progressively embedded in a series of constricting transformations. The listening task is to discern from the actual facts of the mutual engagement, as Freud first did in the specimen case (*Anna O.*) of psychoanalysis, exactly how psyche can be observed to operate in this dyad here and now. Time has shown that listening, like observing in physics, is not a passive, static activity. We end up interacting in a variety of ways as we investigate relatedness styles, modes, and patterns. As we are engaged for the purpose of investigating psyche's imprisonment, what kinds of responsiveness from us will serve to maximize this special opportunity for mutual study?

From Frame Technique to Variable Responsiveness

Determining what constitutes optimal responsiveness on the part of a psychoanalyst has been one of the stickiest and most hotly debated topics over the years.[6] Such considerations beg the question of what one takes our assumptions and purposes to be in psychoanalysis. Ekstein (1984) goes so far to say that we invent theories to justify what we intend to do in psychoanalysis. If so, then the analyst has already decided beforehand what

---

[6]H. Bacal (1983) is generally credited with the term *optimal responsiveness*, which he substituted for Kohut's *optimally failing empathy*.

position and what value systems to endorse and what effects to promote. Freud himself chose to destroy rather than publish a number of his papers on technique, presumably because he was unhappy with what he had been able to say about the kinds of responsiveness that optimally encourage the psychoanalytic process.

Traditional technique has evolved as a *frame*work deliber-ately constructed to bring the targeted neurotic symptom into focus for study. So-called frame technique is based on a medical model that views the illness as an objectively definable entity. There is a history to the illness that must be brought to light, and certain conditions are considered favorable for that purpose. The patient is instructed to say what comes to mind. The analyst is to provide private, nonintrusive, uninterrupted, emotionally neutral, constant, objective, nongratifying, nonseductive, and time-enclosed evenly hovering attention.

The psychoanalytic situation has been written about widely (Stone 1962, Langs 1982). Until recently, virtually all recom-mendations have centered around the traditional assumptions of the medically oriented paradigm designed for curing neurosis. After the inadequacies of this approach had become so glaring that they could no longer be ignored, a series of parameters were proposed as short-term measures to keep the treatment going until the need for the alteration of basic technique could be analyzed (Eissler 1953). It should be noted, however, that a few far-sighted analysts (Jung, Ferenczi, and Alexander, among them) intuitively grasped the severe limitations of application that Freud's classical technique necessarily introduced, and they began experimenting with variation of technique designed to analyze so-called preoedipal personality constellations. Gradu-ally, over time, as the scope of psychoanalytic studies evolved beyond the original paradigms, an array of alternative tech-niques was explored for treating "the more deeply disturbed."

In leaving behind medically styled diagnostic thinking and curative manipulations, the quest for objectively defined mythical beasts, and the belief in the attainability of historical truth, new criteria for "optimal responsiveness" must be developed. Frame technique has proven its virtues in listening to certain kinds of relatedness labeled "neurotic." Kohut has put forward another type of responsiveness, "self to selfobject resonance," for dealing with another set of relationship situations ("narcissistic tensions," which will be discussed later). A number of other writers and practitioners have been experimenting with diverse kinds of responsiveness geared to maximize understanding of yet other types of "preoedipal" or "preneurotic" relatedness situations. The assumptions guiding "variable responsiveness" as technical procedures in a listening situation have to do with our attempt to develop a series of listening perspectives for grasping different aspects of interpersonal relatedness. In order to consider relatedness styles other than those called neurotic, different perspectives with different modes of responsiveness are required.

Parallel to the listening perspectives for receiving information are necessarily a set of ideas about the kinds of engagements that might be anticipated, as well as notions of what kinds of interpersonal responsiveness might serve the listener best in his or her task of understanding how two are experiencing the relationship at any moment. The listening perspectives and their companion notions concerning optimal responsiveness are well defined but perhaps somewhat arbitrary thought positions from which to grasp certain kinds of human relatedness as they appear in analytic discourse.

Listening perspectives with variable responsiveness techniques make no a priori assumptions about the nature of the person in analysis or the unique story and interactions that will unfold. Nor do the listening perspectives make assumptions about the nature of limitations that a person might be experiencing or what he or she may do to gain greater flexibility in living. Rather, they are designed to help the listener maintain a consistent and coherent inner orientation. Listening perspectives function to establish a position of perennial uncertainty, of unknowing rather than making fixed (frame) assumptions that seek to establish a direction of certainty, of knowing. A compass does not guide a ship but orients the mind of the captain who, depending on changing conditions and varying intentions, will make decisions that lead to different destinations. Each member of a psychoanalytic couple has a private agenda for the enterprise. And each has broader, long-term goals. The listening perspective approach is designed to foster neither personal agendas nor any other personal goals per se, but rather to keep the couple oriented to the ongoing nature of the personal exchange that is in fact happening. At last, we have evolved a psychoanalytic approach to satisfy the demands of a postquantum universe. We have a compass orienting us to a broad map of the world of human relatedness potentials. Two set out on a journey together that evolves as a series of glimpses of interesting and curious happenings. They come to weave an unfolding story of their adventures and what they have made note of and called into question while they were together.

But like the compass, the listening perspectives did not simply float in out of the blue. Orientation can be accomplished in many ways. Before the compass, navigators either traveled treacherously close to shore, using visual means by day, or ventured out further when navigation by means of the stars was understood. On dark days or nights voyaging was dangerous. The various means for navigation were not completely arbitrary or based merely on human whim. There were reasons for choosing to orient in certain ways and not in others. Orientation depended upon some familiar configurations, some attractor—the shoreline, the moving celestial bodies, or magnetic north. What strange attractors might we discover in our orientation to elusive psyche? (Briggs and Peat 1989, Gleick 1987). A century of study has led to the emergence of a set of ideas that has made possible preliminary definitions of the listening perspectives in terms fit for a quantum age. We are now in a position to examine the historical considerations that gave rise to the listening perspectives of the relatedness paradigm. We will then explore the listening perspectives themselves. (The notion of listening perspectives as strange attractors will be developed in Chapter 6.)

PART II

SELF AND OTHER

5

The Relatedness Paradigm

THE EMERGENCE OF THE REPRESENTATIONAL WORLD

Freud's first paradigm for thinking about psyche appeared at the turn of the century and highlighted the workings of the dynamic unconscious, wherein slips of the tongue, dream symbolism, various hidden meanings in humor, and other aspects of relatedness were studied for their determining unconscious power. By 1923 Freud had changed emphasis in a paradigm shift that highlighted the importance of considering features of personally constructed and evolving internal structure of mental functions defined along the lines of shifting balances and ratios among instinct (id), moderation (ego), and inhibition (superego) of the forces of life and the inevitability of death.

The third paradigm, relatedness, begins with Hartmann's

conceptual distinction between Freud's concept of the ego, as agent or set of internalized and structuralized functions, and the self, as evolving and integrating subjective center of the personality (Hartmann 1950). Jacobson, in "The Self and the Object World" (1954) and in a 1964 follow-up book by the same title, declared that in working with more "deeply disturbed" or "functionally depressed" people than psychoanalysts usually treated, she did not find Freud's concepts of id, ego, and superego helpful.[1] Rather, she noted that the ways in which more deeply disturbed individuals represent themselves in relation to others provided more illumination for the analytic task. Jacobson credits Rappaport with pointing out that representation as a concept is not experiential but metapsychological (Jacobson 1964). To this understanding I would add that mental representations as a concept must be expanded to include not only those that appear as symbolized cognitions but also those that appear as enduring affect or mood states and those that appear as patterns of interactions and tensions. Thus, representation is expanded to include the verbal-symbolic mode characterized by the attainment of some constancy of oedipal integration and also the affective, interactive, and self-consolidation modes that characterize preoedipal integrations. The metapsychological concept of mental representation thus serves to point toward the various forms of interpersonal communications achieved at different developmental levels of self and other relatedness. Joseph Sandler, working at the Hampstead Clinic, reported in a 1960 study that a search of numerous protocols of child analysis revealed the surprising

---

[1]While Jacobson's landmark departure from Freudian structural theory has liberated psychoanalytic thinking for the elaboration of a new paradigm, it now appears that both previous paradigms need to be fully elaborated *within* the new framework. That is, the conscious, preconscious, and unconscious aspects of id, ego, and superego need to be studied for their differential implications at each of the four major developmental watersheds of self and other relatedness.

finding that child psychoanalysts do not use the concept superego in their work. In a follow-up study, Sandler and Rosenblatt (1962) spoke of self and object representations and the representational world.

These studies opened the way for a rich proliferation of ideas about how humans come to experience and represent themselves in relation to important others in their lives. The extreme usefulness of conceptualizing human interactions in terms of the determining power of self and other representations has been repeatedly demonstrated in the psychoanalytic litera- ture over the last four decades. Notable are the contributions of Margaret Mahler, Fred Pine, and Anni Bergman, in their study of the relationships between young children and their mothers (Mahler et al. 1975), Kohut's (1971) innovative work regarding the development and maintenance of the self, and Kernberg's (1975) creative explorations of the differentiations and integra- tions of self and other representations that can be observed in analytic therapy.

On the surface it might not sound as though self and object representations are a great discovery. After all, it is obvious that people have experiences that they would represent in some form of memory of the ways they experience themselves and others. However, it seems less likely to occur to us that mental organization itself could be fundamentally conceptualized ac- cording to various forms of representations that these experi- ences give rise to. But many ideas have a way of looking self-evident after the fact—of course the world isn't flat, of course the earth travels around the sun. How could anyone have ever believed otherwise? The philosopher Wittgenstein reminds us:

> The aspects of things that are most important for us are hidden because of their simplicity and familiarity. (One is unable to notice something—because it is always before one's eyes.) The real foundations of his inquiry do not strike a man at all. Unless *that* fact has at some time struck him. And this means: we fail to

be struck by what, once seen, is most striking and most powerful. [Wittgenstein 1953, I:129]

It takes a human infant very little time to realize that the key features of its environment to be studied and manipulated are human. Furthermore, infant researchers assure us that babies come into the world well equipped to begin the work at once (Stern 1985). And so it is that the central idea of contemporary psychoanalysis—self and other representations as organizers of psyche—is disarmingly simple to grasp. But learning to discern these representations and to find ways of mirroring them to the speaker for analytic understanding is yet another task with numerous issues and complexities.

LISTENING PERSPECTIVES DERIVED FROM SELF AND OTHER EXPERIENCE

Hedges (1983) surveyed and organized the ideas and findings from a century of psychoanalytic research on self and other representations into four major categories designed to be utilized as perspectives for listening in relatedness situations. But the practitioner must be careful when considering the listening perspectives approach to self and other representations. The listening perspectives approach can easily be misunderstood as simply another way of organizing a complex literature that seeks to define selves, others, and representations. But the liberating twist of the approach is not to be found simply in a comprehensive reorganization of ideas or a redefinition of things. A profound shift of mental organization on the part of the analytic listener is mandated. With the following preliminary pointers toward the listening perspectives, one should be able to begin to grasp the basic notions without being too concerned with the possible reality of such *things* as selves, others, and representations.

I. The Personality in Organization: The Search for Relatedness

This perspective for listening is based upon an appreciation of human intrauterine life and the earliest months after birth, periods during which an infant organizes perceptual, affective, and motor channels toward the human environment. The earliest learning experience of organizing channels for sustenance and intelligibility provides a foundation for the development of subsequent patterns of relatedness. Traditionally, persons overtly functioning primarily or periodically in mental states that resemble early developmental states have been referred to by such labels as psychotic, autistic, schizophrenic, manic-depressive, or paranoid-schizoid. But all humans have experienced this period of primary organization of psyche. All physically normal infants organize channels for reaching out and contacting the environment pre- and postnatally. Infants work to bring the environment to themselves by various means. All future somatic and psychic development depends on how this process goes and how the body-psychic modes developed here expand as well as constrict possibilities in ways specific to the infant, and to the possibilities offered it by the immediately available facilitating environment. Most psychoanalytic work sooner or later focuses on the primary relatedness modes that form the foundation of the person's basic physical organization and emotional life. Hedges terms this the *organizing period* and speaks of *organizing issues* that remain embedded in body structure and in personality. This listening perspective is designed to orient the listener to the ways in which organizing patterns (forms, modes) can be discerned and responded to. How people search for and find satisfying relatedness and how they learn to accept defeat and to expect a loss or breaking of human contact are the focus of study in this listening mode.

II.   Symbiosis and Separation: Mutually Dependent Relatedness

From the earliest beginnings of psyche, as channels are being organized, they form on the basis of response from the mother's body and personality. By the fourth month, we can see the "mommy and me" dance clearly, in mutual cueing behaviors established and visible to the observer. Mahler calls this *symbiosis*.[2] The internal states of the infant evolve according to the expectation of a sort of dance that the two learn to do together, where the response of each depends upon the response of the other. Peaking by the twelfth to eighteenth month, the symbiotic mutuality, merged responsiveness, or forms of symbiotic exchange, remain strong through the twenty-fourth to the thirtieth month. Character structure dates from this period as the constitutional and personality variables of the infant come into play with the environment. This creates the first sense of psychological familiarity and stability. Of course, the possible available dimensions for construction of the merged dual identity dance of the symbiosis must be built upon and are limited by the foundations of available connect and disconnect modes laid down in the physical and psychical patterns of the previous organizing period. The particular emotional and behavioral patterns established in this primary bonding relatedness follow us throughout our lives as we search for closeness, for intimacy, for security, for familiarity, and for love. If some people's search for love seems strange, perverse, or self-abusive, we can only assume that it replicates in some deep emotional way the primary bonding pattern as the infant and toddler experienced

---

[2]Stern, at a UCLA conference on infant research, reported that near the end of her life, Mahler was presented a vast array of research data on the behavior of newborns (first four months of life) and in light of the data withdrew her term *autism* to describe this early, very busy, and in no way autistic period of the neonate.

symbiotic exchanges with his or her caretaking environment. This listening perspective evolved for use with what is often referred to as borderline personality organization (Kernberg 1975), and is essentially a way of understanding various aspects of the preverbal interaction patterns that were established during the symbiotic and separating periods of human development. All well-developed people experience patterns or scenarios[3] related to basic emotional bonding or symbiotic experience that we search for endlessly in later relationships. These patterns become replicated in some form when any two people attempt to engage each other emotionally. The dance that forms can be studied in terms of an interaction, a drama, or a set of scenarios that unfold based on deeply entrenched ways each participant has established for experiencing and relating to another. This listening perspective seeks to bring under scrutiny the predominantly preverbal engagement patterns that mean attachment, bonding, and love, regardless of what individualized forms those patterns may take.

III. The Emergent Self: Unilaterally Dependent Relatedness

Mothers know altogether too well the point at which a child begins to develop his or her own mind—they call this period the "terrible twos." The bonding dance of union, merger, and collusive engagement ends with No!

Freud's 1925 paper, "Negation," establishes negation not only as the beginning of an individual's independent mental functioning, but also as the beginning of language and culture.

---

[3]Hedges (1983) defines *scenario* as a listening device for highlighting the interactive nature of the early bonding experience as it manifests itself in the replicating transference based on an analytic re-creation of relatedness forms, patterns, and modes of the symbiotic period.

The child begins to refuse the (m)other's ways and to experiment and insist on his or her own ways. After the child establishes some right to autonomy, he or she begins the development of what has been called by Kohut (1971) the "cohesive self." After establishing the right to a certain emotional separateness, the child reapproaches the mother on a new basis, this time for affirmation of who he or she is becoming. This consolidation of the sense of self runs from birth to death, Kohut says, but peaks in its emphasis in the third year of life, the subphase Mahler calls *rapprochement*.[4] The listening perspective for this process of ongoing consolidation of the self sense describes a "selfother tension" (Kohut's term is selfobject), or the need to experience the reassuring, confirming, or inspiring other as a part of one's sense of self. Kohut calls these mirroring, twinship, and idealizing transferences based on selfother tensions *narcissistic*. The other is recognized as being a separate center of initiative but is used as a cohesion-building function of the self. A tension motivates the person to seek out the selfother to achieve a sense of wholeness and cohesion.[5]

IV.   Self and Other Constancy: Independent Relatedness

Freud first intuited that it was during the third through seventh years that children faced and worked through the problems of independent psychic life. Borrowing the mythic themes of Sophocles' *Oedipus Rex* and Shakespeare's *Hamlet*,

---

[4]At the 1979 UCLA Self Psychology Conference, Kohut was asked at which of Mahler's phases or subphases would he place the development of the cohesive self. He answered without hesitation, the "rapprochement."

[5]As Kohut was evolving his notions of the other being used to confirm the self, Winnicott was working on a similar concept, that is, "the use of an object" as distinct from and arising later out of "object relating." See Winnicott's "The Use of an Object and Relating through Identifications" 1960a.

Freud discovered in his own self-analysis the power of emotional triangulation. It is one thing to search for nurturance and intelligibility in the world (organizing level). It is yet another thing to establish a dyadic reliability (symbiotic level). It is still another thing to look to the other for consolidation of a sense of self (selfother period). But the most complicated aspects of human life develop when a full emotional awareness of third parties, of contingent emotional relationships, is integrated into psychic functioning. That is, the moment of the oedipal triangulation experience relies on the child's growing realization that each relationship exists within a broader set of contingencies determined by the social order itself. Symbolically and historically the third party is represented as father or The Fathers. But in fact, the third party begins with language and cultural awareness—that which comes between mommy and me—that intervenes and takes us into the broader human community. The presence of the third party is the factor that elevates human life to the level of symbolic understanding, that gives us an outside perspective on every dyadic relationship we try to establish, and that somehow robs us of exclusive ownership of the one we wish to love. The researches a child conducts and the conclusions he or she draws about how triangles work in relationships form a strong emotional web that Freud first understood and referred to as the Oedipus complex. The assumptions developed during this period tend to govern subsequent relationships to such an extent that Freud labeled them "neurotic." The Freudian listening perspective operates on an entirely different plane (the symbolic) than the three that precede it.

DOING WITHOUT OBJECTIVE REALITIES

We are asked by the listening perspective approach to imagine human development in a phase motif that features increasing complexity of relatedness without getting hung up on representations of self and others. We are also asked to imagine listening to the verbal and nonverbal representations of some-one with whom we have a listening relationship, from one or more of these vantage points, which provide understanding of their experience of themselves and us. It is difficult to believe how tricky, how subtle, and yet how crucial this small shift in consciousness is from seeing internal representations (as things) to listening to idiosyncratic and specific patterns or forms a person employs to represent personal experience. Exactly how to make the crucial transition from objectively listening to some-thing "out there" to designing an internal subjective frame for organizing what we hear is the central theme of this book. Most readers will still be saying, along with Piaget's young children, "It looks the same to me." But it's not at all the same. It's a new perceptual world that is difficult to enter. It's easy to say, "Oh yes, Hedges wants us to stop labeling mythical beasts, so we aren't supposed to say, 'This person is borderline' any more." It's slightly more difficult to avoid saying, "This person is stuck at a symbiotic or borderline level of development." Instead, we now have "This person who comes to my consulting room engages me in the most interesting, puzzling, and confounding ways. For the moment, I might tag these interactions I don't understand and find so disturbing as borderline or symbiotic issues. This impres-sion suggests to me that what is of importance here will not be found in the word story that the person is able to tell me, but rather in some emotional dance or mutual engagement the person attempts to get me involved in. Let's see now. What am I feeling? What do I notice I am thinking and doing as I try to be genuine and spontaneous with this person? Something's peculiar here. What is it? What's going on? How am I silently being instructed in my part? What do I seem to have to do in order not to rock the boat here, to get along smoothly with this person? What versions of heaven or hell does this person seem to imbue our relationship with? It seems as though whole parts of me are not free to be alive here. Why not? What's going on? I'm feeling coerced somehow. I'm feeling unnatural or forced in how I have to be with this person. I've got to start paying more attention to the nuances of the demand here, of how careful I am not to upset this person." And so forth. These are the kinds of thoughts that occur to one when beginning to focus on the interaction, the engagement, the exact qualities of the nonverbal play that is happening. Soon we will be asking, "What is desired of me here? First I tried one thing that wasn't too satisfactory. Then I waited and that was irritating. I feel like I'm in some sort of a trap, a scheme, a scenario in which I must play a definite part.[6] What is that part? What am I being shown by this way of relating? Am I to play the part of this person's mother, father, brother, sister, or uncle? Perhaps, but maybe now I see something more. Aha! This rascal is doing to me exactly what was done to him. No wonder I feel so disoriented and confused, so abused, so tricked, and controlled! This ticks me off now. How on earth will I ever get this one straight? And, oh my God, how will I ever show this one to him? The minute I try to claim any space for myself, for any idea I have, he either ignores me or becomes irritated, so I don't dare tell him I hate what he's doing to me. I feel reluctant to say that I feel uptight and inhibited and it seems he is doing it to me. I know he'll say, 'That's what I've been telling you is wrong with me, and now you're complaining too! I thought you were supposed to accept me no matter what! Where is your empathy?' Maybe I'm thinking too much about this. We'll just work on his girlfriend awhile; he always can say something about her. Or we can talk about his mother or his childhood. But no, this thing I'm stuck with—whoops—is my stomach churning? Am I angry at being so trapped? He's had frequent ulcer symptoms. No, I'm sure this is me. There is something familiar to it even though there is also

---

[6]For scenario as a listening device, see Hedges's (1983) chapter on "Borderline Treatment Scenarios," pp.165–196.

something uncanny or alien. And his whole demeanor now, there's something almost fraudulent in it. Like somehow when he gets in these moods he is acting or speaking for someone else. Who? His mother? It will take more time. Maybe I'll discuss this man at supervision group. I'm so confused. I know I didn't get everything worked through in my therapy as well as I might have. After all, I've had stomach upsets before that were not related to this person. Maybe he'll get bored and stop coming. What's that he just said? How insulting, how humiliating. Am I supposed to just sit here and be told that therapy isn't doing him any good? That I always say the same old unhelpful things! Lord knows I've tried. He just doesn't listen to me. If you'd just listen to me, you idiot, try to give me some importance, value me and our process, just a little. Maybe we could get along better. A borderline for sure. I should have set him up on once-a-week supportive work instead of three times intensive. He drives me nuts."

There are ways to contextualize and move out of such subjective dilemmas—in fact, different ways for each listening perspective. In this case, one might pay attention to all of the nuances of the countertransference ruminations, including personal free associations to aspects of one's own history and psyche, in hopes that they will point toward an understanding of the infantile position of the speaker. Discovering that the listener's dilemma is somehow central to the speaker's inner life will give the listener the courage to begin somehow showing the speaker how he or she is presenting the worst of the symbiotic experience of mother—showing how bad it was by doing it to the listener. The listener is being parented the way the speaker had been—all automatically, nonverbally, because that is the level of development in the speaker that is being represented at this time by making the listener feel in his or her subjective place. The mechanism, most simply stated, is that people tend to treat others in ways that they were once treated. People make others feel badly the way they once were made to feel badly. How to listen for such an outcome and exactly how to turn the tide of understanding with the speaker will be dealt with later. The main point of this little fantasy is to give permission to enter a listening mode—free of a search for things and mechanisms, a mode that focuses on listening to what is happening between the two, to what interaction pattern is being picked up, and to how countertransference responsiveness might be working in unexpectedly elegant ways. Someone, for instance, might insist that the relationship move in a certain direction. How does the listener become attuned to such nuances? And, of course, what does he or she do about them? These are central listener responsiveness issues. But first, a problem.

"Thing Language": How Do We Proceed Without It?

The philosopher Wittgenstein said:

The general form of propositions is: "This is how things are."— That is the kind of proposition that one repeats to oneself countless times. One thinks that one is tracing the outline of the thing's nature over and over again, and one is merely tracing round the frame through which we look at it. [Wittgenstein 1953, I:114]

Long before psychoanalysts, physicists began to suffer from needing to name strange and unnameable observations, from needing to form some kind of picture of what is happening in the quantum world, even when the falsifying or misleading nature of the picture could be acknowledged. In a quantum universe we now know that the minute we have a picture of a quantum event we have lost the essence of the finding itself. So too in analytic work. Our general diagnostic pictures about people that we are tempted to form tend to obscure the special, the unique, the idiosyncratic experience that might well emerge if we could refrain from ruining it with a priori notions.

Wittgenstein again:

> The evolution of the higher animals and of man, and the awakening of consciousness at a particular level. The picture is something like this: Though the ether is filled with vibrations the world is dark. But one day man opens his seeing eye, and there is light. What this language primarily describes is a picture, what is to be done with the picture, how it is to be used, is still obscure. Quite clearly, however, it must be explored if we want to understand the sense of what we are saying. But the picture seems to spare us this work: it already points to a particular use. This is how it takes us in. [Wittgenstein 1953, II, vii: 184]

But someone may protest that mental states and processes have a certain reality, mainly that they "happen in me."

> Certainly all these things happen in you—and now all I ask is to understand the expression we use—the picture is there. And I am not disputing its validity in any particular case. Only I also want to understand the application of the picture.
> The picture is there; and I do not dispute its correctness. But what is its application? Think of the picture of blindness as a darkness in the soul or in the head of the blind man. [Wittgenstein 1953, I:423, 424, p.126]

But there is something in the nature of our perceptual processes and conceptual systems that insists on defining and naming things—even when we have a sense that we are better off without limiting and confining ourselves to definitions we know to be misleading, general, or perhaps even false. Practicing physicists who are occupied with making things for profit have not the slightest concern that the names they give observations cannot possibly describe particles or waves but are fanciful labels for imaginary things that relate to procedures they have learned to manipulate in order to produce such things as microwave ovens, laser lights, surgical tools, video recorders, and compact discs. Is it so shocking to find that physicists deliberately falsify processes by insisting on premature labeling closures in the name of production? Is it so surprising to find that there are many irregularities and unknown interferences operating in video screens, computers, and even clock pendulums, but that these mysteries have not stopped physicists from developing reasonably reliable marketable products? Naming observations and events as though they were real and proceeding incautiously because things can be made to work out fairly well seems to be the name of the applied physics game these days. Theoretical physicists, however, are much more concerned with precision and professional integrity, and they are therefore reluctant to accept sloppy and false labels and notions. The applied physicists move forward with what can be made to work; never mind all that is impossible to know about and control. Is there a lesson for us? If so, it might be that as we move forward, it is important to be mindful of the irresolvable theoretical issues that face us and of the philosophical, epistemological, and psychological problems that remain for us to study and understand. But in the face of applied analytic work, how can we pick up and move forward? Some years ago, after Schafer (1980) had provided a set of definitive reasons why the "self" as a systematic and technical term must be abandoned in future theorizing, he added that, for the present, however, he was choosing to retain it because of its "inspirational" value until alternate ways of conceptualizing became available. At least there is an unmistakable ring of practicality as well as honesty in such a statement.

As we move forward the problem is that self and other representations, which are the central metapsychological concepts of the third paradigm of modern psychoanalysis, remain cast in thing language. Yet here I am still advocating that the listening perspectives be organized along an axis suggested by these mythical beasts! And after having made such a case for abandoning mythical beasts! But at this time it would seem that forms that represent self and other relatedness patterns are the best concepts our field has been able to conjure up, and they do work reasonably well when applied systematically. So do we proceed, along with Schafer, because we don't know what else to do and need inspiration to move forward? Or, like applied physicists, do we proceed incautiously because we don't care about inaccuracies? Since psychoanalysis involves human beings, perhaps we need to proceed more carefully and systematically.

So often in fields of study like analysis, debates rage in a quasi-religious manner over which theory or technique is correct, or best, or whatever. Benefiting from the experience of post-quantum science, I am presenting a different type of argument altogether in this book. I have suggested that the quest for certainty and objectivity be abandoned in favor of learning from uncertainties and subjectivity, that the search for cure be converted to a desire for ongoing consciousness raising, that the belief in and search for mythical beasts be suspended, that narrational and interactional relational activities be scrutinized for crucial meanings in place of the illusion of discovering historical truths about one's origins, and that a set of perspectives be defined that can orient us to the listening and responding task. Yet our human ways confine us to language games, structures, and conventions that force us to picture how things are. Such long-held habits of language and thought are not easily changed. But simply searching for inspirational usages and settling for sloppy thinking are not acceptable ways to proceed, given the paramount importance of our subject matter. In short, by now it is clear how we must revise our thinking habits to be more in keeping with the quantum age. But how do we go about the task when our very thought modes keep us chained to thinking and speaking about things and relations between them? Restated, when it is no longer tenable to conceptualize the human soul as a thing filled with other things, relationships, and processes, but our very language system requires that we speak in terms of things (nouns) that act or are acted upon (verbs), how do we shift our position to meet the quantum age? The solution proposed in this book is to begin thinking and speaking a "soft" or "transitional" thing language that will open new relatedness possibilities to us while not overconfining us to restrictive systems of thought. In order to shift our long-held habits, it is necessary to begin speaking of *forms* of relatedness, *patterns* of self and other engagements, and *modes* of human exchange. Forms, patterns, and modes of relatedness (nouns, "soft" things with personal, idiomatic, and idiosyncratic referents) will serve as deliberately created mythical beasts onto which we can project various aspects and movements of psyche as she makes fleeting appearances in human relatedness situations. As a transition between objectivity and subjectivity, between certainty and uncertainty, and between knowing and not knowing, human life can be provisionally conceptualized as a series of individualized relatedness forms, patterns, and modes that can be defined in order to help us grasp more fully and more dynamically our relation to the worlds around us. The listening perspectives approach, which stipulates a range or dimension of human relatedness possibilities, will serve as a compass in our search to ferret out features to be defined and in our endeavor to tell a story that contains an individual's personal adventure in life and analysis. Schafer (1976) suggests that we aim toward considering people as the only nouns in our sentences and what they do and the ways they do it as the verbs and adverbs. Until and unless such purity in thought and speech is achieved, personal forms, patterns, and modes of human relatedness can serve our purposes.

6

The Strange Attractors of Psychoanalysis

PRISONERS OF RELATEDNESS FORMS, PATTERNS, AND MODES

When we want to relate to another person we ask ourselves, "What is this person saying to me, or what is the meaning and nature of this engagement? And, given my desires and purposes for relating, how might I be optimally responsive?" Our language system implies an isomorphism between subject and object in each sentence we speak. That is, the "I" and the "you" in linguistic relating have equal status. The sentence "I want to know you" includes two equal people. Our social and legal doctrines also hold all persons as equal with equal rights and responsibilities. We make exception for persons under what we call legal age. Contemporary psychoanalysis challenges our general linguistic, social, and legal assumptions when entering the area of personal relatedness. We do not always speak or listen from a place of full individuated maturity and personal responsibility—certainly not when we engage in serious relating. If we note carefully for a few hours how we relate to those around us, we will see that much, if not most, of the time we are relating from a one up or a one down position of social, linguistic, or legal inequality. In fact, if we were to be honest and do a frequency count of the minutes during each day in which we engage another human being in a full on, completely differentiated and individuated, equal and mutual relationship, we would find either that they are very few or that we are very self-deceived! So long as the psychoanalytic situation is experienced as sick patient–well doctor or crippled child–mature parent, the relating remains unequal. Analysts might do better by considering themselves more as servants, mercenaries, or hired help—people paid to do the specialized task they are trained to do. The functional designations of speaker–listener have the advantage of placing analysts more in a position of social, linguistic, and legal equals. But perhaps it should be considered whether equality is what is desired in relationships, especially in light of the realization that so seldom do people work toward achieving it. Perhaps the question is, "With all the social, cultural, legal, and linguistic emphasis on equal relating, how is it that in daily relationships equal relating is so rare? Why do we say we are striving for equality and mutuality when our actions speak so loudly to the contrary?" In fact, we structure most of our lives according to extremely limited and constricting social-role expectations with an array of hierarchial implications. Are we afraid of fully differentiated and individuated living? Do we not know how to achieve a living and vibrant mutuality in our relationships? Are we victims of social expectations, habit, convention? Are we prisoners of some sort? If prisoners, then held captive by what? Psychoanalysis teaches that we are indeed prisoners of our own preferred unconscious relatedness modes and that it is we ourselves who hold the keys to our own captivity. It is we who insist on remaining victims of our own blindly held relating habits, and it is we alone who have the power to set ourselves free—free to live the promise that we have created and continue to subscribe to—that all humans are created free and equal. Freud's grand discovery is that it is none other than we ourselves who prevent the realization of our human hopes and dreams. Or, in the immortal words of Walt Kelly's Pogo, "We have met the enemy and he is us."

ASIDE: ON THE STRANGE ATTRACTORS OF PSYCHOANALYSIS

From my earliest studies of psychoanalysis, two realizations possessed me and continue to haunt my musings about our field. First, it is clear that the riches of Freud's genius have yet to be fully tapped by any stretch of the imagination. The face of twentieth-century thought has been profoundly impacted by Freudian conceptions. Yet the longer I study the twenty-four volumes of psychological writings he left us, the clearer it is that we do not yet know how to understand the rich potentials of the thought system he initiated. There undoubtedly will be many more "readings" of Freud as time unfolds. The infinite complexity of his inaugural ideas can only continue to expand.

The second realization that has always gone hand-in-hand with the first is that we must continuously revise and expand the ways in which we think about, understand, and formulate the Freudian insights. Like those of any of the great thinkers of our civilization, Freud's ideas could only be cast in terms, metaphors, and thought modes specific to the era and cultural climate in which he lived. However, living as we do in a time of unprecedented opportunity for communication and dialogue with outstanding thinkers of all persuasions throughout the world, and with unanticipated and unprecedented unfoldings of human understanding and knowledge, the elusive glimpses of

psyche that Freud afforded us must now be continuously subjected to reevaluation and reformulation in terms of the expo-
nentially expanding corpus of human wisdom, creativity, and
concept formation. But I believe that this living reassessment of
the gems of insight that psychoanalysts have slowly wrested from
their studies of individuals who have undergone psychoanalysis
during the last century must be conducted in the wider arena of
expanding human consciousness. This must be done without
losing, compromising, or sacrificing in any way the illumination
that Freud's genius has cast into the dark recesses of human
mental life, enabling us for instants to witness psyche in her
wispy if not ghostly and at times ghastly comings and goings.

My studies, dating from the mid-1960s, of the corpus of
psychoanalytic wisdom led to my own reformulations, which I
published in 1983. At that time I was able to appreciate the
necessity for reorganizing and reformulating psychoanalysis
along fresh lines pointed to by epistemological, philosophical,
and methodological considerations that have evolved subsequent to the notions of science and knowledge that Freud had to
work with at the turn of the century. I followed the lead of the
philosophers, notably Ryle, Wittgenstein, Sartre, and J. M.
Russell in the mammoth undertaking of reconceptualization that
I believe remains successful in pointing toward entirely new ways
of thinking about and living with Freud's psychoanalytic enterprise. By then I was able to speak of the third paradigm evolving
in psychoanalysis—relatedness—and to demonstrate how the
entire set of psychological ideas emerging regarding self and
other experiences were pointing us in a breathtaking new direction
with many fresh possibilities for expanding theory and practice.

What I had no way of knowing then was that thinkers in
many other fields were simultaneously attempting similar transformations of thought inherent in the histories of their disciplines, notably chemists, physicists, and mathematicians, but
also meteorologists, ethnologists, biologists, economists, and
many others, all discovering new ways to study strange phenom-

ena inherent in such things as global weather, diseases in generations and populations of animals, stock market trends, and above all, turbulences and chaotic, apparently random events wherever they occur. The new approaches to study arising from, related to, or reacting against quantum mechanics involve the definitions of phase space, fractals, recursion, the principle of universality, scaling effects, structure in chaos, and most fascinatingly, strange attractors. After assembling *Listening Perspectives*, I was relieved to turn my studies away from psychoanalysis for a while, and I began delving into a series of uncanny and unbelievable texts that had started to accumulate on the shelf by my bed. Gribbon's *In Search of Schrodinger's Cat* was the first of my mind-blowing adventures into quantum physics. These opened my eyes to the many ways in which others were solving similar epistemological, philosophical, and methodological dilemmas regarding the means they were devising to think about whatever realities there may be to observe in our vast universe. By reading about the adventures of other explorers, I could now begin to define more clearly and broadly just what I was up to and where my thinking was headed. The methodological revisions implicit in the title of my book, *Listening Perspectives in Psychotherapy*, registered my awareness of the necessarily participatory nature of all systematic investigation, whether one chooses to call it science or not. The paradigmatic shift I pointed toward was also done without benefit of Kuhn's (1962) magnificent treatise on paradigm shifts that I only came upon in my studies of the history and transformations of scientific thought. But what has tickled my fancy most in these cutting edge experimenters and writers is the multiplicity of findings by scholars from all fields now passing under the rubric of chaos or turbulence studies, all of which trace their origin back to the concept *strange attractor*.[1]

---

[1]The most readable reviews of these studies I have found to date are Briggs and Peat (1989) and Gleick (1987).

While it is clearly premature to begin recontextualizing psychoanalytic findings and theories within these incredibly encompassing canopies of expanding knowledge and methodology, it is never too soon to begin proffering speculations about the implications for psychoanalytic thought of humankind's expanding and ever-changing views of realities. I can only tantalize my readers at this point and perhaps encourage others to ferret out these exciting new ideas and begin relating them to our field.

Heisenberg's uncertainty principle, received from studies of the quantum world, is rich with implications regarding the way we believe we make our psychoanalytic observations and the ways in which we choose to speak about them. I am by no means the first psychoanalytic writer to begin to grasp the enormous implications of this fundamental discovery for our field (see Schwaber 1983). The findings of quantum studies have shockingly demonstrated that the ways our species has come to conceptualize the worlds around us cannot possibly be regarded as comprehensive, complete, or even correct in most regards. Furthermore, the very ways in which we have evolved as a species to notice and organize our perceptions and conceptions have been forever put into question by the quantum findings. But, as every quantum scholar is quick to point out, quantum studies only demonstrate how slippery realities are, that Einstein's space–time relativities are only the beginnings of our awareness of what realities are not, and that we do not yet possess any clear or readable picture of how things are or might be. And, more perturbing, it may even be that in principle, no coherent picture of the realities of the universe exists!

Feigenbaum, discoverer of the principle of universality that states that different systems behave indentically at the point of transition between orderly and turbulent, tells the story this way:

Something dramatic happened in the twenties. For no good reason physicists stumbled upon an essentially correct description of the world around them—because the theory of quantum mechanics *is* in some sense essentially correct. It tells you how you can take dirt and make computers from it. It's the way we've learned to manipulate our universe. It's the way chemicals are made and plastics and what not. One knows how to compute with it. It's an extravagantly good theory—except at some level it doesn't make good sense.

Some part of the imagery is missing. If you ask what the equations really mean and what is the description of the world according to this theory, it's not a description that entails your intuition of the world. You can't think of a particle moving as though it has a trajectory. You're not allowed to visualize it that way. If you start asking more and more subtle questions—what does this theory tell you the world looks like?—in the end it's so far out of your normal way of picturing things that you run into all sorts of conflicts. Now maybe that's the way the world really is. But you don't really know that there isn't another way of assembling all this information that doesn't demand so radical a departure from the way in which you intuit things.

There's a fundamental presumption in physics that the way you understand the world is that you keep isolating its ingredients until you understand the stuff that you think is truly fundamental. Then you presume that the other things you don't understand are details. The assumption is that there are a small number of principles that you can discern by looking at things in their pure state—this is the true analytic notion—and then somehow you put these together in more complicated ways when you want to solve more dirty problems. If you can.

In the end, to understand you have to change gears. You have to reassemble how you conceive of the important things that are going on. You could have tried to simulate a model fluid system on a computer. It's just beginning to be possible. But it would have been a waste of effort, because what *really* happens has nothing to do with a fluid or a particular equation. It's a general description of what happens in a large variety of systems when things work on themselves again and again. It requires a different way of thinking about the problem. . . .

One has to look for different ways. One has to look for scaling structures—how do big details relate to little details. You look at fluid disturbances, complicated structures in which the complexity has come about by a persistent process. . . . The process doesn't care where it is, and moreover, it doesn't care how long it's been going. The only things that can ever be universal, in a sense, are scaling things.

In a way, art is a theory about the way the world looks to human beings. It's abundantly obvious that one doesn't know the world around us in detail. What artists have accomplished is realizing that there's only a small amount of stuff that's important and then seeing what it was. . . .

I truly do want to know how to describe clouds. But to say there's a piece over here with that much density, and next to it a piece with this much density—to accumulate that much detailed information, I think is wrong. It's certainly not how a human being perceives those things, and it's not how an artist perceives them. Somewhere the business of writing down partial differential equations is not to have done the work on the problem.

Somehow the wondrous promise of the earth is that there are things beautiful in it, things wondrous and alluring, and by virtue of your trade you want to understand them. [Feigenbaum, quoted in Gleick 1987, pp. 184–187]

The reader familiar with recursions and universality will immediately understand how rich with implications these remarks from Feigenbaum are, but for present purposes we will confine our attention to his emphasis on the necessity of abandoning our familiar scientific methodology in favor of thought systems that have the potential of assembling information according to different, more complex principles than the search for data and laws will ever be capable of yielding.

The new science provisionally labeled "chaos" is multidisciplinary in nature and seeks the elucidation of orderliness in apparent chaos or randomness by searching for identical patterns that exist to describe complex, naturally occurring events simultaneously at all levels of scaling. Mandelbrot's (Briggs and Peat 1984, 1989, Gleick 1987) incredible mathematical set, which generates infinite complexities at all levels of magnification that are nearly but not quite identical, illustrates graphically the functions of recursions and fractals. All of these ideas are rich in implication for mental life, especially the nature of thought and consciousness. But of special importance to present speculations is the discovery and progressive elucidation of the phenomenon of the strange attractor.

The story of the strange attractor begins with Edward Lorenz, a meteorologist working with a small computer at the Massachusetts Institute of Technology, attempting to predict global weather patterns. The key to his discoveries was

> The average person, seeing that we can predict the tides pretty well a few months ahead would say, why can't we do the same thing with the atmosphere, it's just a different fluid system, the laws are about as complicated. But I realized that *any* physical system that behaved nonperiodically would be unpredictable. [Gleick 1987, p. 18]

The reason for this unpredictability became known as the beginning insight in the new field of chaos, the "butterfly effect," a principle stated only half jokingly as the notion that a butterfly stirring the air today in Peking can transform storm systems next month in New York. The facts behind such a shocking notion have to do with Lorenz's mathematical finding that "for small pieces of weather—and to a global forecaster, small can mean thunderstorms and blizzards—any prediction deteriorates rapidly. Errors and uncertainties multiply, cascading upward through a chain of turbulent features, from dust devils and squalls up to continent-sized eddies that only satellites can see" (Gleick 1987, p. 20). But Lorenz discovered a fine geometrical structure—order masquerading as randomness. He turned his attention to steady-state systems that almost repeated themselves but didn't. Weather is one such system. Interestingly enough, even such stable systems as the swinging of a pendulum, which appears so regular and steady-state, also proved not to be. His beginning three nonlinear equations described many a system. Nonlinear equations are nonsolvable and represent the features that people want to leave out when they want a good, simple understanding. For example, the equation that expresses friction in a hockey puck must account for varying amounts of friction, depending upon a series of other variables and how each variable behaves dependent on others. Lorenz's equations described convection in liquids, the movements that are visible when some cold cream is added to a hot cup of coffee or cigarette smoke rising breaks into swirls. The first strange attractor emerged from Lorenz's study of a water wheel, a small device like a Ferris wheel into which a steady stream of water was introduced so that each cup or car moved the wheel by the relative weight of water that cascaded into it. The stream of water could be varied in volume, causing the wheel to turn faster or slower, and each car also could be made to leak a stream of water at preset rates. One might think that the back and forth turning of the wheel would eventually reach some steady state but Lorenz demonstrated otherwise. He showed that the wheel would move in one direction until the weight in the cups forced a reversal, until the weight of the water forced another reversal, and so forth, according to an incredibly complex pattern that he could describe in his three nonlinear equations. When plotted in three-dimensional space, the action of the wheel produced a magical image resembling an owl's mask or butterfly's wings, which soon became the emblem for the Chaos movement. (See Figure 5–1.)

From Lorenz's first strange attractor, scientists adduced that many such strange attractors must exist and set about demonstrating an array of breathtaking designs that describe patterns inherent in all forms of chaos and turbulence previously consid-

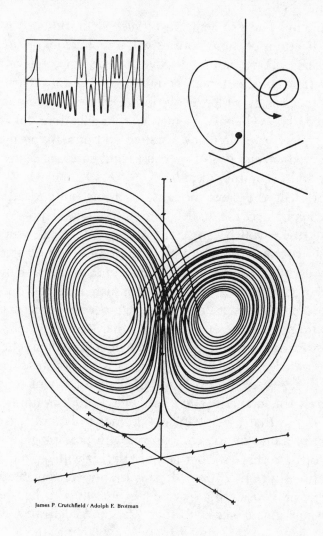

James P. Crutchfield / Adolph E. Brotman

FIGURE 5–1. The Lorenz Attractor. Because the system never exactly repeats itself, the trajectory never intersects itself. Instead, it loops around and around forever. Motion on the attractor is abstract, but it conveys the flavor of the motion of the real system. For example, the crossover from one wing of the attractor to the other corresponds to a reversal in the direction of the spin of the waterwheel or convecting fluid. From J. Gleick, *Chaos* (Penguin Books, 1987), p. 28. Reprinted by permission of Viking Penguin, a division of Penguin Books USA Inc.

ered random. The proliferation of such definitions continues. The applications of these notions will undoubtedly prove world revolutionary. For example, discovering the properties of turbulence in fluids of the human body not only will give new clues to the processes by which evolution of plants and animals has proceeded, but will have tremendous implications for understanding the entire circulatory system and unmasking many of the observed effects, if not the causes and cures, of many kinds of heart and respiratory disorders.

How will the new thought regarding strange attractors become applied to the understanding of mental phenomena? Certainly there will be another order of biological structuring that will reasonably represent an offshoot of whatever attractors become useful in describing animal consciousness. How will human consciousness be a reflection of such attractors operating at other scales? How do our thought processes represent emanations from recursive orderings on other scales? What will be the strange attractors that describe the operation of psyche? Will they be scaled-up extensions of animal consciousness or more complex because of the evolution of human thought tools?[2]

Surely the loud cries can already be heard, not unlike those that maintain that psychic events are not to be understood on the basis of a one-to-one comparison with physiological events and so forth. Perhaps so, but perhaps not. It will depend on the way such definitions evolve. It is certainly conceivable that a new way of considering psychic events is in the making. Feigenbaum encourages us to shift gears and begin new ways of thinking if we are to enter this new explanatory arena where methodologies and thought systems take entirely different forms.

Whether or not actual equations can be evolved to describe events of human consciousness, thought, or language, the

---

[2]The Soviet neuropsychologist, Vygotsky, believes human consciousness is distinctly different from animal consciousness because of our use of thought tools. See Vygotsky (1962, 1978).

strange attractor notion may yet have its usefulness at a metaphoric level, and it is to this possibility we can address ourselves now. For Freud, the strange attractors would have originally been the systems Unconscious, Preconscious, and Conscious. His later thinking would feature the Id, Ego, and Superego as strange attractors of human mentality. Thoughts, affects, and behavior would constellate along these patterns. In the third paradigm, the strange attractors might be the four levels of self and other integration implied in the listening perspectives approach. Should it prove possible to map in some way such strange attractors, what will they look like when visually displayed, and how might abstract movement through phase space be represented? One possibly unwelcome aspect of this entire line of thinking is that just when we have succeeded in liberating ourselves from one set of mythical beasts, the diagnostic categories, and the tripartite structural elements, are we now ready to discover new mythical beasts in the form of strange attractors? And, on a final note, as a psychoanalyst I find it interesting that the butterfly effect of Lorenz, a notion chosen half jokingly, later appears as the very image of his strange attractor, as though chosen through intuition. Even cosmologists have unconscious mental processes!

FORMS, PATTERNS, AND MODES OF HUMAN RELATEDNESS

Thinking of human relatedness in terms of culturally derived forms that become structured as emotional patterns and modes puts listeners hot on the trail of what those forms might be or how they might look as we encounter them in ourselves and in others. Listening to the speaker's verbalizations only captures one level of forms—the verbal-symbolic forms that can be most meaningfully understood as the triangular contingency forms that are embedded in the realm of the symbolic. But as listeners we also need to be prepared for resonating with selfother forms, interacting with symbiotic and separating forms, and contacting organizing forms. The listening perspective approach conceptualizes human relatedness as embedded idio-syncratically in an array of forms, patterns, and modes. This approach has the advantage of being able to guide our listening and responding in certain directions. Forms, patterns, and modes of relatedness as concepts serve as "soft" or "transitional" things that we can define and speak of as deliberately created mythical beasts, but that we can use to project human related-ness issues onto so they can be seen and listened to more fully.

The approach of listening for various forms, which have been derived from a study of child development, considers the array of expanding human realities to be constructions that are a function of the human capacity to perceive, organize, and integrate various stimuli through the medium of forms. Vibra-tions emanating from the environment are thought to be received as sensations, impressions, or shapes on the organism's receptor apparatus. They are centrally organized into forms, patterns, or modes according to genetically determined and/or socially generated probabilities and consequences. According to this way of thinking, sensory impressions thus become actively experienced, represented, or constructed as personal forms. The idea that humans have developed a highly sophisticated capa-bility for receiving and emitting forms from various experiencing or processing centers provides a fresh view of biological, psycho-logical, and cultural evolution.

According to this way of thinking, human forms of a wide variety are considered an integral part of all personal experience and mediate between private sensorimotor impressions (shapes) and more public consensual realities. The idea of human realities as essentially an interplay of environmentally deter-mined forms assumes that we possess a highly developed capacity for reception, storage, and transmission of basic information.

Further, the interplay in both genetics and culture is complex enough to require a series of alphabetic characters and codes for the passage, processing, and storage of information. Campbell, in his *Grammatical Man* (1982), demonstrates that humans display a remarkable capacity for many types of information reception, storage, and transmission. We are like highly sophisticated computer systems with extensive capacity for receipt, codification, storage, transformation, and transmission of many kinds or modes of patterns and forms (*information*).

The unique event in human history has been the development and utilization of our symbol- and myth-generating capacities. Through projection of private experience into shared forms, as well as active reverberation with creative symbolic and imaginary forms, humans through the ages have continued to create fresh realities that are as lawful and as powerful in their effects as are other environmental realities known through the *power of form* (Rose 1980).

TOWARD A RECOGNITION OF THE POWER OF FORM

What exactly do I mean when I speak of "form realities as human constructions"? In its most differentiated and sophisticated sense, "form" includes any and all human endeavors, creations, or products. A painting or a line of music or poetry is form. A dance step or game has form, pattern, rhythm, and expectation. Myths, fairy tales, parables, rules, and ritual represent various cultural forms. A Catholic mass is form, vestments are form, penitence is form. Lessons, vigils, styles, pilgrimages, duties, bullfights, baseball games, "looks," talk shows, and computer programs all take on or present distinctive patterns and forms. Feeding pigeons in the park, taking a stroll along the beach, having coffee in the morning, or savoring the smells and tastes of chicken soup are all common forms. Children learn forms in play and storybooks. "Ducks waddle and go 'quack, quack'"; "Lions roar and rule the forest"; "Rabbits are quiet, cute, and cuddly"; "Pigs go 'oink,' are fat, and eat all the time," are auditory forms that are paired with visual forms to captivate and delight a child's imagination. We are often amused when precocious children use their forms to imitate those in the adult world to which they are exposed. We see in vivo the acquisition of solid, kinesthetic forms.

Important forms are not solely of human origin. Basic forms exist in nature—the wind, surf, and stars. Earth, fire, and water take on various forms. Astrology has developed forms that link human emotion and destiny to the temporal patterns and forms in the heavens. Thus in the broadest sense, forms may be said to represent or be represented in all that we see, hear, smell, taste, feel, and think. A "blue mood," a "rapturous sunset," a "black day," or an experience "full of sunshine and light" all present affective forms. Meaningful narrations of personal experience are full of forms. Meaning and narration are forms; experiences have form. Actions and activities that comprise experience take on and arise from forms.

But here someone will ask, "What's the point of attempting to isolate a concept of form realities if all we perceive and do is referred to as form? If all human activity is said to emanate from, to represent, or to be mimicked or modeled upon structures, patterns, rhythms, expectations, rituals, or symbolic forms in the human environment, what clarifying views can the concept of form realities possibly offer?"

My thesis is that each person may be considered a complicated and elegant collection, collage, or amalgam of various forms. Personhood itself may be usefully thought of as no more and no less than a unique and intricately woven set of complex forms for getting along in the world of other people. The human personality may be thought of as evolving slowly from the moment of conception through a series of intelligible and changing patterns and forms. That psychoanalytic research points toward more or less distinct categories of human relatedness forms suggests that we may benefit from considering these types of forms as strange attractors, along much the same lines as mathematicians and chaos theorists have noted peculiar nonlinear configurations that they have chosen to define as strange attractors.

We learn from Freud that aspects of human experience that may appear unintelligible reflect shortcomings or limitations in our ability to notice and to *formulate* the intelligibility of the human personality. For example, Freud's notion of the "unconscious" is one of many attempts he made to bring intelligibility to human activity. The entire history of psychoanalytic thought may be considered a series of attempts to bring order out of apparent chaos, to create forms or patterns to be noticed and placed in specific contexts. The personal narrations and narrational interactions that develop in the course of psychoanalysis may be said to be the creation or construction of new *formulations* about oneself and about others, and our various formulations as constellating around four strange attractors. The listening perspectives approach seeks to define our own observational positions vis-à-vis these strange attractors of human relatedness forms.

FORMS IN ANALYSIS: THE PSYCHOANALYTIC STORYLINE

I have introduced the concept "form realities" in order to consider in a fresh way a long-standing and specific human enterprise. Freud's version of this enterprise is called psychoanalysis, but countless other versions have been reported throughout recorded history.

The storyline is basically that one troubled soul reports to another who assumes a socially defined role or form of an authoritarian oracle, a wizard, a witch doctor, a physician, a counselor, a father confessor, a psychotherapist, or an analyst. The seeker provides some type of narration or narrational interaction in an effort to describe a sense of subjective concern, disorientation, or distress. The person fulfilling the role of cultural oracle listens from a specific context handed down from ancestors and considered wisdom. The distress subsides or the concern diminishes as the private narration becomes satisfactorily recontextualized in terms of the acceptable and understandable forms provided by the culture. Personal experience and meanings become systematically recast within a broader framework of received wisdom.

New understandings obtained from this process of submitting the shakings of one's soul to a knowing oracle typically produce relief and gratitude. At times, of course, the contributions of the oracle are enigmatic, inadequate, corrupting, simplistic, or misguided, and new troubles emerge, disaster strikes, or better advice is sought. A "great soul" may find the wisdom of the ancients inadequate in light of new cultural circumstances, and find it compelling to transcend the current oracular contribution and to invent new wisdom. This may be considered genius, insight, creativity, reformation, invention, or revelation, or may be seen as open rebellion, treachery, or various forms of evil. History tends to glorify those perceived as contributors to the received traditions and wisdom. History stigmatizes as detractors or infidels those whose contributions threaten to undermine the traditions and their wisdom.

This particular glimpse of the story line, which provides the underpinning of psychoanalysis, follows one of Freud's main theses. Freud (1930) cast individual pursuits into conflict with collective possibilities in such a way as to predict permanent unrest. Responding to this unrest as it appears in individual lives is the task of psychoanalysis. The traditional format where there is a troubled and unknowing seeker and an unchallengeable "one who knows," has suited authoritarian-based cultures of the past. The speaker–listener designations of participants in contemporary psychoanalysis captures more of the consciousness-raising democratic spirit of our times in which we may all be knowers of different things, each in our own time and way.

FORMS AND THE HUMAN RELATEDNESS DIMENSION

One set of human forms that has attained special importance in the psychoanalytic enterprise may be conceptualized as modes characterizing the human relatedness dimension. I have delineated (Hedges 1983) four major variations of the sequencing of the human relatedness potential. They will now be summarized in a manner suited to the present discussion of form realities as imaginary or transitional "things" to be considered in the relatedness paradigm.

Organizing Forms: The Search for Relatedness

From the moment of conception, the human zygote evolves through a preestablished genetic program in accordance with possibilities provided by its immediate environment. Various control centers coalesce to organize and establish channels for the extraction of necessary supplies. Stated in broadest terms, evolving regulating centers function to establish an organismic equilibrium in conjunction with various channels being established for exchange with the intrauterine environment. At birth, the neonatal environment requires fresh adjustments. The early months of life are characterized by the organization of reliable connections with new environmental features and sources of supply. Cultural variables necessarily affect the types of channels and the manner in which various connections with the environment are established. Tustin (1984), in her work with autistic children, has demonstrated the relation between the earlier perceptual stimulation, said to be received as private patternings or perceptual *shapes*, and the gradual shift into social or consensual *forms* through the effect of social interactions.

Psychoanalysts have called this early epoch the era of the part-self and part-objects, in that the earliest psychic organizations are thought to center around such events as noticing and manipulating fingers and toes, thumbs and nipples, smiles and rocking, tension and calm. We have yet to specify what channels or aspects of intrauterine life we might point to that leave indelible marks on later psychic formation. The infant is thought to be organizing his or her perceptions of, experiences with, and relations to important features of the environment. Continuous care and available psychological contact are required to assure a general continuity of harmonious experience and to prevent traumatic losses of equilibrium. Human babies are generally successful in signaling and robust in demanding continuity of care and harmony of experience. Gradually the perceptual-motor and cognitive-affective fields are thought to organize around the possibilities provided the infant. Empathically presented and reliably maintained human forms from the psychosocial environment thus come to govern the way in which the infant organizes his or her perceptual-motor and cognitive-affective activities, and is thereby transformed.

Symbiotic and Separating Forms: Mutually Dependent Relatedness

As the child acquires the capacity to sustain attention and to tolerate periods of mild disequilibrium (tension), the optimally responsive parental environment begins to supply tolerable doses of frustration that serve to prolong attention and connection. More forms from the culture are thus introduced in a fashion that encourages intentional or goal-directed communication, in contrast with previous more or less genetically prepatterned and/or inadvertent communication. The process of mutual cueing between caretakers and child dominates the period of eight to eighteen months, although its functions are clearly observable from four to twenty-four months. During this period, most children tend to show a distinct preference for relatedness with one particular caretaker, usually the biological mother if she is available and willing to permit the symbiotic bonding. Just why symbiosis is so important and often tends to be accomplished primarily with one particular person is not altogether clear. But it can be said that this set of interactional forms established with early caretakers constitutes the foundational sense of reality, truth, and love, and remains, almost as imprinting, habitually active in subsequent social and affective life. We might suppose that the personality of the elected symbiotic other provides a certain consistency of response leading to the establishment of a reliable mutual cueing process. This simplifies the learning of forms and integration of affect and behavior within a reliable set of forms presented by a single human source. But many babies who are offered more than one very invested other are systematically responsive to those others. Babies show a remarkable capacity to distinguish what can be provided by each significant and available other. They also demonstrate a capacity to establish mutual cueing according to different forms with each important other. But in the final analysis, at least in our culture, "Mommy and I are one" still retains a special power. During this epoch, the most striking feature from the standpoint of a discussion of forms is the highly intricate and idiosyncratic communication network that characterizes the so-called symbiosis. Each (m)other–child dyadic combination evolves its own private idiom or culture. Affective responses tend to be ambitendent, that is, at any moment in time the other and/or the "I" are experienced as all good or all bad because the dance, as the child wishes and expects it, is working or failing in its purpose. I have chosen for the sake of clarity to speak of various sets of scenarios that mark or distinguish the exact nature of these form-filled idiomatic expectations and exchanges.

Various scenarios characterize the symbiotic and separating eras and define the personal (character) foundation for subsequent interactions. The symbiotic exchange is thought to provide the basis for virtually all early organized ego functions, including the synthetic function of thought processes, and the regulation of affective stimulation. It even influences, often drastically, the contours and formations of body structure, somatic functioning, and self. I have formulated that when, for whatever reason, the symbiotic bond fails to provide control (adequate behavioral formatting) of the thought processes or to foster culturally determined standards for the regulation of the affective processes, the person is likely to remain unduly influenced or dominated by pre-symbiotic organizing modes, medically diagnosable as schizophrenic and manic-depressive psychotic. Since there are many variations of effects of personal relatedness patterns established at the organizing level, I speak of relatedness possibilities that either do or do not receive adequate or effective stimulation for activation and the subsequent implication for these organizing issues. Most of the previous organizational foundations from the intrauterine and neonatal eras ordinarily become subsumed within the culturally influenced symbiotic organization. But intense yearnings of the organizational era that had to be cut off, dissociated from, or denied because they were unmet by the human milieu, influence heavily all subsequent relatedness possibilities, regardless of the overall level or context of personality development.

It will be important later in this work to realize that, while in some sense, various evolving organizations tend to subsume previous organizations of experience in what might be called a continuous manner, many discontinuities inevitably occur during the repeated reorganization and resynthesis of experience into new *formats*. Such discontinuities must be taken into account during the psychoanalytic enterprise. For example, we tend to expect issues in later development to emerge with greater clarity earlier in analysis. However, the peculiar gaps, inconsistencies, discomforts, and tensions inherent in the later developmental formats of experience tend to point toward earlier motifs that form the developmental underpinning and that are likely to emerge in analysis as somewhat discontinuous with formulations based on integrations and organization of later experience. Not infrequently, when the underlying or predisposing *forms* can finally be experienced and defined in the analytic process, the narrations of subsequent developmental experience become revised to include what was left out, set aside, denied, split off, repressed, or otherwise not noticed or integrated in subsequent developmental epochs. By way of illustration, a woman experienced great relief when she finally could say, with violent shaking and tears, "I am nothing." At a pre-birth level, she believes she was not desired by either of her parents and that she was emotionally handed over to another family member before she was born. To her parents she was "nothing." Her instinctive or unconscious knowledge of this situation, perhaps even *in utero,* governed all subsequent "layerings" of self and other experience. Most of her childhood developed as a reaction formation of extreme determination to be something or somebody everywhere she went. Through good-enough parenting she became a well-developed woman, but every aspect of her relatedness potential bore the mark in one way or another of "I am nothing." At every juncture in analysis the "nothing" appeared as indeed something very important to define and analyze in its impact. This general point clarifies the historical concern that has arisen when an otherwise well-developed person needs to explore a more primitive aspect of self. Analysts at times have been inclined to stop the analytic work and shift to "supportive" work because a "borderline or psychotic case" has

emerged. Shifts in developmental levels now regularly characterize the analytic process.

I do not view the symbiosis as a state of harmony and bliss.
The psychological structures built during this era may be
regarded as retained relatedness modes from the early mutual
cueing processes, overlearned ways for two to interact. While
the split affects characteristic of this period tend to make one
search for heaven and fear hell in relationships, the subtleties
and peculiarities of each symbiotic dance are what interest us
most in analytic study. The search to define one's symbiotic
modes is always unique, for they are always highly idiosyncratic,
strange, and usually shocking to our higher sensibilities. One
man was finally able to state with conviction, "My deepest
passion is to be beaten, raped, robbed, and left for dead."
Another, "I have a hard dick for women who can't be there for
me." Or another, "I wish to be passive until I am finally
abandoned altogether." Or, "My deepest longing is for an empty
teat." These statements of a person's scenario reflect years of
psychoanalytic work and in each case are radically condensed
into an almost bizarre bottom line that captures the deepest
and worst of one's perverted relatedness desires and potentials
based on some of the earliest relatedness strivings. This kind of
deep realization about one's passionate involvements with others
is usually reflected in unconscious sexual longings of a perverse,
masochistic nature. Unconscious masturbation or orgasm phan-
tasies, as they come to light in analytic work, always strike one
as perverse or self-destructive in one way or another but regularly
point toward one's deepest relational strivings. Short-term or
non-analytic therapies rarely produce narrations of such basic
symbiotic structures. Ingmar Bergman's films have been particularly adept at capturing the essences of these perverse characterological passions that originate in symbiotic interactions. It is
as though an infant learns that the excitement or passion of
being with mother results from relinquishing certain crucial

aspects of his or her instinctual longings or true self. This painful surrender of aspects of self comes to punctuate regularly all of our relatedness strivings, especially in our intimate love relations. Adult sexuality in its many (polymorphous perverse) variations becomes witness to the early (masochistic) necessity of giving up selected aspects of self need or striving in order to have and to enjoy the excitement of being with the other. Thus all passionate attachments can be expected to bear the stultifying influence of our personal conditioning and histories. Bergman's *The Passion of Anna* graphically depicts the unfolding of Anna's compulsive desire to maim, kill, or sacrifice the object of her passion, thus leaving her lost and lonely. Bergman shows how that scenario interacts with Peter's reciprocal passion toward being crushed, crumpled, and distorted in love. Peter's definition of his long and tenaciously held deformed version of potency and his desire for undistorted phallic potency is depicted in the last scene in which he is caught against the horizon, pacing back and forth between the image of a bent, gnarled, deformed tree and a tall, straight, healthy tree. Peter is frozen between the two trees, between the self-destructive passion of the old and the prospects of escape to new forms of self-potency as the final scene fades. As usual, Bergman has succeeded in capturing a universal human dilemma.

Cohesive Self Forms: Unilaterally Dependent Relatedness

Peaking in the third year of life, a strong sense of self may evolve which, however, remains intimately tied to stylized ways of experiencing others during this era (e.g., mirroring, twinning, and idealization). Hedges (1983) has discussed various ways in which the importance of the symbiotic network begins to wane during this period in favor of newer formats of self experience. Kohut (1971) has elaborated various possibilities through which archaic and compulsively sought "selfother"[3] constellations gradually shift toward more mature and personal ones. His idea is that the young child's sense of personal selfhood evolves through using others for confirmation of developing talents and skills. Kohut's concept of the selfother captures the essence of this particular developmental peaking. Others in the immediate environment are recognized as such, but are emotionally used for purposes of affirming, confirming, or inspiring aspects of self-development. Only as self-cohesiveness evolves is it thought possible for the growing child or person in analysis to develop a full cognitive and affective appreciation of others as separate centers of initiative. Forms for selfother resonance are available in our culture as we seek empathically to understand another's feelings of having been let down, disappointed, or disillusioned by us. Kohut elaborates the shame that characteristically serves as resistance to taking narcissistic pride in ourselves and resistance to analysis of selfother transferences. He also elaborates the vengeful nature of narcissistic rage when selfother functions are not adequately met (Kohut 1972).

Self and Object Constancy Forms: Independent Relatedness

Following the establishment of a cohesive organization, the self begins to assume a certain reliability or constancy, and others are distinguished more sharply from the self and assume more reliable, predictable, or constant forms. One result is that the child is able to research the problem of triangulation in relationships in new ways. Simultaneously held positive and negative reactions from and toward all known and concerned persons and the self come to be understood as contingencies. For

---

[3]I have elected to change Kohut's term *selfobject* to *selfother* in order to be more consistent in relinquishing the medical approach upon which Kohut's theories are built.

example, "How is (m) other's love contingent upon the presence or absence of father (or someone else), what are the relational implications, and how do I feel about them?" Earlier dyadic forms of envy give way to the various jealousies, loves, and hatreds (ambivalence) Freud called the "Oedipus complex." Intolerable positive or negative impulses or attitudes tend to be systematically disavowed to unconsciousness in the process of repression. The task is to analyze the verbal-symbolic structures which, as a result of repression, have constellated so as to neurotically deprive a person of his or her full personality energy and functioning.

The waning of an established Oedipus complex has now come to be thought of as a lifelong process. Under favorable developmental conditions, basic attitudes and beliefs, crystallized in early childhood and described as oedipal, are said to constitute an infantile neurosis. Various repressions of intense positive and negative strivings leave in their wake a series of unresolved ambivalences. Repressed policy decisions not to experience intense lust or aggression and not to spell out or to represent those strivings in consciousness form unconscious verbal-symbolic *forms* which, though repressed in deference to social proscription, are thought to operate as motivators in subtle and unconscious ways. Freud's brilliant formulations of "unconscious impulses" and "structural conflicts" have made more intelligible the enigmatic experiences (forms) that emerge as compromises between instinct and prohibition in dreams, slips, jokes, and sexuality and that are traceable to this era. Analysis has a record of producing subjective relief from distressing neurotic/oedipal/triangular conflicts through verbal interpretation of the operant verbal repressive forms.

The foregoing summary of the supposed epigenesis of childhood relatedness forms that continue to be influential in various ways from conception to death may be thought to comprise a series of form realities that are tailored by each growing child to meet the demands and contingencies of his or

her environment. The impact on analytic thought of conceptualizing in this way is that personal conflicts, tensions, concerns,
and discomforts are considered to arise from narrowness or
limitations in form experience. The function of the analytic
listener is to find an artful way of empathically presenting
*form*ulations of the speaker's stream of consciousness activities
that are more encompassing or comprehensive than those
currently in use and that may stimulate the creation of greater
personal flexibility than those implicit in the previously established narrations and narrational interactions of the speaker.

THE FORM OF THE ANALYTIC POSITION

The chief technical concern of psychoanalysis emerges as a
paradox of how the analytic listener is to offer forms that de facto
exert an expanding influence—in the least influential way
possible. This problem has always been an issue in skilled and
empathic parenting that seeks to interfere minimally in the
development of the child's own nature. In analytic work, the
problem is one of being sensitive to emerging individual concerns and, through empathic responsiveness, providing different
and perhaps more encompassing formats for organizing those
concerns. At the same time, the parent or analyst attempts to
encourage the child or person in analysis toward maximum
individual creativity and evolution within expanding contexts of
new forms. In some instances, the formulations offered by the
analytic listener may be received as naive, inadequate, corrupting, despicable, and/or may stimulate various forms of oppositionality, reformulation, and revision.

At the present time, the more comprehensive forms available to the analytic listener are likely to be variations of the
foregoing developmental metaphors that provide perspectives

for organizing the listening task. The most comprehensive forms currently available are those related to the analyst and the analytic position. Implicit in the oracular role or form called "the analyst" is a sensitive understanding of all human relatedness possibilities that range from primitive organizing aspects through symbiotic scenarios and self-cohesion strivings to the establishment of self and object constancy. The real person who assumes the role of analytic listener may or may not be fully cognizant of or privately and vitally experiencing all of these aspects. This may not be as critical as the cultural assumption or the fantasy that he or she is, which is implicit in the oracular or omniscient form of the analytic position. Although in the current approach to the psychoanalytic task the attempt is to get away from the knowing and authoritarian tradition implicit in the role of the analyst, the listener is still likely to be endowed with an omniscient role at times, partly because of cultural tradition and partly no doubt due to an infantile belief that mother knows everything. Also, the analytic listener has a certain advantage over the person who is free associating. The listener can be thinking, reasoning, making sense of things most of the time, while the speaker is obligated to continue his or her stream of consciousness and spontaneous interactions. It is only to be expected that the listener develops a variety of ideas about what is coming up in the associations or about what the forms of interaction are that the speaker might be demonstrating.

As in the acquisition of all forms, the emergence of subjective distress (concern, conflict, disorientation, or tension), when met with empathic recontextualization in the psychoanalytic situation (contact, delay, frustration, understanding, and so forth) tends to engender increased attention and responsiveness to the nuances of wisdom implicit in various cultural forms and in the *form* of the analytic position. That is, analytic experience fosters differentiated definitions of one's relatedness experiences, and accordingly produces increased

flexibility among the various possible forms of human relatedness which, in turn, serves to expand one's personal purview and
interpersonal capabilities.

BRIEF EXAMPLES OF THE POWER OF FORM

A simple but perhaps illuminating example of the kind of
phenomena under consideration might emerge as one ponders
buying a new car. To what extent does a mother of several
children see herself as a hauler of children and supplies and
therefore wish to drive a large station wagon or van (forms). Or
to what extent does the purchase of a station wagon or van then
catapult her identity into new variations?

Or consider the junior executive hesitating about a Mer-
cedes, hardly daring to step into a new status. How may the
possession of the car subsequently affect his experience of
himself and the kind of feedback he gets from his social
environment? And how many of us at one time or another,
shopping for a new car, have chuckled when we found ourselves
considering various identities that are associated with different
makes of cars and trying to see which identity fits us best?
Similarly with clothing, colors, textures, style, furniture, and art
work in our offices, living rooms, and bedrooms. Circularly, we
choose and arrange things to express our supposed identity in
some way and then we identify with the image or form our
lifestyle creates for us! Stanislavski's method acting approach is
to get the actor to posture and move correctly as expressive form
with the assumption that the feeling and emotion generally
associated with that expressive form will follow (Stanislavski
1936).

Much of our form searching activity is unconscious, but
much of it we are aware of and are quite deliberate about.

Conversely, we are also aware that in many ways we make judgments or decisions about other people based on the identities inherent in the forms that they present or project to us. A "messed up" person is someone whose identity symbols are obviously chaotic, a "compulsive" person betrays him/herself with neatness and sterility, an "hysteric" presents with the dramatic and flamboyant. Our choices of social and professional groups and philosophies reflect the same dialectical process.

We deliberate and participate in these more obvious choices concerning who we believe we are or intend to be. But how do we consider the many more subtle modes and styles that operate unconsciously? The words we choose to express ourselves, the emphases and inflections in our voices and patterns of speech, the ways our facial expressions convey meanings, the way we walk, play tennis, listen to a symphony, dance in public, and on into the infinity of personal responses and styles. We say that these things are just how we are. Dimly we understand that our habits and expressions are carefully chosen modes with forms and identifiable patterns that serve to communicate who we are. We squirm even at the word *choice* in many of our ways of being since we prefer to think that "we are what we are" and to acknowledge little or no choice or responsibility in many characterological features and stylistic devices that we believe constitute ourselves.

These relatively commonplace illustrations will perhaps serve to direct our attention to the pervasive presence of forms and organization of forms in our lives (Rose 1980). Consciously and unconsciously, we structure our lives according to the way we address and interact with culturally determined forms. Depending upon the available array of forms and the values assigned to them in a particular context, we adopt forms to express our personal preferences and to make various statements about ourselves. We are aware of people who are pretentious and ostentatious, or who are understated. A sixteen-year-old sporting punk dress might be making an effective independence statement which his/her parents will respect. On the other hand, parents who demonstrate a general lack of acceptance of individuality and independent expression may force a provocative and rebellious style.

These are all truisms we know too well. All aspects of our lives are filled with identifications, so we need not dwell further at this level. More to the point in a psychoanalytic inquiry is the speaker who narrates a story, ending with some expression such as, "I feel so guilty about that" or "It makes me sad to think about it." The listener, however, did not receive the impression that the person felt guilty or sad, but rather, perhaps, triumphant or relieved. The narrowly interpreted cultural storyline for the reported circumstance requires one statement, but it does not fit the person. One supposes that a new storyline will make the inconsistency more intelligible. For example, "You think you should feel guilty about what you did, but it sounds as though under the circumstances you feel triumphant about your decisiveness." Or, "One would think that you would be sad about such a loss, but considering the tension you have been under for so long, you sound greatly relieved."

I recently heard of an adolescent girl who was taken to therapy for "wild and rebellious behavior." She began one session by telling her therapist that there was a major disaster this week. It seemed she was late and missed the train to San Diego, where she was going to spend the day with a church group sightseeing and having a nice picnic. Not wanting to tell her mother she was late again and missed the train, she spent the day in a Jacuzzi with several of her boyfriends—boys of whom, incidentally, her mother did not approve. In some important sense the girl believed her own disaster story and was quite put off at the therapist's suggestion that perhaps she finds the church group somewhat boring and her friends more exciting.

FORMS AND THE UNCONSCIOUS

Freud's early studies of unconscious processes in dreams (1900), slips (1901), and jokes (1905) are replete with such examples. That which is unconscious is to be found in the chain of associations. One consciously intends to say or do one thing, but links in the signifying chain are such that the wrong word or phrase is used and the speaker is misled. Or a listener is misled by words early in the joke and caught by surprise at the end. In dreams one symbol may represent a series of related meanings that are condensed or displaced through what Freud called primary process abstractions. Analytic experience unravels the various unconscious meanings in human actions and activities. There must be many ways to think about storylines or chains of signifiers in human life. People often speak of being passively subject to influences from "an unconscious," rather than viewing consciousness as a special emanation or tool of a highly developed, highly evolved unconscious system. The example of the girl with the church picnic disaster is a case in point. Her behavior could not be called neurotic or oedipal in any sense of the words. She was committed to a "terrible twos" stylized relationship (i.e., a separating scenario) with her mother. One of her mother's friends saw the girl headed for the Jacuzzi and reported to mother. The mother's trap at the end of the day forced another lie and mother once again was victorious in proving her moral superiority and the naughtiness of the girl. The girl's storyline showed access to the mother's version of the symbiotic interaction as she sincerely and dutifully reported the "disaster" to her therapist. She was thrown into a state of confusion by her therapist's refusal to blame her and his inquiry into her rights and preferences under the circumstances. Her mother canceled her next appointment because "funds were short." Experience tells us that it will be a long time before the child permits herself to address the therapist's more comprehensive understanding of her behavior. Further, we know she will only be able to do this fully and successfully when and if her symbiotic partner can tolerate a diminution of the entanglement aspects of her scenario, or when she ceases to care what effects her growth has on her mother.

ANCIENT MYTHS FOR THE LISTENING PERSPECTIVES

Each of the four ways of listening to human relatedness potentials has precedence in ancient mythology. Freud's first mention of the Oedipus complex and its relation to Hamlet as universal themes characterizing the family romance occurs in a letter to his friend Wilhelm Fliess on October 15, 1897, when Freud was in the thick of his own self-analysis.

I am not thinking of Shakespeare's conscious intentions, but supposing rather that he was impelled to write it by a real event because his own unconscious understood that of his hero. How can one explain the hysteric Hamlet's phrase "So conscience doth make cowards of us all," and his hesitation to avenge his father by killing his uncle, when he himself so casually sends his courtiers to their death and dispatches Laertes so quickly? How better than by the torment roused in him by the obscure memory that he himself had meditated the same deed against his father because of passion for his mother—"use every man after his desert, and who should 'scape whipping?" [Freud 1954, p. 224]

The oedipal themes have served well to highlight certain listening situations of neurosis through time.

Kohut (1982) introduces an alternate myth to characterize parental attitudes toward their offspring. Kohut points out that since Oedipus's parents abandoned him at birth, no wonder his competitive rage at his father and incestuous longings for his mother, which were bound to result in disaster. When parents are able to accept the instinctual destinies of their children and to affirm with joy and pride their assertiveness and libidinous adventures, we have a different result indeed. He cites Homer's story of Odysseus.

> When, as told by Homer, the Greeks began to organize themselves for their Trojan expedition, they drafted all the chieftains to join them with their men, ships and supplies. But Odysseus, ruler of Ithaca, in the prime of young adulthood, with a young wife and a baby son, was anything but enthusiastic about going to war. When the delegates of the Greek states arrived to assess the situation and to compel Odysseus' compliance, he malingered, faking insanity. The emissaries—Agamemnon, Menelaus, and Palamedes—found him ploughing with an ox and an ass yoked together, and flinging salt over his shoulders into the furrows; on his head was a silly, conically shaped hat, as usually worn by Orientals. He pretended not to know his visitors and gave every sign that he had taken leave of his senses. But Palamedes suspected him of trickery. He seized Telemachus, Odysseus' infant son, and flung him in front of Odysseus' advancing plough. Odysseus immediately made a semi-circle with his plough to avoid injuring his son—a move that demonstrated his mental health and made him confess that he had only feigned madness in order to escape going to Troy. [p. 404]

Kohut holds the semi-circle of Odysseus up against the father murder of Oedipus as

> . . . a fitting symbol of that joyful awareness of the human self of being temporal, of having an unrolling destiny: a preparatory beginning, a flourishing middle, and a retrospective end; a fitting symbol of the fact that healthy man experiences, and with deepest joy, the next generation as an extension of his own self. It is the primacy of the support for the succeeding generation,

therefore, which is normal and human, and not intergenerational strife and mutual wishes to kill and to destroy—however frequently and perhaps even ubiquitously, we may be able to find traces of those pathological disintegration products of which traditional analysis has bade us think as a normal developmental phase, a normal experience of the child. It is only when the self of the parent is not a normal, healthy self, cohesive, vigorous, and harmonious, that it will react with competitiveness and seductiveness rather than with pride and affection when the child, at the age of 5, is making an exhilarating move toward a heretofore not achieved degree of assertiveness, generosity and affection. And it is in response to such a flawed parental self which cannot resonate with the child's experience in empathic identification that the newly constituted assertive-affectionate self of the child disintegrates and that the break-up products of hostility and lust of the Oedipus complex make their appearance. [p. 404]

In providing an alternative to the myth of Oedipus, Kohut reminds us that the instinctual life of a 5-year-old can be met by his or her parents in such a way as to produce a consolidating, cohesive effect on the self, rather than to foster excessive repression of the more archaic and less integrated aggressive and lustful aspects of human impulse life.

In considering the younger 3- or 4-year-old child, both Kohut and Freud have set before us the myth of Narcissus who, in order to consolidate himself, fell in love with his reflected image in a pond. Other versions of the myth say that he fell in love with his twin sister. Freud's original formulations on narcissism (1914) are based upon the child's feeling that his libidinous urges are deflected from the object of his desire, the parent, and onto the self. In these early formulations primary narcissism was allied with psychosis. That is, love directed at an object led to psychoneurosis while love turned in upon the self led to narcissistic neurosis (i.e., psychosis). Secondary narcissism became associated with the 3- and 4-year-old child who tends to search out others in order to use their admiring reflections to affirm the developing sense of self with its growing array of skills and talents. The self-aggrandizing, twin identities, and idealizing trends of the so-called phallic periods of psycho-sexual development, if met with adequate parental understanding, serve to consolidate a firm sense of self prior to the onset of the oedipal period, in which the contingent relationships of independently interacting selves are studied by the young child. Whether the narcissistic structure takes the flavor of the grandiose self, the alter-ego or twinship selfother, or the idealized selfother (Kohut 1971), the function of the other is one of affirming, confirming, and/or inspiring the development and consolidation of the self-sense of the narcissistic developmental period.

The mythical theme I associate with the symbiotic period of development (four to twenty-four months) relates to Janus, the Roman god of all beginnings, who later came to be associated with doorways (*januae*) and archways (*jani*). Janus was the first god invoked in liturgies, the beginnings of days, weeks, months, and years being sacred to him. January yet begins our year. The portal to human life is the symbiotic exchange through which the affective relation to human intelligence prepares the way for the later emergence of the symbolic. Entering the north portal of the forum, Janus was portrayed as a beardless youth, but once inside he was portrayed as a virile, fully mature man. The notion of "two-faced" is a recent corruption, not belonging to the Roman god of beginnings. But the split or divided self portrayed on opposite sides of the portal continues to haunt our thinking about the nature of human beginnings: the split or differences between the generations, between the sexes, between self and other, between good and bad—all are preoccupations of symbiotic beginnings and remain active to some extent in all the forms and patterns of later life.

I associate the yet earlier "organizing" period before initiation proper into human social structure with the myth of Proteus.[4] Aristaeus was a beekeeper, the son of Apollo and a water nymph, Cyrene. His bees had died from unknown causes and he went to his mother for advice. She told him that Proteus, the wise old god of the sea, knows the secrets of all things and could advise him on setting up a new bee colony and averting disaster in the future. Proteus, she explained, is the god of the tribes, schools, and flocks of the sea (the unconscious social instincts). He knows all things past, present, and future (the timelessness of the unconscious) and is capable of assuming all forms ever known (the infinite transformation, displacement, and condensation known to us in primary process). In order to speak with Proteus and to gain his knowledge, Aristaeus must seek him in his favorite haunt, the island of Pharos or Carpathos where he daily naps in the sun on the rocks with the seals. He must be seized and chained to a rock. Since he is capable of changing into all manner of things, his captor must be resolute, as Menelaus had found in attempting to speak with him upon returning from the Trojan War. If he could be held firmly through all of his changes he would speak with his captor and answer what he was asked. Aristaeus did as he was bid by his mother, holding fast while Proteus went through all of his monstrous forms until, discouraged, he returned to his own shape. In response to Aristaeus' questions about bees he told him to sacrifice to the gods and leave the carcasses of the animals in the place of sacrifice. Nine days later he must go back and examine the bodies. Aristaeus did as he was bid by Proteus and on the ninth day discovered a marvel, a great swarm of bees. After his encounter with the god of all forms and of the flocks of the sea, who was well known to his mother, Aristaeus' bees were never again troubled with blight or disease.

---

[4]I owe the association of the myth of Proteus to William Young, Ph.D., who, upon hearing my lecture on listening perspectives, suggested the formlessness or formfulness of Proteus as the forerunner of symbiotic forms.

The protean experience is one of taming the unconscious social instincts, of wresting from an array of endless shapes, specific forms (sacrifices to the gods leading to the establishment of a colony) that make possible the harnessing of instinct in the service of social order. Out of the protean unconscious beneath the sea, the secret of all things and the capability for all forms—past, present, and future—are given to Aristaeus, son of Apollo, great god of the sun, and the water nymph Cyrene. It is his mother who prepares him for the wisdom to be offered by the god of all forms, Proteus. The organizing period might be considered a movement from water toward the sun by means of harnessing the social instincts in the service of forms prescribed by the gods. This mythic theme describes the organizing period.

ON EMPATHY

Kohut (1959) formulated that the data of psychoanalysis have always been personal introspections and that the mode of observation in psychoanalysis is vicarious introspection, which he termed *empathy*. Introspection and empathy form the limits beyond which psychoanalysis as a science cannot go.

Kohut bitterly complained to the last days of his life that people misused his notion of empathy to mean something like syrupy sweet kindness or sympathy and that people were attempting to exalt empathy as something inherently good. He delighted in giving the example of the sirens that the Nazis put on their dive bombers to strike terror into the hearts of their victims as an instance of perfect empathy being used for evil or destructive purposes. Empathy is to be understood solely as a mode of observation. Only late in life was Kohut reluctantly pushed into conceding that empathic observation in psychoanalysis does, in fact, have a certain beneficial effect beyond its usefulness as a research tool. Since the development of concepts concerning self-cohesion stood in the center of Kohut's investigations, he stated the benefits he saw in terms of the consolidating and firming effects on the self of admiring, confirming, and inspiring responses from empathic selfothers.

And now to broaden the purview of empathy. It seems useful to consider psychoanalytic narrations and interactions as a successively expanding compilation of forms for expressing experience. Experience itself is comprised of yet another set of forms for providing versions of activities. Consciousness must be classed as a network of forms for communicating, sharing, or comparing experiences of activity.

In the present context, empathy is taken as one person's private and personal ways of sensing, imagining, and thinking about how another person organizes and narrates his or her understanding of personal actions and activities, in a world partially or largely thought to be his or her construction. Much of the activity of empathy is likely to be unconscious, especially at the beginning of the analytic relationship. Gradually, however, the analyst constructs various versions of what he or she considers to be the person's narrational contexts.

The chief limitation on Kohut's work is that self is only one of a number of important interwoven strands involved in individual human development. His insightful work on self-to-selfother resonance is one, albeit an important one, of perhaps many potentially definable forms in human life and activity. My own work has sought to separate out four clearly definable categories of human experience and activity. I have elaborated four corresponding listening perspectives as modes of psychoanalytic inquiry, or as guidelines for considering different modes of relatedness. Each of these distinctly different modes of relatedness is associated with different forms of empathic response. The modes of empathy can be summarized now within a context of form realities.

FOUR EMPATHIC MODES

1. *Organizing Forms and Activities* are perhaps best met with what may be called interception or interceptive contact. The most basic forms of orienting, organizing, and ordering of affective and sensory-motor response seem facilitated by their being contacted while in active exploratory or manipulative extension. An infant's, child's, or adult's tentative extensions into the environment may result in a variety of consequences. Those that put him or her into safe and reliable contact with the human environment are those that are met with various forms of reliable, warm, human responsiveness. Orienting, organizing, and ordering extensions not warmly or safely met in a timely fashion result in psychological enclaves of autosensuousness (Tustin 1984) leading to forms of entanglement with dangerous, threatening, seductive, nonhuman, mechanical, or erratic environmental figures or features. Many culturally defined forms exist to encourage patient waiting until an infant is in a position of extension in which he/she may benefit from human contact (interception of movement). The psychoanalytic tradition has evolved a variety of patience-inducing concepts that represent analogous forms for providing availability and responsiveness for the organizing aspects of personality. In persons or areas of a person where there has been an early traumatic history we will be concerned primarily with the way contact, once established, is broken off. The exact mode or style of destroying life giving (form providing) contact represents a transference from earliest experiences in which contact was either not maintained satisfactorily or was traumatically disrupted. Systematic study of the breaking of potential thought links is an important part of knowing about a person's organizing forms.

2. *Symbiotic Activity* implies a real or fantasized partner who shares a private culture and relates through a highly personal idiosyncratic idiom known only (or mainly) to the dyadic

participants. As people live out their symbiotic structures in intimate relationships they tend to assume that their way is the right way, the only way, or the most appropriate way. Infants who have available more than one very invested significant other may have a more varied series of symbiotic scenarios derived from diverse mutual cueing experiences. Empathic, interactive contact with symbiotic activity in psychoanalysis may be described as "replication" (Blanck and Blanck 1979) or as the "replicating transference." Much of symbiotic activity is preverbal, and the sense of replication of personal symbiotic modes is likely to arise from active or passive nonverbal patterns of interaction that develop in the analytic dyad.

The detection of a replication of a symbiotic mode often occurs via some experience of the countertransference. Conceived broadly as all affective and/or cognitive responsiveness to the person on the part of the analyst, countertransference may be said to represent the "royal road" to understanding various replicated scenarios of the merged dyadic experience. Many culturally determined forms for providing responsiveness to symbiotic yearnings are available to parents and therapists. Responding on cue to important desires and asserting counter cues may ultimately lead to mutual interpersonal boundary definition. This separation–individuation experience can only follow on the heels of an experience of intense symbiotic merger. The separating phase is often accompanied by depression and/or anger, registering the person's resentment that the dyadic symbiotic mode that spells attachment, connection, bond, or love is being violated. Even if the old modes were dreadful or abusive, people tend to cling to them out of addictive habit and experience severe withdrawal when giving them up as a result of immersing themselves in a new relationship.

3. *Self-Cohesion Activity* is thought to be performed in relation to another, the "selfother." Mirroring, twinning, and idealization activities constitute forms in which the other functions in an affirming, confirming, or inspiring manner.

These self-cohesive activities initially performed by an other are thought, through positively experienced repetitions, to become part of the activity repertoire of the growing person. The developmental continuum from archaic to mature forms of selfother resonance might be characterized as a shift from compulsive searching for (archaic) selfothers to the development of a capacity to generate and to use creatively affirming, confirming, and inspiring engagements with others for many kinds of personal enrichment and for personal sustenance during times of stress.

Perhaps Kohut's most useful clinical contribution is the manner in which he viewed tension regulation in relation to self-consolidation. He defines a cycle in which insults to self-esteem lead to tension increases and a search for tension relief. Tension related to issues of self-esteem and self-cohesion is typically lowered when a selfother is available for some sort of affirmation, confirmation, or idealization. But the significant moment in analysis is one in which selfother empathy fails in some regard, thereby producing increased tension. Kohut formulates that a temporal breakup of previously established cohesion tends to produce crude lust and aggression as fragmentation byproducts. However, with the restoration of selfother empathy comes the restoration of self-esteem and the resultant lowering of tension. Repeated experiences of empathy failures followed by favorable selfother tension relief (restored empathy) are thought to lead toward the personal establishment of a capacity for lifelong creative and comfortable self-to-selfother resonance.

Practically speaking, the listener may be doing the utmost to be there, to attend, to understand, or to provide whatever the speaker seems to need as the tension runs high. But sooner or later the empathy fails and the speaker feels let down, disappointed, discouraged, and perhaps even depressed or enraged at the empathic failure of the listener. Kohut argues that what is crucial is the listener's capacity to perceive the failure and to remain steady, understanding as well as possible all aspects of the reaction to the empathic breach. The selfother or narcissistic transference is from a failing parent figure who was not able to understand the failure and empathize with the bad reactions disappointments bring out in us. Kohut has teased out and defined an array of forms through which selfothers regularly are able to respond to disappointment with affirming, confirming, and inspirational activity.

4. *Constancy Activities* are thought to arise out of the establishment of an experiencing self that can be more or less reliably differentiated from various experiences of others. Even so, repressed unconscious fantasies regarding one's personal relationships are thought to play a significant role in how one continues to perceive and chooses to engage others in all manner of triangulated interpersonal relatedness (e.g., the Oedipus complex).

Ascendancy to full oedipal experiencing involves relinquishing to a large degree organizing, symbiotic, and separating modes of relating to others. Full freedom to engage in the complex oedipal activities of lust, competition, fear, and injury also involves the relinquishing of predominant reliance on reassuring selfother modes in deference to more complicated contingent and triadic forms of relatedness. A readiness to tolerate the intense stimulation associated with feelings of attraction, rivalry, jealousy, and injury permits the assimilation of social codes on a different plane than previously possible—the so-called crystallization of the superego. Full emotional capacity to consider others as separate centers of initiative with separate interests and motivations introduces the realistic possibility of personal injury (e.g., so-called castration) and gives rise to various forms of distrust. That others' personal and narcissistic investments constitute a danger is a reality to be reckoned with, Kohut says. Not to notice in oneself or in others unacceptable forms of attraction, aggression, jealousy, or injury is the dominant way of dealing with these intense forms of stimulation in the oedipal mode. Freud formulated this policy as one of not noticing, as unconscious defensive activity, which he categorized as various forms of repression. In order to master the intensity of the Oedipus complex, a person must learn to sublimate or at least not to notice stimulation that would disrupt the continuity of the sense of self.

Historically, empathic contact with repressed oedipal activities through carefully timed and tactfully delivered verbal-symbolic interpretations has been the central thrust of the psychoanalytic enterprise. Freud's insistent advocation of a strictly verbal-symbolic, interpretive approach and his gradual limiting of the population of the analyzable to neurotics has led to much dissension. At present, Freud's obstinate consistency can be seen as limiting to analytic work with preoedipal issues, but as clarifying with regard to the value of abstinence and verbal interpretation for understanding and analyzing personal (neurotic) activities constellated and integrated in the abstract symbolic mode of Oedipus, who blinded himself, symbolizing his wish not to see (be overstimulated by) relating others.

Kohut (1982) has argued convincingly that optimally empathic oedipal figures are successful to a large degree in limiting overstimulation during this period, thus preventing the formation of excessive defensive activity and neurotic constellations. It can be added to Kohut's observation that empathic responsiveness to self-cohesion modes from important others prevents excessive fragmentation during self-consolidation. Furthermore, appropriate empathic responsiveness forestalls extensive good-bad splitting in the symbiosis and separating modes as well as needless searching and floundering in organizing modes. Kohut (1971) has maintained that the traditional psychoanalytic emphases on lust and destruction have overshadowed the positive trends of stimulating love and assertiveness that are possible with positively resonating parental selfothers. In addition, emphasis on self fragmentation, good-bad splitting, and chaotic or bizarre behaviors have also tended to overshadow the positive aspects of developmentally determined modes and activities when more appropriate forms of empathic responsiveness are available from the parents and/or the analytic listener.

EMPATHIC MODES AS FORMS "FROM ABOVE"

The gradual refinement of developmental theory and technique has made possible the extension of the concept of empathy to at least three preoedipal modes that do not include verbal-symbolic interpretive activity as a consistent response. Interception of organizing activity, replication of symbiotic and separating interactions, and repetition of selfother resonance all represent major modes of listening to and empathizing with various preoedipal aspects or features of personality. These empathic modes have evolved to supplement the traditional empathic mode of verbal-symbolic interpretation. In order to avoid confusion, a mode is conceptualized adverbially as a way of seeking contact with another. However, a mode usually stems from preestablished forms or patterns and/or rapidly becomes a form of address to the other.

In many instances, what passes for empathic response differs little from sympathy and by itself has no useful effect in psychoanalysis. Everyone has seen or heard of instances in which an analyst has continued for a protracted period of time in genuine sympathetic immersion with a person who has realized only limited personal gains as a result. The effect is at best benign or helpful in promoting an ameliorated life adjustment. One might liken such a situation to transitivism or sympathetic parallel play in young children who, though they may enjoy one another and may react intensely to each other's play, are quite unable to elevate their level of mutual relatedness without intervention of the kind that recognizes or implies higher (more comprehensive or flexible) relatedness options.

Children can be told to be considerate and they can indeed be taught not to create a ruckus with one another, but differentiated capacities for self-confirmation and mutual consideration come from somewhere else. Where? Clearly from something that can be described as a learning, modeling, or identification effect. That is, empathy if it is to be transformationally effective, must come "from above." And what can this mean?

Returning to our main topic to shed light on the problem of empathy, we can only consider others fully when we know what it means to be considered. We can only know how to confirm another struggling self when we know what it means to feel confirmed. We can only tolerate separating opposition when we understand how crucial it is that our opposition be received tolerably. We can only permit ourselves to be drawn into a symbiotic replication when we know how important it feels to have someone fully involved in our subjective world. We can only know how to wait for and to discern extensions that can be momentarily met if our own extensions have been adequately met. Different modes of empathy are necessarily derived from identificatory experiences of others listening to us or being with us in increasingly broader, more flexible, or more comprehensive ways, or as it were, "from above," in a hierarchy of complexity in human responsiveness.

A Kohutian truism, which is confirmable in the more differentiated self and otherness states, relates to the consequences of empathic failure. Kohut predicts increased tension, fragmentation, and loss of self-esteem following an empathic failure. This prediction indeed appears to hold true when it is the self that needs confirming. However, in symbiotic and organizing activities, the results of empathic failure may be manifold and are generally not well described by merely referring to them as increases in tension, fragmentations of the self, or losses in self-esteem. For example, one person may experience a relief at a certain type of symbiotic failure in empathy because, as with the original symbiotic partner, failure means that the experienced battering or abuse (connection) comes momentarily to an end. Conversely, for someone else, certain kinds of intrusion or abuse might signal interpersonal contact and a consequent relief from a terrible period of isolation and loneliness. By the same token, either an empathic connection or failure to connect to organizing features might, depending upon the original caretaking situation, either permit or prevent a withdrawal into hallucinatory experience, a flight into manic elation, or an escalation of depression or paranoid rage. A placid interval may mean to a mother that the baby is content, while it may represent to the infant a state of depletion resulting in disappointment or failure to attain his or her subjective aims.

Contrary to Kohut's general assertions regarding empathic resonance at the level of self-cohesion striving, it is not possible in the short run to predict with certainty the consequences of empathic contact or empathic failure in pre-cohesive self-states. Paradoxes and surprises abound in preoedipal activities in which a person's strivings may resemble a young child's attempting to master the nuances of a complex environment with certain limitations in knowledge or communication skills. Misunderstandings between child and caretaker are common occurrences rather than exceptions. However, a persistent baby and a devoted caretaker in time do develop a mutual cueing system (the symbiosis), which is a fairly reliable communication system. How many instances have we all encountered of well intentioned empathic response that failed to meet the mark in terms of tension release.

Empathy, if it is to be accurate and comprehensive, and if it is to promote greater flexibility, must come "from above," that is, be derived from more encompassing, more abstract, or more flexible forms of understanding. The empathizer must be able to convey a sense of understanding of and tolerance for the personal concerns and positions being expressed, sought, or presented for interaction or interception. That a baby will be happier and healthier with a clean diaper is no consolation to the angry, kicking, screaming child who has been interrupted in absorbing pursuits. Mother's understanding and tolerance of the rage and its causes will make it possible for her to survive the infant's attacks without retaliation until soon the two are laughing and cooing together to the smell of fresh talcum and the sense of a clean diaper, a nice baby, and a happy mother. The expectable provocations of "the terrible twos," and "adolescent rebellion" are common examples of personal activities that try a parent's (or therapist's) patience. In these cases empathy can only mean a willingness to engage in a fray so that the opposing self can experience an independent consolidation. There are also various seductions that must be accepted and lived through in some suitable manner. Whether the seduction is to some form of organizing contact, merger, self-confirmation, or incestuous activity, empathizing means receiving the wishes and impulses openly and being prepared to be available, supportive, and responsive when inevitable limits and disappointments arise.

Empathy is not enough if it only means sympathy or if it is limited to the understanding of certain forms of relatedness. Comprehensive psychoanalytic empathy is based on an assimilation of a variety of developmentally determined modes and forms. Indeed, the role of the empathizer is a form. The role inherited by the analytic position is endowed with several thousand years of form-filled tradition in addition to the specific rituals and requirements that twentieth century professional life has added. Empathy is not enough until it includes an understanding of the full human repertoire of developmental patterns, modes, codes, and forms. The analytic position is a specially contrived form with a variety of modes for understanding established patterns of personal activity. Sustaining the analytic position inadvertently fosters the systematic expansion of personal realities through an enhanced process of personal reverberation with the form-filled human milieu via the living presence of the analytic listener.

7

Working the Countertransference

THE VARIETIES OF COUNTERTRANSFERENCE

Freud's impediment theory of countertransference (1915a) assumes that emotional responsiveness of the analytic listener derives from unconscious infantile sources that are inaccessible to conscious processing. Consultation or personal analysis is the traditional remedy for countertransference interference. Numerous analytic writers have taken issue with the impediment theory. Considering analytic interactions with the symbiotic structures, I came to speak of the countertransference as "the royal road to the merger experience" (Hedges 1983). While the symbiotic engagement is the focus in this chapter, countertransference to the replicating transference needs to be viewed within the broader context of the varieties of countertransference expectable within the overall listening perspective approach.

149

I. Countertransference Responsiveness to the Search for Relatedness

To imagine what kinds of listener responsiveness might be expectable to organizing states we need but recall the kinds of reactions that parents have in the earliest months of their new baby's life. Yes, think of the happy Gerber baby and of the Holy Family, the joyous and beatific Madonna and Child. And yes, the thrills of new parenthood are many. But too often the horrible relatedness strain that parents and families of newborns experience is forgotten. Even in the best of circumstances, with a longed-for baby who is normal and healthy, marital and familial stress characterize the last months of pregnancy and the first few months of life. Feelings of abandonment, rejection, loss, disruption, jealousy, envy, and resentment—to mention only a few—characterize the general relatedness atmosphere before and after the new arrival. The couple's social and sexual relations are usually disrupted by the upheaval occasioned by the emotional preparation for new ties and new relationships that the baby's arrival creates. But as if the strain of all the shifting relatedness patterns is not enough, actually working out the ways and means of accommodating a highly dependent human being into daily schedules, family budget, sleep and feeding routines, and emotional awareness patterns takes just about every ounce of energy of everyone concerned. Sibling and oedipal rivalries (actual and transferential) are stirred up in everyone. Irritation and fatigue become the expectable rather than the exception. By the end of the baby's fourth month there are bags under both parents' eyes, severe feelings of deprivation and irritation reign supreme, marital and familial tensions are at an all-time high—in short, everyone is just about sick and tired of their lives being intruded upon by this "blessed event." Fortunately, not all is gloom and doom, for everyone is observing, nourishing, and in direct ways reaching out to find and know the new person in the family. Every day the baby does something new and endearing. Even the interruptions of sleep routine are bearable because everyone knows that the strained period will soon come to an end. The newly arrived creature will soon be showing signs of socialized and civilized behavior—like being able to stay on a reasonable feeding and sleeping schedule, like not crying interminably when no one and nothing can seem to provide reassurance. First we try one thing and if that doesn't work we try another. When one person becomes exhausted attending, another takes over. Parents begin to look lovingly into each other's eyes again, have an evening out, and use help in managing the daily tasks. "Look, he's becoming a regular person!" "See how she looks at me, watch her eyes move and her lovely smile." These responses from caretakers mark the beginning of the mutual cueing process, the internalization of a structure called symbiosis, the onset of a mutual dance in which two interact with one accord. In a family with more than one heavily invested caretaker, each dyadic exchange gradually assumes a characteristic life of its own.

But prior to the gradual establishment of mutual understandings and reciprocal behaviors between baby and caretakers, there is chaos, strain, confusion, bodily tension and stress, sleep disturbance, eating difficulties, and any number of psychological and physical disturbances. All of these and more can be expected in the countertransference responsiveness to organizing states. Searles (1979) has been most courageous and influential in his writings that portray the disruptive, confusing, somatic, tension-filled, emotional responsiveness to his deeply disturbed patients. Likewise, Giovacchini (1979) and Little (1981) write of the many disturbing experiences they have undergone while working with primitive transferences. Accounts of various kinds of therapist disturbances abound at centers that specialize in the treatment of psychoses (Ekstein and Motto 1966, Silver 1989). No one to date has been able to specify systematic ways in which the countertransference can be put to use in understanding organizing, autistic, psychotic, and schizoid states.

One important cue toward systematic study of organizing level countertransference has been provided by Bion (1962, 1963), a British analyst, who for years studied the origins of the human thought process by studying psychotic states. Bion's overarching question revolved around the problem of how it is that one primate thinks and speaks while the others do not. Using a metaphor of container and contained, Bion noted how the human thought process begins. An infant is born into the world with a capacity for sensations (beta elements). On the basis of received sensations the baby gives out some cue regarding the state of the body/mind. The mothering person, drawing upon accumulated cultural wisdom regarding infantile needs, elects to do something that has the effect of altering the baby's bodily states and sensations. It is the (m)other who first thinks, thereby passing on some aspect of a complex cultural thought system that alters the sensation or tension states of the infant. After repeated instances of this containing of a state by the thoughts and actions of the mother, almost by classical conditioning the infant acquires the first elements of thought (alpha elements). These elements might be some sense of anticipation based on mother's movements, some paired association of milk sensations with the smell of mother's breast, or some other pairing with the sound of her voice, or the warmth of her touch. By means of the establishment of these rudimentary cycles from sensation-mother to thought-alteration-of-state-sensation, the whole complex web of human affectivity, movement, and thought evolves. Bion speaks of the "linking" of thought elements, initially accomplished through mother's body–thought system and later through complex interweaving of logical and symbiotic thought. Extrapolating, it might be said that the formation of the symbiotic system of relating is comprised of a set of such baby–mother linking cycles that build and expand until the two come to move and live psychologically as though they were one. This at-one-ness might be considered as an attempt to re-create on a psychological plane the original sense of intrauterine union, and to note that in various ways for the rest of our lives we seek state alterations that move toward replication of the interaction patterns by which we managed to achieve this sense.

The aforementioned developmental sequences point toward a way to think about normal and expectable processes. Infant researchers are now discovering and defining many ways through which these early processes operate. But even in average expectable rearing situations, how often do baby's sensations go unresponded to, go unlinked to a greater thought system? When we observe organizing states in the analytic listening situation, even in the context of well-differentiated self and other constellations, we might surmise that in various areas the linking was inadequate or incomplete. In persons who tend to be considered psychotic in lifestyle, we might surmise massive failure of linkage, whereas in most babies many links were satisfactorily made and only certain areas have remained unresponded to. It is these areas that present themselves for analysis and often are referred to as a "psychotic core." I prefer to speak of "organizing" features or issues.

This way of thinking about links from bodily sensations to cultural thought systems (through mother's intelligent handling) that have the power to be transformative, points in the direction of a crucial problem area.[1] Babies come into the world well equipped to search out and call for the kinds of help that they need in order to survive and thrive. Further, a certain special intelligence operates in maternal care that transforms sensation states into thought systems. Massive or partial failures of this transformational process are universal. When studying various organizing states analytically, we note that focus on the ways in

---

[1]Bollas speaks of this transformational process being accomplished by the baby's attachment to a transformational object. He further remarks that Freud's invention of the analytic situation unwittingly and forgivably represents an acting out of this early transformational setting. The implication is that even change at "higher" levels of integration requires the holding and containing of the early life processes to effect change (Bollas 1979).

which people orient for interpersonal contact and the ways in which they compulsively break off or prevent transformational contact from occurring yield crucial transference information. That is, transference memories become available for scrutiny in the analytic listening situation. These memories bear witness to the ways that the (m)other once was and was not available for transformational experience and, eventually, for symbiotic exchanges that have the power to bring somatic states into the realm of psyche. Now, a few countertransference implications.

Considering early somatic states as idiosyncratic and ever changing according to principles that are at first unfamiliar to caretakers, we see that the key event in the organizing period is how the infant manages to reach out to others for transformational experiences. When these experiences have worked well to form connections to the other, patterns of symbiotic exchange form. When early sensations and yearnings are frustrated or go unresponded to in any of a variety of ways, the exact manner of the failure is recorded in body memory, and this early template for experience will be faithfully repeated as transference to the (failing) other. Winnicott (1949) makes this point in terms of early "persecutory experiences" that serve as patterns for the receipt of all later frustrations. The task of the analytic listener is first to discern these subtle patterns as they ebb and flow during the course of a clinical hour. That is, transference experience based on rupture and failure in regard to the earliest linking processes manifests itself in the fine details of a clinical hour as contact is invisibly sought and lost. Next, the listener must find ways of identifying and bringing under mutual scrutiny the moments in which and the means through which contact is transferentially broken. The listener, maintaining the sense of contact and continuity with the content of the interaction, will generally fail to discern when the speaker has silently and invisibly left, vanished, abandoned the emotional impact of the relatedness. The reason is simple enough. Most analytic listeners have themselves enjoyed favorable enough developmental experiences that they automatically assume contact or engagement if the person is talking, emoting, or otherwise apparently interacting. Close scrutiny of clinical sessions with people functioning at the organizing level at the time usually reveals, however, that the speaker is mimicking relatedness, thereby giving the listener the illusion (or delusion) that they are connected. It is my impression that most therapy that continues for protracted periods of time (ten, fifteen, or twenty years) has been conducted under these conditions. That is, the therapist was caught up in the content of the psychosis, rather than in pursuit of the process by diligent study of points of contact and transferential moments where that contact is broken. The content of the psychosis could be hallucinatory or delusional as in schizophrenia, or affect loaded as in the affect disorders. In following the material on people referred to as multiple personalities, as well as many of the eating disorders, perversions, addictions, and schizoid withdrawals, it appears that too often the analyst becomes caught up in the ebb and flow of the content, i.e., the symptoms and conceptualizations of private life, so that the object relation process becomes completely lost from view and little reconstruction is possible. My term for the break in contact is the "appearance of 'the psychotic, overwhelming, or noxious mother,'" or the "breach" or "blockage" of the organizing channel to characterize the bringing to life in the transference moment the failure of the environment to meet some extension of the nascent self. It is only by scrutinizing many such interactions that the listener may begin to pick up on the moments of the break in contact.

The countertransference to organizing states will expectably be disorganized, chaotic, frustrating, anger provoking, fearful, dismaying, and generally filled with various emotions on the part of the analyst–listener that threaten to become disorienting and out of control. No wonder analysts have tended not to treat the organizing level, since their own personality is likely to be threatened with disruptive fragmentation! It seems that analysts empathically tuned in to the opening and closing of organizing channels of connection regularly and expectably become disrupted in their functioning. From observing the chaos generated in analytic listeners (my own included), when becoming aware of the abrupt and subtle ways in which people functioning in organizing states withdraw from or cut off connectedness, I believe that our own unmoderated, unmet organizing states are activated. Restated, a listener subjected to idiosyncratically and/or misunderstood connections and disconnections from the engagement typically fails to notice what is happening, much in the same way that people occasionally find themselves automatically doctoring up a narration of their experiences so as to make a seamless fit to self-concepts, self-esteem, and the present narrational context. People catch themselves actually lying, subtly exaggerating, distorting, or otherwise altering facts in order to fit the perceived needs of the present context. So analytic listeners, in order to retain their sense of humanity and a sane orientation to the speaker, go to the greatest lengths to understand the content, thereby avoiding the deep-seated chaos and disorganization that would result if one were suddenly aware of being abandoned or rejected. People who live most of their lives in organizing states learn to imitate or mimic human interaction patterns so as to "pass" in most everyday situations and thereby to delude the therapist into thinking them still connected. I refer to this self-structure based on imitation and mimicry the "mimical self." This structure contrasts sharply with Winnicott's notion of the "false self," which is a structure of later symbiotic life based upon relinquishing of a true, instinctively based self in favor of conforming to demands of the nurturing environment. Jerzy Kosinski's *Being There* (1970) depicts such a mimical self as Chance, the gardener, becomes catapulted toward wealth and fame by being regarded by those around him as Chauncy Gardiner. In the movie version, Peter Sellers portrays the mimicry of the hapless fellow who only knows how "to watch." In one of the great sex scenes of all time, the millionaire's wife, played by Shirley MacLaine, is intent on seducing him. She asks how he likes it, not realizing that he hasn't the slightest notion about sexual interaction. He responds "I like to watch," referring to television since he doesn't understand human interactions, but can only imitate. There follows a bizarre scene in which he proceeds to imitate stretching exercises he is watching on television, ending up standing on his head. All the while, she, in a black negligee, thinking she is exciting him, proceeds to masturbate to orgasm on the skin of a big black bear whose open jaws stare into the camera. *Being There* is a brilliant novel that not only captures the plight of the organizing state but the amazing extent to which people go not to notice psychotic disconnection. Only the black maid speaks the truth when she sees him being interviewed on network television as a celebrity, an authority on international economics. She turns to her family and declares, "This sho is a white man's wo'ld, that man ain't got nothing but bread puddin' 'tween his ears!"

People with organizing personalities often manage to develop good intelligence and skills and may be successful and highly placed in business, industry, politics, and the professions. But careful examination of their capacities for interpersonal relatedness places them at below the 4-month level, mimicking human life but knowing they are different, weird, strange, crazy, somehow not quite human.

While there is at present no known way to relate these disruptive countertransference reactions to the various contents and symptoms of organizing states, the responsiveness of the listener can point to the search for contact as well as the moments and means through which contact is regularly and compulsively thwarted. Transference has been the central tool of psychoanalysis from the beginning. In organizing states, the transference records the movement toward transformational experience and the breaks in contact that foreclose the transformational process. The literary work of Franz Kafka depicts beautifully and graphically the organizing struggle to reach out and make connections to a world that is unresponsive (Hedges

1983). By working together to learn to identify the times and styles of contact breaks, listener and speaker can analyze the transference to the psychotic or inadequately responsive mother that has been preventing the person from freely forming links that could move toward a fuller mutual cueing process of the symbiosis. It was Searles (1979) who discovered that the reconstruction process in psychosis entails forming a symbiosis *de novo* with the actual person of the analyst. From here, self-identity and cohesion have an opportunity to develop for the first time. Some countertransference responses to organizing issues seem to represent the listener's retreat from the overpowering instinctual stimulation of the speaker. Other withdrawing or approaching countertransference responses seem to represent the listener's personal response to his or her failing or overwhelming mother of the organizing period. Yet other forms of countertransference to organizing issues represent listener empathy with the terrifying features of contact moments for the speaker. Here it is the listener, acting as proxy for the speaker, who withdraws from or breaks contact as an empathic response to the fear of the speaker.

Freud's formulations regarding transference identified a person's tendency to experience the current analytic relationship in terms of crucial relationships from the past. He was able to demonstrate successful analysis (understanding) of triangular structures formed during the oedipal period. Kohut demonstrated that a different technical notion was needed to analyze selfobject or selfother transferences from the phallic-narcissistic period of development. Many current approaches, including "interpreting the countertransference" advocated in this book, are demonstrating the viability of analyzing the replicating transference to psychic formations of the symbiotic period. The organizing transference forms on the basis of early organizing channels being broken off.

II. Countertransference to Mutually Dependent Relatedness

Listener responsiveness to relatedness when aspects of symbiotic bonding are being revived in transference has posed a major problem in psychoanalysis from the first glimmerings Freud had of it in the specimen case of Anna O.'s work with Joseph Breuer. The classical position has been to abort the formation of the symbiotic transference by not permitting replication of the at-oneness sense to become a part of analytic relatedness. This is sometimes deliberate (by declaring the person unanalyzable) and sometimes inadvertent, but in either case it is occasioned by the analyst's not having available conceptual tools that would provide adequate technique for handling the transference. Without transference, of course, the analytic engagement fails to produce transformation of the relatedness dilemmas central to the speaker's psychological existence. Freud (1915a) on more than one occasion voiced his fear of analysts losing their balance in the love relationship called transference. His doctrine of abstinence served to maintain firm interpersonal boundaries between speaker and listener but at the same time foreclosed the possibility of analyzing deeper or earlier merger developmental structures, whether in the context of a diagnosis of borderline psychosis or in his more neurotic patients. Kohut (1971) demonstrated that other kinds of transference constellations to preoedipal issues can be secured for analysis. He demonstrated that the rigidity of separate boundaries fostered by the traditional frame technique does not allow for the analysis of narcissistic transferences (based on a blurring of boundaries as ordinarily understood) that are necessarily involved in the study of selfother tensions. Schwaber (1983) has written most clearly and convincingly on the need to abandon the idea of transferences as a distortion in favor of acknowledging the realistic participation of the analyst in the emergence of transference formations. Kohut's (1977) suggestions engaged the analyst in new ways by focusing his concern on the "self to selfobject relational unit." That is, the way in which the speaker uses the person of the listener and the setting of the analysis for personal expressive purposes is highlighted in the approach that involves studying what Stolorow, Brandchaft, and Atwood (1987) have referred to as the "interpersonal field." It took Winnicott (1982) to distinguish between wishes expressed at the oedipal-symbolic level that could be analyzed with words, and needs at the symbiotic level that required responsive listener participation. More traditional approaches have sought to define persons as analyzable if they presented a neurosis based upon internal conflict and unanalyzable if they presented narcissistic or borderline states based upon blurring of interpersonal boundaries and deficits in ego structure. Classical frame technique has been recommended for the former while some form of modified or supportive psychoanalytic psychotherapy has typically been recommended for the latter. Kohut's (1977) argument for the analyzability of narcissistic or selfother transferences is based on the notion that even if one pole of the personality retains deficits, there is another pole that could functionally compensate for the deficits, so as to make termination of analysis, that is, full separation–individuation from the analyst, achievable. The Hungarian analysts from Ferenczi forward put forth various formulations of how preoedipal analysis was to proceed. Jungians and Kleinians have always supposed that analysis of preoedipal issues is a possibility. All writers, however, seem of accord that complications of the analytic process, as well as the strain on the analyst, increase when preneurotic issues take center stage.

In the listening perspectives approach, the self and other configurations dating from the symbiotic period of human development, which expectably come into focus sooner or later, are secured for analysis through the replicating transference (Hedges 1983). Writers such as Winnicott, Ferenczi, and Balint hold that special provision needs to be made in the analytic relationship for these earlier relational issues to be seen and analyzed. Following Blanck and Blanck (1979), I speak of the transferences from this early period of development as more than mere transfer of instinctual feelings from oedipal parents (Hedges 1983). Symbiotic or early bonding experiences occurred at a time in the speaker's life when infant and caretaker engaged in a mutual cueing process in which two lived and experienced each other as one. Anyone who thinks that symbiosis is a mere metaphor can readily observe in mothers who are deeply attached to their infants how difficult it is for them to be away for any length of time. The power of the early bonding process hooks the mother and invested others by its deep and abiding power. As the analytic engagement proceeds, this same hook begins to be felt by speaker and listener, often noted carelessly as dependency feelings, regression, or fragmentation.

The replicating transference can be expected to be a reliving at an unconscious or preconscious emotional level of patterns, styles, and modes of relatedness once known in relation to the symbiotic other. In the original symbiosis, the mother is hooked by the power of the relatedness. In replication, the analyst must be equally hooked at *an emotional level* for the nature of the bond to begin to become apparent. Frequently in case conferences I hear a therapist making remarks such as: "I am going to present this case because somehow I find myself doing things I don't ordinarily do in my practice," "This person has a way of manipulating me that I find upsetting," "I feel like I'm being set up for something, that something isn't right, that I don't know what's going on with this person, that somehow I am being duped." Such expressions register the sense of interpersonal boundaries being tapped or stretched from the therapist's ordinarily expectable personal and professional guidelines and limits. Studying how the listener experiences these boundary demands or violations (Searles 1979, Giovacchini 1979) begins to give clues to the preverbal emotional replication being lived out in the analytic interaction. Searles (1979), Giovacchini

(1979), and Little (1981) provide plentiful examples of this boundary stretching process and how they have been able to make it work in the service of analytic understanding. That is, in the countertransference responsiveness, emotional configurations come into play that are at once alien to the listener's personal preferred ways of experiencing relatedness situations, and at the same time often somehow deeply familiar within the listener's personality. Another way of thinking about this is to say that the speaker has the project of attempting to communicate preverbal memories. In doing so he or she tends to ferret out and use various aspects of the analyst's personal emotional responsiveness for the purpose of arranging an emotional replication of the way things once were. To the listener it often feels as though his or her Achilles heel has been found, that the speaker has learned how "to push my buttons." In teaching I have often said that if I were to ask students to write three pages on their personal philosophy of life regarding how people are, how relationships should and should not be, and what they want and expect in interpersonal relatedness, we would no doubt be able to decipher many of the relatedness assumptions from their own symbiosis. That is, the earliest bond, the first love, and the foundational realities of our lives are derived from the assumptions we make about the environment and important people in it. This set of attitudes, beliefs, assumptions, and relatedness modes becomes so firmly entrenched that all intimate relationships for the remainder of our lives can be expected to touch upon how we experience the world and the realities of relatedness through symbiotic templates. The merged sense we have regarding how intimate relationships "should" be is so automatic and entrenched as to be readily confused with reality. Little (1981) even goes so far as to argue against the use of the term "symbiosis" to describe the sense of this early state. She prefers "basic unity" because it is a one-body instead of two-body notion. In the replication of the merger sense, there is an urgency for the analytic listener to behave or to respond in certain ways and to desist from responding in others. A very definite set of expectations and relatedness difficulties arises and the speaker is adamant in insisting that such and such is the way things must go between us, or that such and such doesn't go here. I like to stigmatize these moments as the search for heaven and the avoidance, fear, or hatred of hell in relationships. Gradually the analytic listener feels closed in on all sides or backed into a corner until he or she can find a way to make an effective interpretive intervention, a way to "stand against the scenario" (Hedges 1983). The resistance is often so severe as to make relinquishing of the sought-for pattern almost an impossibility.

The first problem is for the listener to be able to place the difficulties in an interactive, symbiotic format so that exactly what the relatedness demand is comes into bold relief. Not only is this a cognitive task involving problem solving with new ideas, but the relatedness dimension itself necessarily has engaged the listener in many unconscious or automatic ways, so that the listener's own character defenses become activated and obscure the precise nature of the engagement. But even when observing a listener skilled enough to be able to see the relatedness dimension insisted on by the speaker, and even when the defensive structure of the listener can be more or less laid aside for the moment, making verbal interpretations of complex nonverbal experiences poses an entirely new set of problems. Therapists have been known to talk themselves blue in the face and what they were saying was well formulated but somehow it still didn't hit the mark. The patient might even agree, even cognitively elaborate the therapist's ideas, or make behavioral changes in accordance with the interpretations, but still there is no connection to the deep, nonverbal emotional layers that the interactive dilemma springs from.

In my experience, verbal interpretations of preverbal symbiotic relatedness patterns are not effective until the issues are in active replication in the analytic relationship or a parallel relationship and unless the interpretation functions as some sort of active confrontation of the relatedness mode in the here and now present relating. "Confrontation" is used here cautiously, and does not mean that the person or behavior is being confronted, but rather, the forms, modes, or patterns of relating that arise from experiencing emotional relatedness templates from the past. As a device to aid in the interpretive process I have introduced the listening device of a scenario. Since the symbiosis consists of a set of stylized relatedness patterns and modes that cannot be spoken, if they are to become known they will manifest themselves in the non- or paraverbal exchanges between two people. As the exchange proceeds, a pattern of relating will emerge with regular expectations of how listener and speaker are to interact under varying conditions. The "mommy and me are one" dimension becomes inadvertently or unwittingly lived out in the exchange, beginning with the dependency or care aspects implicit in the analytic situation. By looking for a recurring pattern or scenario that is regularly a part of the person's relatedness, the listener becomes aware that the "mommy and me" interaction pattern gradually appears in each of its particulars as it is lived out in relatedness expectations. Too rigid or too loose boundaries on the part of the listener may thwart the process. Unlike the study of neurosis, in which a series of rules or policies (the frame) are established to bring the neurotic longings sharply in focus, the study of symbiosis requires that the listener maintain whatever minimal limits and boundaries are needed to preserve personal and professional integrity, and then watch to see how the speaker chooses to structure the relatedness and attempts to play with, stretch, or violate the boundaries. What can then be observed and opened to comment are the idiosyncratic ways in which the relationship becomes oriented and structured by the needs and demands of the speaker. That is, the replicating transference can be expected to be nonverbal and interactional in its impact, a silent development in the spontaneous relating of two human beings.

A great deal of talk may occur as the listener attempts to inquire and offer ideas, but the crucial event of transformation will not occur as a result of verbal work, but rather of non- or paraverbal action or interaction.

Two major forms of the replication are to be watched for: the passive version and the active version. The passive replication, though often unnoticed for long periods, is the experience in the transference of the listener and the listening situation in some particular way like the preverbal interaction with an early caretaker. For example, the demand for a fee or for regular and timely appointments becomes experienced like some demand from a symbiotic parent for time and energy to be directed not as the infant/speaker would have it but as the parent/listener insists. An array of reactions might emerge: irritation, injury, rage, spite, excitement, rebellion, conformity, lust—each would represent the revival of some emotional relatedness mode from early childhood. Speaking these things is often welcome and well received but typically goes nowhere. In the replicated transference, in the passive or active forms, a certain emotional climate is set up by the speaker and the listener is expected to be in agreement or to conform to it. So long as the listener is living his or her part well, things go well. But when the listener fails to obey (inadvertently or through active confrontation of the scenario) the relatedness rules that have been laid down, a disturbance in the relationship ensues. This splitting of good and bad affective experiences keeps the listener on target in understanding the exact nature of the relatedness hopes and expectations.

Over time studies have led to consideration of active replication of a symbiotic dimension in which a role reversal is entailed. That is, the speaker is "doing unto the listener what was done unto him." A position of passive weakness or trauma is turned into active victory in the role reversal. The speaker acts instead of the parent, foisting onto the listener relatedness demands that the speaker once experienced being foisted upon him or her. Freud's (1915b) formulation is that of turning passive trauma into active victory. Anna Freud's (1937) formulation is "identification with the aggressor." Her interpretation rests on the truism that no matter how good the parenting process, the parental ministration is frequently experienced by the infant as an aggressive intrusion into his or her space for instinctual expression. Klein (1946) formulates in terms of "projective identification," noting that early incorporated "bad objects" are made available for analysis by projection into the person of the analyst. Alice Balint (1943), in a brilliant tour de force, has detailed the process of primary identification and holds that we identify with what cannot be readily used and incorporated into the nurturing process. That is, it is the negative, the traumatic that poses a problem for the infant. In attempting to solve the problem of negative intrusions, the infant more or less builds a mental model of the parental emotional response that must be understood because it is intrusive. As the early model is built, it becomes a foundational and functional part of the early structure of the child's mind. In active replication transferences, these living modes based on primary identification emerge with clarity in the analytic interactions. These primary identifications, because of the global nature of infantile responsiveness, often manifest themselves in bodily constrictions, posturings, or gestures.

Symbiosis is considered a two-way street based on mutual mimicry and mutual exchange of affect tending to mirror each other. It is the disturbing aspects of this early mirror of mother that arise in and become identified with the replication transference so that the speaker acts in order to mother the listener in the same emotional ways in which he or she once felt mothered. Again, we tend to "do unto others what was done unto us." It is important here to remember that a scenario, thus constructed from observing the emotional exchange between speaker and listener, is not expected to be a recreation of historical truth as it might have been viewed objectively at the time. Rather, the interactional patterns that become discerned, defined, and observed (shifting through analytic time) produce truths of an interactional-narrational sort. These reflect the internal experience of the infant as recorded in the body and the style of affect engagements with the other, rather than visual or cognitive memories of any real or discrete events. The pictures, affects, and words that emerge as a joint creation of the two participants serve to define real experiences of some sort and are often cast into a language of literal memory or of inferential reconstruction of past reality. It is certainly conceivable that early historical events may be recalled with accuracy, but it is also certain that we have no way of distinguishing the actual from the narrational based upon a reliving of the surviving affects.

Often a speaker will wonder if such and such an event that seems so true or is becoming so vivid in memory ever really happened. And if that memory is of a seduction, the speaker will frequently voice a sense of doubt about the badness of the supposed seducer and a sense of guilt for having in some way invited or enjoyed the seduction or abuse. It does little good to speculate about the veracity of the memory *per se* and certainly trusting the listener's gut level belief that it really did happen cannot be safe, since so much countertransference is being evoked at such times. The crucial aspect of the seduction hypothesis that Freud put forward early in his career is that each of us was actively invaded in many ways by caretakers. And, depending on the nature and extent of such seductive intrusions, narrative, cognitive, and visual memories can be expected to emerge in the course of analytic work. Freud's mistake was to get hooked on the question of whether the picture created in analysis was real or not. Others continue to do the same thing. There can be no doubt that seductions and abuses are widespread and that whether or not a particular event can be depicted as happening on a particular date in history, a violation or series of seductive intrusions did occur, even if only in the overall atmosphere of caretaking that existed at the time. *But of much greater importance than the actual veracity of a certain seduction or abuse, and perhaps the reason so many get sidetracked on the question of its reality, is the question of how that seduction or abuse is being replicated in the here-and-now transference– countertransference engagement.* Speaker and listener often get caught chasing red herrings about the past so that both cannot notice the abuse that is being experienced by the speaker at the hands of the listener in the here and now. Resistance and counterresistance obscure the replication as it is being actively lived out in the relationship. For this reason it is essential that therapists develop consultative resources for regularly reviewing their cases and searching for outside feedback on the state of the countertransference and the counterresistance to noticing how the symbiotic replications are developing. Replicating transfer- ences are bound to develop with all people who have been fortunate enough to have experienced a symbiosis and who have developed the capacity for affective relatedness. The question in an analytic process is when and how it will reappear and what will the listener have done or failed to do to facilitate its emergence. In a later chapter actual transcripts of case confer- ences will be presented that illustrate how groups of therapists can help elucidate the replicated transference in which the therapist is unwittingly engaged.

By now, most dynamically oriented therapists are fairly adept at noticing and verbalizing aspects of the passive replica- tion. Therapists have learned to use parent–child metaphors to draw pictures, scenes, and adventures that may depict the ways in which the speaker is experiencing the listener as a parent. There are concepts such as "good breast" and "bad breast," that give an image of the current experience to think about. Most therapists at this point in the history of psychotherapy are sensitive enough to the notion of transference to be able to endure rageful attacks and lustful seductions as a part of what people in analysis must communicate about their private lives.

Much has been written on tactful and effective ways of handling such transferences when the speaker experiences the listener as parent or significant other. Still, we too often fail to speak what seems perfectly clear from the interaction as true, for fear the speaker will have an untoward reaction or reject the interpretation out of hand. Even if the idea is accepted and responded to, there is a sense that it did no good in terms of bringing relief to distress or a diminution of symptom–complaints.

But what is especially lacking are ideas, guidelines, and techniques on how to listen for and respond to the reversals, the active replication of the symbiotic issues. That is, when the "bad child" is being projected into us, when the aggressive parent imago seeks to attack or limit us, when we are the passive target for the victorious identificatory aggressions and seductions from the speaker's infantile history—how then do we receive and define the intrusions, the abuses, the identifications and projections that were once experienced? Moreover, how do we find words to begin capturing the experience we are having in the countertransference as a result of a successful replication of symbiotic patterns? Once again the parent–child metaphors will come to the rescue in trying to form pictures to depict what it feels like to be limited, abused, provoked, teased, tantalized, argued with, seduced, and so forth. But even if we have been more or less successful in fixing on crucial aspects of projected replication experiences and putting our experiences into words and pictures for ourselves, we face once again the problem of how to communicate our understandings so that the speaker can make use of them for transformational purposes. Whether the aspect of the countertransference life we are trying to bring to light is the passive or active replication, we repeatedly find that in trying to put preverbal affective experience that has a quality of relational reality into pictures, scenes, and words that might define that experience, our words and pictures essentially fall on deaf ears. Therapists often liken it to a mother speaking to an infant, explaining things that the infant has no way of grasping.

The infant may listen intently, study mother's face and the sounds of her voice, and respond in a variety of ways, but the verbal understanding cannot be affectively received. For this reason, I believe therapists should attempt to verbalize their ideas whenever it seems sensible to do so, whether they seem to fall on deaf ears or not. Kohut declares that a self develops because a mother addresses the child from the first day of life as though the child had a self. We need to keep in mind that many of our verbalizations are to keep ourselves oriented to the task at hand and may not yet be comprehensible to the speaker. Mother must find some other way of delivering whatever complex messages she intends to be fully received by children in the symbiotic period of development—through action or interaction of some sort. Mothers become geniuses at this nonverbal, interactive communication with their babies and it is this particular aspect of maternal care that may account for why this work is generally easier for women to learn to do. From early on little girls know that some day they are going to grow up and have a baby. They show intense interest in the mothering processes that often tend to pass completely by most little boys, whose developing masculine identifications are occupying their energies. By the time a woman trains to be a therapist she has likely participated in the emotional life of many babies, perhaps even her own, and is generally much better prepared to grasp the subtleties of nonverbal, active, and interactive communication than her male counterparts. We are hoping that enlightened parenting is serving to change some of this early sex role stereotyping, but as of today we remain profoundly affected by it.

The crucial twist that Bollas (1983) clarifies is that much of countertransference responsiveness can be considered a registration of the speaker's infantile past. Bollas holds that finding creative ways of speaking the countertransference is tantamount to putting words on preverbal experience that the speaker cannot at present verbalize. Speaking the countertransference represents interpreting the early mother–child idiom of being and relating. For a series of typical or expectable scenarios that are encountered frequently by therapists in their efforts to grasp the nature of the symbiotic exchange, see Hedges 1983, "Borderline Treatment Scenarios." Before looking at some ways to begin conceptualizing this unusual interpretative task, the problem of resistance needs to be considered.

RESISTANCE

As previously mentioned, Freud encountered a force that he called resistance that at first seemed to operate against the establishment of transference in the analytic relationship. Resistance is now understood as a form of memory that is also transference. Broadly stated, the person resists relating to the analyst and to the analytic situation with openness and freedom because in previously longed-for relationships that are now being remembered by resistance, various problems for the person once arose. Kohut points out that resistance to the establishment of narcissistic transferences takes the form of shame, shame that one wishes to be so grandiose or is so infatuated with the twinship or idealization aspects of relating. We have been taught that it is wrong to like to "toot our own horns" or to consider ourselves the center of the world or to overidealize people. Yet these are natural inclinations that become resisted through feelings of shame, humiliation, and mortification. At the organizing level, the resistance to experiencing connectedness to the analyst takes the form of a fear of falling into a black hole, the blackness and disorientation of despair, fragmenting explosions, and outer space, the black hole of relatedness that was once traumatic and from which the person has withdrawn. Tustin (1984) develops these images of resistance to object relatedness based upon her thirty years of study with autistic children.

Resistance to the establishment of the replicating transference often takes the form of fear of a real relationship with the analyst in the form of dependency, neglect, or some kind of seduction or abuse. The memory aspect here is not too difficult to see and interpret. A form of resistance to the neglectful, seductive, or abusive replication, which is often equaled by the strength of the counterresistance, is that of noticing how the replication is already happening between the two. But perhaps the most difficult resistance at this level is to seeing the destructive and masochistic aspects of the replication in such a way that the person feels impelled to relinquish the relatedness modes that form the core of his or her identity, the relatedness memories that have come to spell love, or mother, or safety, or familiarity. The symbiotic relatedness modes are so foundational to the way we organize and orient our entire beings that a wholesale shift in lifestyle and interpersonal relatedness will be required. People are not only reluctant but terrified to give up ways of being that are basic to how they experience reality. The cry of resistance is always heard in one form or another, "I can't do it, you must do it for me!" It can take many forms: "I can't change without a completely safe relationship," "Unless I can be held and allowed complete internal integration of my true self I can't possibility develop," or "Your style of working or person-ality simply will not allow me to do what I must do. I need a therapist who. . . ." The bottom line is "I can't (or won't) give it up." Symbiotic scenarios are like addictions; they fill in with something where complete satisfaction of the original yearnings is no longer possible. We can't return to the womb where all is safe or to the familiarity of a stable symbiotic dance. So the cry of "mother do it for me" in a thousand versions expresses our helplessness to have what we once knew was good and our refusal to develop ego strengths to cope with the world and to compromise our wishes with its demands. We only want to regress, to be allowed the safety and comfort that we know we once had and we still want to believe is possible. We do not want to hear the interpretation of active and passive scenarios because it would mean having to give up a way of relating dependently, safely, or familiarly with a maternal object who could be relied on for a set of responses—be they good or bad. To relinquish long-held ways of relating is tantamount to giving up our mother, letting her die, being without our main ways of greeting the world. No wonder no one wants to individuate; it means a crumbling of ego function that was built on the old style of relating. And in the way of progress there is tremendous disruption, disorientation, and grief that our once-stable object relations are collapsing and we are fragmenting and losing our footing and our grip on what we once thought was real. I have observed the most painful and horrendous regressions in the service of therapeutic progress. More than once I have heard a person say, "Where is my old self? I used to be able to function even though I was screwed up," or "If I'd known how painful and disorganizing this process would be I don't know if I would have started." I have watched many therapeutic processes abort just on the brink of a major relinquishing of symbiotic relating—and all under some form of the guise "You must do it for me," or "I must feel good and you must provide those feelings for me." Sometimes speaker and listener find ways of rationalizing the failure and cheering each other up with a Hollywood sunset termination. Preferable is the greater honesty inherent when both end up feeling defeated that they have tried their best to make it safe for the fragmenting loss to occur, but as the psychotic aspects underneath are activated, the fears are too strong to continue. In principle, I believe the relinquishing as well as a working through of the psychotic or organizing aspects is possible, but in practice we have to consider the personal resources available to the speaker at the time, the strength of the conditioning factors as originally laid down, and the analyst's preparedness to experience organizing regressions that a crumbling of symbiotic structures in the speaker is likely to stimulate. Freud's discussions of "negative therapeutic reactions" rest upon lifelong dependence, on overidealization, and on a penchant for moral masochism that the continued living out of the character scenario gratifies. And so the person on the threshold of cure abruptly aborts the therapeutic process, often disillusioned or enraged with the analyst (Freud 1923, 1924, 1932). The interpretive response to the insistence that "you must do it for me" is based on an understanding of how ego advances are accomplished in general but prototypically during the symbiosis when so many skills are being learned. Everyone learns for another. Children learn for mother and later for teachers, for love, and finally for the love involved in self-esteem. But mother's presence is required for venturing out at the symbiotic level. I believe likewise that in some way the real presence of the analyst in a supportive and reinforcing way is required at the point that a scenario is being relinquished. This is not the kind of support referred to in supportive psychotherapy, a giving up on the analyzability of something or someone. Nor is this support or active reinforcement focused at the level of behavior or getting better *per se*. The active and supportive intervention needs to be conceived like a mommy and me project of learning to walk, to tie shoes, to draw, or to write. The nascent ego in exploration and extension must be actively supported momentarily by an auxiliary ego until success in the new skill is achieved. At first this sounds like supporting behavior change or as though it may be too great a departure from the analytic stance (to break down structure) in the direction of a constructive or educative stance (to build up structure). In fact, nothing could be further from the intent or outcome. From the study of long-term intensive psychotherapy with learning-disabled children, we find that many basic ego functions involved in perception, balance, coordination, orientation, and the later reading and writing, computational, and comprehending skills built upon basic modes remain defective until the object relations problems associated with the failure for the skills to mature have been solved. I have repeatedly watched numerous special education techniques produce minimal effects for several years until the object relations aspects are worked out in psychotherapy. Then the skills take a sudden leap, and even major jumps in IQ and achievement scores can be expected.[2]

But all people resist vigorously giving up their earliest and most foundational love bond in whatever form its memory is retained. And when it begins to crumble, suicidal and death fears abound that are properly interpreted as "You are dying; the only self you have ever known is being killed off. You are afraid because there is nothing in your life experience to suggest that things will ever be any different."

CONTACTING THE COUNTERTRANSFERENCE: AN EXPERIMENT IN IMAGINATION

In order to demonstrate more clearly how this shift in thought can be made, I frequently introduce this visualization experiment to audiences. I ask them first to close their eyes, since we imagine better with our eyes closed. Then I give a series of instructions. Since you cannot read with your eyes closed, I suggest that at this moment you slow your thought processes and allow yourself to shift mental sets toward imagination. To experience the full emotional impact of this approach follow the instructions in the next chart very slowly and carefully. I have presented them in chart form as you may wish to refer to them whenever you are thinking about countertransference with a particular person. Experiment for yourself now using Chart 7–1.

---

[2]My ten years of school consultation, especially at the Mardan Center for Educational Therapy with Mary Walker as play therapist, demonstrated repeatedly the urgency in handling the psychotherapeutic aspects before gaps in ego deficit can fill in. A brilliant book, *Disturbing Teenagers*, by Carolyn Crawford, a long-time teacher there, is still in manuscript form. It will be valuable in demonstrating this point as well as in revealing the numerous countertransference responses and how to work with them.

When I turn to audiences of therapists and ask what they came up with, we are regularly astonished at the strength and

---
CHART 7–1
DEFINING COUNTERTRANSFERENCE FEELINGS

Imagine someone with whom you have fallen into a very difficult relational situation, someone who overwhelms you with countertransference responsiveness. Take your time and mull over each item.

What exactly is happening that you find disturbing in your relationship with this person? Imagine addressing this person with these sentences to complete:

1. When I'm with you I feel. . . .
2. You make me want to . . . when I'm with you.
3. The thing I fear most when I think of our relationship is. . . .
4. What I most wish from you is. . . .
5. The trouble with you is. . . .
6. I hate it when you. . . .
7. You make me furious when. . . .
8. I practically become disoriented when you. . . .
9. The best part of our relationship is. . . .
10. I feel the most positive toward you when. . . .
11. I would feel safe, warm, and comfortable with you if only. . . .
12. When we struggle together it reminds me of. . . .
13. What I most want from you is. . . .
14. I feel most manipulated by you when. . . .
15. I feel most seduced by you when. . . .
16. I feel most mistreated by you when. . . .
17. We could really get somewhere if only. . . .

intensity of responses. Here are some responses one audience I taped came up with.

> It frustrates me that you won't let me help.
> I fear being incompetent and overwhelmed.
> I want to hold you.
> I feel inadequate, frightened.
> I'm frustrated because you say you know all these things and yet you won't change.
> I can't find you.
> Nothing I do will make a difference.
> I want to protect you.
> Why won't you listen to me?
> Don't go crazy on me!
> If you'd stop talking you'd feel a lot better.
> I fear non-identity.
> I feel seduced.
> I'm working harder than you are!

What did you come up with that you would like to say that expresses your gut-level spontaneous reactions to this person? It's worth taking a minute to ponder.

Next I ask audiences again to close their eyes and now to imagine that they are very small—12 months old. Though they have no words, they have a deep sense of being and an expressive wish. The other person is now their mother and they need to express their feelings toward their mother in all of their smallness and helplessness. What does it sound like now? Try it yourself. Speak to the person you are considering as if he or she were your mother. You are a hapless child stuck with this mother. What will help? What do you need to say to her? Try it now; give yourself a minute to let deep responses arise.

INTERPRETING THE COUNTERTRANSFERENCE

To the extent this little exercise got you to a deep place with the speaker you were imagining, you no doubt realize that you just encountered a special and somewhat different understanding of this person from inside his or her skin, from the infant self that has been presented to you through your history of spontaneous interaction with this person. I believe that now you must find a way to speak what you just spoke in your imagination to this person. And you must begin speaking as soon as timing, tact, and your nerves permit. You can guess the stir that goes up in audiences I address when I charge them with this task. However, I am quick to reassure them that now I am going to tell them how to speak these powerful and potentially upsetting things to the other person. I hear sighs of relief, chuckles, and a shuffling of pencils and paper as we move to issues of how to begin speaking what you somehow know deep in your gut is true.

1. Focus: The Symbiosis or Basic Character Structure

The method of considering countertransference advocated in this section has a very specific and in many ways quite narrow application. We are considering countertransference responsiveness to issues that are thought to have their origins in the 4 to 24 month period of life. This is the era of dual symbiotic relating in which one's basic sense of human realities forms and the time in a child's life when his/her character or personality structure is forming. Countertransference responsiveness to transference manifestations dating from other developmental epochs clearly requires different considerations. Symbiotic or characterological expressiveness is at the basic level of engagement characteristic of intimate love relations with significant others. The countertransference feeling begins to have echoes of the kinds of things that spouses, intimate friends or work colleagues, and other family members often say in anger, devaluation, advice, exhortation, or accusation to the speaker. The things that begin to form in your mind as listener to say to the person may seem quite rude or unempathic at first but somehow still ring true. You are feeling the person, the speaker in this relationship, stuck in some basic mode of relatedness that he or she is attempting to foist onto you or insert into your relationship. It may be that you feel controlled, managed, misused, limited, manipulated, tantalized, exploited, abused, seduced, taken advantage of, tricked, cajoled, restricted, disciplined, persecuted, or even tormented. Or you may come to feel that the person is behaving toward you in an authoritarian, tyrannical, fixed, narrow, ingratiating, invasive, entitled, seductive, controlling, frightened, or overly precise manner. The point is that a specific style of relatedness is emerging. There is a method in the madness.

Whatever is happening between you two deserves careful consideration and study in terms of words, images, and metaphors that come to mind to describe the relatedness sense that is evolving. You may be having a novel set of feelings, but more than likely you will at first begin to notice some familiar aspects of responsiveness that you know to be characteristic of your deeper self. You may even have a series of personal associations that relate what is happening in the transference/ countertransference engagement to your own personal life or past emotional history. Its familiarity may throw you off by causing you to think that only your own biased feelings are involved and getting in the way of true empathy with the other person. However, as the feeling persists, refines itself, and reveals itself to be the kind of reaction that others have or might well have under the circumstances, you may begin to suspect that something invisible is being done to you, that your reactions, while clearly your own, are also being somehow projected into you. Other speakers in relationships seldom make you feel this way or require such accommodation or consideration in these ways as this person does. When you find yourself doing these things with this person especially in mind, it may well be going beyond the level of mere empathic attunement or consideration to the level of some form of primary identification with that person's parent or infant self that you are beginning to assume. Passing feelings brought up by specific situations seldom provide enough emotional impact to warrant this kind of countertransference interpretation; but persistent, strong, recurring reactions that clearly seem to be stimulated in a certain way by this particular person's characteristic forms, modes, and patterns of relating are the target for this type of interpretation. Speaking emotional reactions that arise as a consequence of your relatedness interactions with this level of personality formation is tantamount to interpreting either how the person once felt as a young child or interpreting the parent's position *vis à vis* the symbiotic child.

2. Atmosphere: One of Free, Thoughtful Exchange

In order to begin speaking such sensitive feelings, the therapist generally will need to create a special type of interpersonal atmosphere in which he or she can, on occasion, claim the right to speak freely, tentatively, loosely, creatively, and spontaneously, so as to throw partly formulated or even somewhat misstated or faulty possibilities into the arena as food for thought and material for mutual discussion. This kind of interpreting requires that a communication atmosphere be established in which the listener is not seen or felt at all times to be an authority or an oracle, but at times may need to play aloud with notions that can be toyed with jointly in a lighter than usual, perhaps even humorous or silly way. The listener's need for such a free, less serious atmosphere at times can be directly explained to the speaker in a variety of ways. I might, in an offhand, casual manner begin by saying something like, "You know how sometimes you come across an experience, a thought, or a dream that you find puzzling or confusing or hard to speak about but you try to tell me about it anyway? And then for a while we both look blankly at each other without the slightest notion of what it may all be about. Then we talk awhile and then one of us has a flash of intuition and we are off to the races, suddenly filled with many possibilities that seem to make perfect sense all at once. Well, I often have such half-baked ideas, fantasies, and dreams myself. And at times such notions are bound to be about you and about our relationship. I may not even know at first that the thought relates to you, but then I may have a sense that even though I don't understand it, my feeling or some picture that keeps popping up in mind is in some uncanny way related to you. Well, when that happens, sometimes I may feel it important to bring up what I am thinking, even though I can't make much sense of it, so I can see what we can do with the idea as we discuss it together. At times I'm sure we will have to throw it out as off the track, or merely the musings of my mind that aren't too relevant to what you are thinking or doing. But at other times my bet is that I am onto something, that I have a good intuitive hunch, but don't know how to make good sense of it, don't know how it fits what we are discussing. At such times, I need your permission to think a little loosely, to be quite uncertain in what I offer you and perhaps at times to even bring up thoughts that may at first seem rude or unempathic until we get hold of what I am feeling. In coming to grips with some of my own mental processes that arise here I need to be able to count on you to help me sort out what is useless from what may shed light on what we are working on together. Why, just the other day the most bizarre thought crossed my mind about something you had mentioned some time ago. At first I thought it was a silly notion, but later it came to mind again. I couldn't figure it out, and I'm still not sure, but I thought I'd throw it out and see what it stirs up for you."

Such an atmosphere is more easily created with some people than with others. What you can get away with saying will certainly differ depending on the person involved and the state of the relationship, but I have come to believe that people are more flexible and open to ideas about themselves, even half-formed ones, than we generally suppose—especially if the idea is offered with a grain of salt so it can be quickly cast aside or picked up on and used for the person's own creative purposes. The key here seems to be cultivating a spirit of mutual collaboration in which you are relying on the other person to take what you say and make the most creative use possible of it and to serve as the final court of appeal on what it may or may not mean. We all do this to a certain extent in the service of establishing better and more flexible communication. But some of the countertransference interpretations get quite heavy and difficult to deal with, so the greater the spirit of collaboration and mutual creativity you are able to establish in advance, the easier your decisive work will be when the time comes.

3. Avoid: Ventilation, Discharge, and Confession

As listeners we have all been taught correctly that ventilation of our own feelings, discharge of affects, and personal confessions and disclosures *per se* have no rightful place in analytic work. However, in my experience, when the early glimmerings of ultimately interpretable countertransference responsiveness begin to make their appearance, the temptation is to ventilate, blow up, tell secrets, or whatever. But at the time we have no way of discriminating between what may be of value and what may be intrusive or at best a detraction. We need to make use of the sense that we are ready to blow our stack, or that what the other person just said made us think of something our mother once said. That is, while our work requires honesty and spontaneity in order to be truthful and worthwhile, our preverbal, affective life emerges spontaneously in ways that we frequently have no sense of at all. Our reaction could be to what is happening now with this person or to something spilling over from another intense emotional involvement elsewhere in our lives, or perhaps even from the flow of the day, or a disturbing conversation we had last hour or between sessions with an office colleague. Since the variety of responsiveness under discussion is to preverbal, affective experiences and exchanges with the person, it may take us a bit of time to get some balance and perspective on what is coming up through our body-sensory-emotional selves for review. Again, the key is whether the feeling we are having begins to persist or make sense in definite or recurring ways that seem to touch the basic modes of engagement offered by the other person. If we aim to understand the person's basic character structure, the sense will be one that comes up often enough in different ways so that missing it the first time will not matter. There will be plenty of opportunity for mutual reflections on these basic aspects of relating. On the other hand, we may have been tracking a particular sense for some time and suddenly a eureka is triggered; then we may be prepared to begin speaking our insight immediately.

4. Abort: Any Sense of Blame or Accusation

When you consider that the kind of emotional insight we are talking about achieving is a deep one into a person's character armor or earliest relation to his or her caretakers, and ultimately into the most perverse and private aspects of one's being, especially the self-destructive, masochistic, and sadistic ones, you can be sure that numerous other people in this person's life before you have seen the same qualities or experienced the same abuses or seductions. Many times what you may begin to feel is worth mentioning will be the same thing that has been hurled accusingly and insultingly at this person throughout his or her life: "The trouble with you is. . . ." The most important countertransference interpretations are bound to feel intrusive, accusatory, hurtful, invasive, persecutory, and perhaps at first even out-and-out wrong. So when you begin to get an idea and muster the courage to offer something that may be difficult to take, be prepared for the speaker to hear you as yet another person saying the same old, stupid, insensitive, insulting, hurtful thing.

I know how pleased we can sometimes be with ourselves when we get a bright idea. I also know how good it feels to offer a half-formed insight and to have it greeted with affirming enthusiasm. Our narcissistic preoccupations get stirred up when we know we are right about something. We also feel perturbed, insulted, irritated, and disappointed when our ideas are rejected. But when interpreting countertransference responsiveness, we can depend that the more right we are, the deeper and truer our insight is, the less acceptable, the more disturbing and interfering our intervention is likely to be perceived. Knowing this in advance about this kind of interpretation, we can take several precautions to insure more effective communication. I have already suggested precreating as favorable an atmosphere as possible. To this I now add being prepared on an instant's notice to nip in the bud any feeling of being blamed or accused that is likely to arise. For example, "I feel that what I have to suggest today may not sit well with you because it goes along similar lines to what you report your husband often accuses you of. But we here have no time for accusations. So listen carefully to my idea and see if you can help me reword or reframe it in such a way that we can consider what value may be here. It came to me as an accusation, which is why I failed to mention it earlier. I thought it was just a bit of impatience that sometimes takes hold of me in different situations. But upon reflection it occurs to me that there is something important here for us to consider. . . ." In this kind of work, simply instructing the person not to get into bad feelings of blame or accusation because we have more important things to do now usually suffices to keep communication channels open. Of course, if various abreactions become persistent, then they too must be looked at as part of what must be characterologically interpreted. Likewise, resistance that needs to be analyzed may manifest itself as a sense of the analyst blaming or accusing the speaker.

5. Beware: False Self Conformity

Since the focus of this kind of countertransference interpreting is on persistent personality features from the symbiotic era of life, we must keep in mind that one common feature of the dyadic interplay of mother and child is a mutual willingness to conform to personality demands of the other. Winnicott (1960b) has given us the term "false self" to refer to habitual or stylized reactions that compromise our basic integrity. Our more true, instinctive self-investments may run in one direction, but because we need love or fear rejection, disapproval, or abandonment, we choose what the other wants or demands in deference to choices that would represent us more honestly and clearly. Babies and toddlers quickly learn which side their bread is buttered on and play to mother's wishes. This is particularly so for parts of us that never quite moved clearly beyond some mommy and me symbiotic scenario that is, after all, the developmental level that gives this kind of interpreting its emotional impact. So we must assume that all interpretations of this kind may be subject not only to a sense of accusation and blame, but also to conciliatory agreement and conformity. The person may fear our abilities and power in the situation or envy us the position that we have, and readily, or at least intellectually, be prepared to agree with us. Since, of course, we knew we were right all along, we are tempted to accept this conformity, this agreement, this ingratiating response as truthful and honest when it is not. The person may not even be aware of the false-self response until we call to her attention that she agreed, but somehow we felt it rankled her. The person may be at first startled by our comment that such and such a response didn't seem to be as deep and as syntonic as some are; perhaps it was not as true to her self as it might be. But in fairly short order false self conformities can be effectively identified by both people in the relationship.

6. Preface with the Anticipated Reaction

Since most valuable countertransference interpretations of the symbiotic level will be difficult for the speaker to deal with, it may be important to invent a little prologue for introducing your ideas. Recall for a minute the exercise in imagination you did earlier. As you thought of trying to speak your frank and untoward thoughts and feelings directly to the person, you were also able to anticipate what sort of abreaction the person would be likely to have. The kind of decisive interpretations that arise as a result of working this way seldom just pop up out of nowhere. You will generally have been thinking and reacting for some time in an emotional way you didn't quite have a handle on. Your early fantasied images and comments will give way to more refined notions and metaphors until you sense you are near to saying something important, but that it is going to deliver an emotional wallop when it arrives. Give the potential adverse reaction some advanced attention so that when you have an opportunity to speak the countertransference, you will know with confidence the general sense you are trying to convey and are ready for adverse reactions to what you are considering. I suggest "frontloading" a bit either well in advance or by prefacing your remarks with comments like, "I know what I have been thinking about won't sit well with you, but it seems we can't avoid looking this one straight in the face." Or "I have been thinking over something for some time now, but I feared mentioning anything for fear of how much it might hurt. But I know my intention is not to make you feel bad, so I need your attention and cooperation as I try to take the bull by the horns and go for something difficult and painful." Or, "I know how irritated you get at me when this subject comes up, and I have considered your complaint that I don't know what I'm talking about, but somehow this keeps coming up for me, and we have to get to the bottom of what is bothering me and why it makes you so angry for us to talk about it." The preface, of course, should be based on what your anticipation is of what the patient's affective reaction to your remarks is likely to be. Again, the goal here is to increase the likelihood of a good communication in an area that may seem too hot to handle.

7. Error: The Feeling Is My Own

We are altogether too eager to avoid painful, angry, or seductively tinged showdowns that put us on the hot seat. Too often in this area our tendency is to put off or avoid interpretations that could be mutative because in so doing we move ourselves, our most personal beings, right into the thick of it. The most often used rationalization I find is that the feeling coming up in the countertransference is my problem, my material, my hangup from my childhood. Interestingly enough, I find that virtually every one of these pay dirt interpretations is full of personal derivations from our own personal material. I realized early in supervising therapists that speakers in analytic relationships activate their best creativity in order to communicate unconscious, preverbal issues to their listeners. In so doing they must engage the listener at deeply personal emotional levels for the meanings of the replicated transference to become accessible. This means, in principle, that the most effective replications will involve the emotional life of the listener very personally and very deeply. But to use this fact of personal engagement as rationalization for failure to do our work is sheer laziness or cowardice. Persistent reactions on the listener's part almost invariably point toward a symbiotic replication, the exact nature of which must be ferreted out of the emotional qualities of the listener's sense of how he or she is being engaged or hooked into relating.

8. *Caution: We Can Never Be Correct*

Since the kind of preverbal, affective character scenario that stems from the symbiosis cannot be told to us in words, we must be sensitive to the communication potentials of affectively tinged interactions and engagements in which we find ourselves with the speaker. We will slowly begin to feel ourselves tugged in various directions. We will be aware that this emotional pull is familiar in some sense, like we have been here before. It may even be so clear as to be readily recognizable as one of our own Achilles' heels—that we always somehow seem to get ourselves into such and such a position. But persistent study will begin to reveal exactly how this person has accomplished this feat of pushing our buttons, and suggest to us the nature and quality of the emotional replication. Then there may be a dream, ours or the speaker's, that provides some clarifying images; possibly one of us will have a eureka. But no matter how strongly or clearly an idea strikes us or how much apparent confirmatory information we may have, I believe that our interpretive formulation will never be quite correct. Why not? Because we are talking about preverbal, affective interactions that are being replicated in the later or adult emotional lives of two unique people. In some sense the interpretation is always filtered through the medium of our personality. This is not like neurosis, where with enough dream material, slips of the tongue, and other primary process material we can come up with a fairly sensible and correct interpretation. With the symbiotic structure our affective senses are at stake. Emotions rarely translate well into words in the first place. And how much more so when the infantile emotional life of another or of his or her mother is projected into our emotional life, filtered through our symbiotic relatedness with our mothers, and affected by other strong emotional relationships in which similar issues have come up for us, and then all of this processed further by our personal system of words, symbols, and metaphors. How could we ever be accurate, how could we ever provide a narrative of a complex interaction that would be a perfect fit to what the other is experiencing? We have to be prepared to consider our interpretations as adventures in relating that evolve over time. One day we may try something one way and it will be corrected and improved. The person then has a dream that further refines it, then a bit of a row in a parallel relationship that opens up the area for more discussion, and so forth. Our attitude needs to be one of tentatively throwing out an idea for mutual working over. "I had this strong reaction that I thought for sure was just an old familiar one of mine, but then it kept happening and suddenly I thought I might be having a reaction that you had to your mother in your earliest childhood. That I might be feeling as helpless and hopeless as you once felt. Does that go anywhere for you, ring any bells, sound familiar in any way? What do my ideas stir up in you?" Often I have had to tell people that a major position they have taken on some issue has suddenly struck me as fraudulent, dishonest in some strange way. The stance around such and such an issue isn't quite consistent with other things I know about them. Then it struck me that the place it puts me is very similar to the way they felt when their father or mother did such and such to them. They are not reacting here on their own behalf but fraudulently acting in place of mother, giving me the business in a similar manner to which it was once given to them.

9. Timing: Whenever Communication Is Possible

In principle, if we were smart enough and quick enough, we might be able to interpret countertransference feelings the first hour with a person. In practice, I'm afraid I wouldn't advise it and, furthermore, there is no need for it. Important symbiotic issues will be ever present and always interpretable. These webs of symbiotic replication take months and often years of subtle interactions for two to fully appreciate the subtleties of an interaction that has deep interpretive potential. Moreover, like any good communication, a bridge of mutual understanding must be slowly built before anyone has the slightest sense of what the other person is about, and even then we have to get help in sorting out what is ours from what may be interpretable. The timing depends, as always, on when we can get away with saying very difficult things to a person and have some assurance that our communication will be received in the spirit in which it was intended. Since we are dealing with putting words to what Bollas (1987) has called the "unthought known," the climate of understanding is all that much more important than if we are dealing with feelings that were known once and then repressed.

10. Uncertainty: We Can Never Be Sure How Much Is Our Own

How often am I "right" in my countertransference interpretations and how can we distinguish countertransference that is our own narrow private material, from reactions that are appropriate to the developing situation, from the kind of projected symbiotic structures of which I speak? The answer is that we cannot be at all confident in this regard. We must remain uncertain. Classical analysis has always cautioned against premature interpretations before enough data is collected to be sure of their correctness. In the business of interpreting symbiotic, replicated transferences by means of countertransference responsiveness, we are always on thin ice. All the more do we need to create a tentative atmosphere where possibilities can be freely considered and used or thrown out as the speaker sees fit. All the more reason must we be sure that defensive reactions are not set off by our words sounding like a blaming attack or a demand for some sort of false-self agreement. It must be made clear that there are some aspects of interpersonal relatedness that two people must jointly collaborate on defining, but that any truly useful ideas will be ones that describe recurring, life-long reactions and feelings that come up somehow or other in all important relationships. It must also be made clear that the person in analysis shoulders the burden of responsibility for determining what may be the best avenues to explore and what images, words, and metaphors shall be counted as important in describing recurrent patterns. We are free to work the counter-transference in much the same way that a farmer works his fields, tilling, planting, and harvesting repeatedly, always leaving some ground fallow while selectively feeding yet other crops until maximum use is made of all possible fertile ground. Chart 7–2 below summarizes the ten factors to consider when interpreting the countertransference.

Interpreting the countertransferences means finding ways to communicate those deepest and most abiding emotional reactions that arise in any intimate relationship as a result of the natural human tendency to replicate in love, empathy, and aggressive engagement those primordial affective communica-

---

CHART 7–2
INTERPRETING COUNTERTRANSFERENCE

1.	Focus:	Symbiotic/character structure
2.	Atmosphere:	Free, thoughtful exhange
3.	Avoid:	Ventilation, discharge, confession
4.	Abort:	Any sense of blame or accusation
5.	Beware:	False-self conformity
6.	Preface:	With anticipated reaction
7.	Error:	The feeling is my own
8.	Caution:	We can never be correct
9.	Timing:	Whenever communication is possible
10.	Uncertainty:	How much is our own?

tion patterns and interactions that first served to introduce us into the world of human relatedness possibilities. We can bring to light and find ways of bringing new narrative definitions to our primordial templates for intimate interaction by *working the countertransference* for all it's worth!

III. Countertransference Responsiveness to Unilaterally Dependent Relatedness

Kohut (1971) indicates that, as might be expected, the analyst's major responses to idealizing transferences are rooted in his or her own narcissism, especially in areas of unresolved narcissism. He discussed the case of Miss L., who began an intense idealizing transference to her analyst at the outset of treatment. One of her early dreams contained the figure of an inspired and idealized priest, relating to her Roman Catholic background. Though not in direct response to her dream, the analyst did subsequently indicate that he was not a Roman Catholic. He did so in a move motivated by her supposed need to have a minimum understanding of the realities of their situation since her grasp on reality was in his opinion somewhat tenuous. Kohut discerned the beginning of a stalemate in the analysis dating from this remark. He interpreted her dream as an initial tentative transference step toward reinstating an attitude of idealizing religious devotion from adolescence, an attitude that seems to have had its origin in early childhood. Later material from the analysis indicated that these early idealizations had been an attempt to escape from the threat of bizarre tensions and fantasies caused by traumatic stimulations and frustrations from her parents. The analyst's remark that he was not Catholic, not like the priest of her dreams, and therefore not an idealized good and healthy version of herself, was received as a rebuff leading to a stalemate.

The analytically unwarranted rejection of the patient's idealizing attitudes is usually motivated by a defensive fending off of painful narcissistic tensions (experienced as embarrassment, self-consciousness, and shame, and leading even to hypochondriacal preoccupations) which are generated in the analyst when the repressed fantasies of his grandiose self become stimulated by the patient's idealization. [p. 262]

The analyst's uneasiness at being idealized is especially likely to occur if the idealization is early in the analysis and rapid. Discomfort with such idealization is to some extent universal and proverbial: "Praise to the face is a disgrace!" Even analysts usually comfortable with their own narcissism may be tempted to fend off the patient's admiration. The rejection of the idealization may be blunt, or subtle, or premature, or may express itself in no more than a slight overobjectivity or coolness in manner, or in a tendency to be jocular and to disparage the idealization in a humorous and kindly way. Kohut maintains, "during those phases of the analysis of narcissistic character disturbance when an idealizing transference begins to germinate, there is only one correct analytic attitude: to accept the admiration" (p. 264). An automatic emphasis on the analyst's realism in contrast to a patient's idealization is no more justified than an analyst's protestation at the first hint of an oedipal striving that he is not his patient's parent.

In later phases of analysis, the idealizing transference begins to be worked through. Whereas in the early phases of idealization the analyst may feel oppressed by the stimulation of his narcissistic fantasies, in the working through phase he may resent being belittled by the very person who had earlier idealized him. Exaggerated fault-finding and belittling can also occur as defenses against the establishment of idealizing transferences. But the attacks that occur during the working through period may be especially oppressive as the angry disappointment that follows disillusionment and that precedes the waves of withdrawal of idealizing libido from the analyst often fasten onto some aspect or another of the analyst's actual emotional, intellectual, physical, or social shortcomings. According to Kohut (1971):

> The analyst thus becomes aware of these alternations between admiration and contempt and will be capable of viewing with optimal objectivity the attacks which are directed against him, because he can comprehend them within the context of the analysand's needs during the analytic process. He will grasp the dynamic interplay between the patient's attacks on him, the loosening of the idealizing cathexes, and the gradual strengthening of certain internalized narcissistic structures (e.g., of the patient's ideals). [p. 269]

The rewards of watching such a growth process support the analyst when the process proves to be especially stressful.

According to Kohut (1971), the analyst's responses to the mirror transferences are determined by the level of professional experience in handling narcissistic issues, the state of his or her narcissism, and the current state of mind. In the narrow mirror transference the analyst is "the well-determined target of the patient's demands that he reflect, echo, approve, and admire his exhibitionism and greatness" (p. 270). However in the alter-ego or twinship transference, the grandiose self experiences the representation of the analyst as a part of itself, thus blotting out the person of the analyst so completely that he is deprived even of that minimum narcissistic sense that is afforded in the reflective function of the mirror transference. The analyst's optimal responses to the unfolding of the mirror transference are (1) interpretations of resistances against the revelation of his grandiosity, and (2) demonstrations that not only did grandiosity and exhibitionism once play a phase-appropriate role, but that they must now be allowed access to consciousness. It may be difficult for the analyst to tolerate a situation in which he or she is reduced to the seemingly passive role of mirroring infantile narcissism in order to unconsciously interfere with the establishment or maintenance of the mirror transference. When the listener attempts to respond to the twinship transference, the most common danger is boredom, a lack of emotional involvement with the person, and precarious maintenance of attention (with or without drowsiness), including secondary reactions such as irritation, overt anger, exhortations, forced interpretation of resistances and other rationalized forms of acting out the tensions and impatience arising from minimal narcissistic stimulation.

True alertness and concentration during prolonged periods of observation can be maintained only when the observer's psyche is engaged in depth. Manifestations of object-directed strivings always tend to evoke emotional response in those toward whom they are directed. Thus, even while the analyst is still at sea about the specific meaning of his patient's communications, the observation of (object-instinctual) transference manifestations is not usually boring to him. The situation is, of course, different in the case of the analyst's defensive boredom. Although in these instances the analyst understands the transference meaning of the patient's communications only too well, he does not want to understand it. He may, for example, be unconsciously stimulated by libidinal transference appeals and therefore defend himself, by an attitude of disinterest, against the patient's attempt to seduce him. In all these instances we are dealing not with genuine boredom but with the rejection of an emotional involvement (including preconscious attention) which is currently present below the surface layer of the analyst's personality. . . .

The verbal and nonverbal behavior of analysands who suffer from narcissistic personality disorders, however, does not engage the analyst's unconscious responsiveness and attention in the same way as the associative material of the transference neuroses, which consists of object-directed instinctual strivings. [Kohut 1971, pp.274–275]

With idealizing transferences, the analyst's attention may become engaged more easily than with mirror and twinship transferences, in which the grandiose self merges with representations of the analyst. This can become tantamount to total enslavement, making it difficult to be attentive for long periods of time. Many such difficulties are amenable to amelioration through supervision, in which the consultant is able to demonstrate the very important function that the analyst is performing. Thus, countertransferences to mirroring, twinning, and idealizing transferences may act as facilitations to understanding the nature of the transference and in providing optimal responsiveness. Other difficulties of a more chronic nature may require more analysis of the analyst's narcissistic vulnerabilities. Deep fears of merger that need personal attention may account for tensions of some analysts. According to Kohut (1971):

> As is the case in the transference neuroses with regard to object-instinctual drives, so also with regard to the narcissistically invested object in the analysis of narcissistic personality disturbances: the analyst does not interfere (either by premature interpretations or by other means) with the spontaneous mobilization of the transference wishes. In general, he begins his interpretative work concerning the transference only at the point when, because of the nonfulfillment of the transference wishes, the patient's cooperation ceases, i.e., when the transference has become a resistance. [p. 291]

The analyst is aware that a long period of working through lies ahead, during which there will arise an insistence on compliance with the person's wishes prior to the person's experiencing in the transference the disappointment and rage arising from similar disappointments in the infantile past.

IV. Countertransference Responsiveness to Independent Relatedness

Classical psychoanalysis, based upon Freud's original formulations regarding psychoneurosis, is clear on the problem of countertransference. According to this strict and narrow definition, countertransference is always unconscious in nature and springs from the infantile neurosis of the analyst. As such, its emergence into the analytic arena always constitutes an impediment, an interference with the unfolding of the transference of the person in analysis. Since countertransference is by nature unconscious, there is no ready access to it except through consultation with a supervisor or through further analytic work by the analyst.

Freud wrote, "We have become aware of the 'countertransference,' which arises in [the analyst] as a result of the patient's influence on his unconscious feelings, and we are almost inclined to insist that he shall recognize this countertransference in himself and overcome it" (Freud 1910, p. 144f). This moralistic attitude of Freud is echoed in his only other direct published reference to it (Freud 1915a).

> Our control over ourselves is not so complete that we may not suddenly one day go further than we intended. In my opinion, therefore, we ought not to give up the neutrality towards the patient, which we have acquired through keeping the countertransference in check. [p.164]

In a letter to Binswanger dated February 20, 1913, Freud expressed that the problem of countertransference is one of the most difficult ones technically in psychoanalysis. "What is given to the patient," Freud said, must be "consciously allotted, and then more or less of it as the need may arise. Occasionally a great deal. . . ." Later Freud set down the maxim: "To give someone too little because one loves him too much is being unjust to the patient and a technical error" (Binswanger 1956–1957). Kohut (1971) used this notion of Freud's to authorize his own expanded analysis of countertransference responsiveness in the analysis of selfother transferences.

Reich (1951) bolstered the Freudian position by eliminating ordinary feelings from what is to be considered countertransference. She maintained that extremely intense positive or negative feelings for the patient are always countertransference and worthy of more psychoanalysis for the analyst or referral of the patient.

In the listening perspective for use with independent relatedness strivings, or for understanding triadic, contingent relationships, disruptive affects from the personality of the analyst may indeed be dilatory to the development of the analytic enterprise and are probably best handled the way Freud and others have suggested, i.e., through consultation or more personal analysis. The chief difficulty arising today with adherence to these precepts is being able to distinguish among countertransference responses arising in relation to independent relating, responses arising appropriately in relation to selfother transferences, and responses that may relate to replications or organizing endeavors. At present the only gauge seems to be by estimation of the general issues characteristic of the person involved and what sort of material is currently being explored in the analysis. Lacking other criteria upon which to make a judgment, the analyst ought to explore cautiously the earlier developmental possibilities first in hopes that, if in error, the analyst will be experienced as merely irritating or misguided. If one assumes first that it is one's own material, much may be missed and much damage done to the analysis.

8

Countertransference, Empathy, and Interpretation

COUNTERTRANSFERENCE RESPONSIVENESS

From the earliest years of the psychoanalytic movement, people like Jung, Ferenczi, Abraham, and later, Klein and Winnicott all developed their own approach for focusing on early or preoedipal experiences that seem to require concepts and techniques of working beyond the verbal-symbolic mirroring technique advocated by Freud. But not until the last two decades has developmental psychoanalysis been able to generate an array of concepts that permits the systematic study of countertransference by practicing analysts. The contributions of Searles and Giovacchini in particular stand out, but neither has been able to provide widely understood and practiced ways of directing responsible and systematic attention to the counter-transference.

The purpose of this chapter is to spell out the developmen-

199

tal concepts that have evolved in recent years to make the study of countertransference more feasible. The major points are:

1. Countertransference responsiveness may be viewed as closely related to empathy and the interpretive process. All three may be considered along a continuum of developmental metaphors.

2. The central issues considered in analytic investigation pertain to the ways in which one human being experiences, represents, and relates to another. The transference–countertransference dimension affords an opportunity for experience with and interpretation of various forms of personal relatedness styles and concerns.

3. Developmental metaphors can cast into bold relief a series of relatedness issues that present themselves for empathic reflection, resonance, and reverberation in the course of analytic relationships.

4. Countertransference responsiveness tends to take on strikingly different qualities when viewed in light of available developmental metaphors. For example, empathic resonance—and therefore countertransference response—has one set of qualities when relatedness issues commonly encountered by oedipal-age children appear. Countertransference takes on quite different qualities when the manifest relatedness issues resemble those encountered in the developmental periods of phallic narcissism, opposition and separation, stylized symbiotic at-oneness, or early organizational strivings.

5. Empathic resonance is taken to mean the analyst's capacity for and willingness to engage in a personal relatedness experience with the person who comes for analysis. Traditional analytic technique has been based on the general assumption that the chief concerns to be brought to analysis pertain to neurotic-oedipal personality constellations. Oedipal level issues involved in neurosis are embedded in a verbal-symbolic matrix and are therefore subject to verbal interpretation. Empathic responsiveness to earlier developmental issues and concerns

necessarily takes on different forms. Kohut's understanding of
the paraverbal communications that transpire in narcissistic or
selfobject constellations has opened the door for systematic
understanding of yet other para- and preverbal forms of analytic
relatedness. When the personal concerns revolve around issues
that have deep roots in early symbiotic bonding experiences
or the separation/individuation processes, countertransference
takes on the additional role of an informer of the nature of the
yearned-for merged and/or separating experiences. When issues
around early organizational strivings occupy center stage, the
countertransference response takes on yet different meanings.

6. The historical evolution of psychoanalysis now makes it
possible to consider empathy, interpretation, and countertransference in a variety of new ways. This book seeks to challenge
analysts and analytically informed consultants to consider more
systematically the range of countertransference responses in
relation to empathy and interpretation.

OVERVIEW OF THE VARIETIES OF COUNTERTRANSFERENCE

As an informer, countertransference responsiveness functions differently regarding personal issues at different points
along the developmental relatedness axis. For example, intense
countertransference response to highly differentiated oedipal
issues will likely interfere significantly or consistently with the
analyst's more or less objective assessment or understanding of
the issues that have become crystallized in the network of a
highly evolved and integrated verbal-symbolic matrix. At this
level of differentiation and integration, impulses come to be
experienced as unacceptable and are systematically barred from
becoming spelled out in consciousness. Feelings of disgust, fear,
confusion, anger, and other forms of countertransference arousal

in such a setting may relate more to the personal life of the analyst than to analytic material that remains repressed, or to the means by which the repression continues.

In contrast to potentially interfering kinds of countertransference, Kohut (1971) has observed that countertransference responses such as boredom, irritation, and drowsiness may well be appropriate and therefore facilitating reactions to narcissistic issues in which the analyst is not being experienced or related to as a whole or real person. Rather, the analyst may be serving as an extension of some limited or archaic sense of self. Kohut's conceptual schema centers around analytic observation of the self-to-selfobject relatedness unit. Within this listening context, countertransference responses can be meaningfully considered as facilitating informers of the current ebb and flow of the state of the self. Empathic resonance with confused or fragmented states or experiences of self might be expected to take on quite different characters from what would be expected if the resonance or attunement called for were with conflictual issues of a well-established and highly differentiated Oedipus complex.

In further contrast to what have been traditionally considered interfering responses to issues of the Oedipus complex are a wide variety of countertransference responses to relatedness issues that metaphorically might be said to have roots in the symbiotic or separating phases of human development. A quick look at the range of emotional interactions between infants or toddlers and their caretakers shows the vast set of potential responses that might be expected to arise in the analytic situation when the empathic attunement required is with actions and interactions arising in early human development. For example, a parent not prepared to battle it out in some way with a child experiencing "the terrible twos" is simply not in tune with the crucial developmental role of "no" and "opposition" in the ongoing saga of separation and individuation. A parent or analyst not prepared to offer or to engage in a merged symbiotic exchange in which a mingling of separate desires and actions are given the opportunity to achieve a sense of "dual unity" or "at-oneness" within the orbit of two, is simply unaware of the need for or unable to engage in the most basic forms of human bonding. Basic human attachment has an endless array of forms and expressions that are highly idiosyncratic and that may evoke a variety of reactions in another. This is especially true in the analytic exchange when early symbiotic and separating issues become focal. Each person brings to the analytic relationship a personal set of experiences that constitute a sense of primary connectedness, called variously love, attachment, passion, bonding, consideration or the like. The analyst unprepared to engage in a mingling of desires and actions will not be in a position to discover, and later, to help cast into words and actions, the exact forms of interpersonal engagements required to fulfill the primary bonding needs of the speaker. More importantly, an analytic listener not willing or flexible enough to be engaged fully in replicating various interaction patterns or scenarios derived from the early bonding period, will certainly not be in a position to stimulate specific forms of interpersonal opposition that have the potential of leading toward separating and individuating experiences from previously unrelinquished idiosyncratic forms of bonding relatedness.

Organizing relatedness issues stem from the earliest attempts of humans to establish reliable and, therefore, meaningful contacts with the intrauterine and extrauterine environments. Far more often than we think, people tend to perpetuate various rooting, searching patterns from their earliest attempts to relate to needed human elements. Kernberg (1984) refers diagnostically to this group that generally does not display dramatic evidence of their idiosyncrasies in thought or mood as "asymptomatic psychotics." Central to those issues that might be considered functional or psychological—in contrast to manifestations that can be specified as organic or constitutional—are repetitive, searching attempts to find satisfying human contacts that might lead toward a bonding experience or a symbiosis with another human, thus stabilizing or solidifying the personality organization. The presence or absence of psychotic symptoms is not an essential ingredient in these formulations. In this context, psychotic symptoms are taken to represent retained, faulty, or abortive attempts to continue constituting reliable meanings in an environmental milieu which, for whatever reason, cannot provide the needed experiences of human consistency. Entrenched functional psychotic pictures demonstrate a presumably learned tendency to avoid or to destroy links and connections that might be useful but that are viewed as treacherous or frightening (Bion 1962, Tustin 1972). The literary work of Franz Kafka illustrates clearly many aspects of the organizing processes of early infancy and of those ceaseless organizing attempts that may be carried into later life. His work even illustrates the tendency to fear and to destroy potentially organizing links and processes. Previously, and in greater detail, I have defined the functional schizophrenic, manic and/or depressive pictures as derived from a faulty match between the infant's system of potentially organizing needs and the capacities of his/her caregivers to be systematically and reliably responsive to those needs, so that the infant's experience might become organized into consistent systems of meaning. Systems of meanings that comprise rudimentary mental structures are referred to by Glover (1932) as "ego nuclei" and Kernberg (1976) as "ego states, the basic building blocks of personality."

In the analysis of organizing issues, countertransference responsiveness is invariably intense and chaotic, as the analyst strives to discover configurations of meaning that are regularly cut off and destroyed by the person who can only rely on an array of searching patterns, but not upon a consistent availability for contact by others. The difficult task of a parent during the earliest weeks and months of life can be compared with that of an analyst attempting to locate such basic points of contact or schemas of meaning. However, the analyst's work is infinitely more taxing because the early (almost imprinting?) period of connections is no longer active, with the result that the work is very long, tedious, and frustrating. In addition, the therapy work is consistently thwarted by previously established tendencies not only to destroy links, but to encapsulate or wall off from human contact, or to perpetuate entanglements with early forms of chaotic contact that the infant learned to utilize in strange and limited ways (Tustin 1981).

In therapy with organizing issues of personality, the analyst should refrain from a nonproductive search for highly evolved meanings and symbols, instead monitoring every movement for moments of potential contact that might build meaning. A symbiosis *de novo* must be formed with the analyst. Previously established symbiotic trends or threads of relatedness and tendencies to destroy links, to encapsulate or to entangle have to be analyzed and relinquished before the consistent availability of the analyst can be relied upon. This kind of work provides endless frustrations for the analyst, who will likely experience many kinds of chaotic and intensely stimulating forms of countertransference. While many countertransference responses to organizing issues can be compared to a parent coping with a colicky or unpacifiable infant, Bion's concept of container-contained and Tustin's work with autistic children suggest that much of even this type of countertransference may be open to interesting study.

DEVELOPMENTAL FORMS OF EMPATHY AND INTERPRETATION

Restating the previous line of thought from the standpoint of the interpretive process, we realize that an analyst cannot engage in narrational-interpretive activity without having some coherent or adequate means of empathically understanding and communicating what about the person's life can usefully be put into words and when and how interpretive verbalizations can be realized as an integrated aspect of the person's life experience. The classical study of psychoneurosis initiated by Freud has generally assumed that a person experienced oedipal-level issues with various conflicting impulses, concerns, and inhibitions that were once felt toward significant others during that developmental epoch. The further assumption has been that those impulses and conflicts called oedipal have entered the developmentally determined realm or sphere of verbal-symbolic communication, and that through mastery of the tools of symbolic representation (including language), oedipal-level relatedness issues have undergone repressive transformations. The assumption of the classical approach to transference analysis of oedipal issues is that a person's concerns can reasonably be expected to be analyzed in a verbal-interpretive mode such as the one Freud and his followers chose to employ with such illuminating results.

However, as analytic experience has by now amply demonstrated, when the relatedness issues involved have not yet been fully, affectively, and conatively integrated into the verbal-symbolic matrix provided by human culture, it is folly to assume that the relevant dimensions for a person's analysis can be elicited and processed, at least initially, in the verbal sphere—no matter how bright and articulate the person may be in regard to other human endeavors. Kohut (1971) has been our mentor in this regard—at least in the consideration of the self-to-selfother relatedness unit. His major clinical contribution has been the definition of a class of narcissistic or selfother transference constellations in which perfect empathic attunement is sought around issues of personal grandiosity, twinship identifications, and various forms of idealization. Kohut's by now well-known approach to analyzing these selfother constellations highlights the analyst's extension of empathic attunement and the awareness that it will only be a matter of time before imperfections in that attunement will be signaled by various adverse reactions on the part of the person in analysis.

These failures in empathic attunement and their fragmenting consequences are then open to systematic study in terms of the vicissitudes of self-cohesion and fluctuations in self-esteem.

Kohut's opening to the ways in which preoedipal, paraverbal transference reactions can be understood and explained, while primarily limited to the study of the vicissitudes of the self-to-selfother unit, points toward the possibility of formulating fresh analytic approaches to a variety of pre-cohesive self-relatedness forms and issues. Analysis of these metaphorically earlier issues, termed by Mahler (1968) "symbiotic" and "separating," relies on the capacities of the two participants to engage in a replication of the early idiosyncratic bonding experiences. In contrast to oedipal transferences and selfother or narcissistic transferences, the strong interpersonal relatedness required for the elucidation of symbiotic and separating issues merits the terms "replication," "replicating transference," or "replicated scenarios," since much more than mere transfer of neurotic or selfother experience to the analyst is involved.[1] Likewise, reformulations of the concepts of empathy and interpretation, as well as redefinitions of the role of countertransference in the analysis of basic relatedness issues, now seem requisite. The mingling or merging in the replication/counterreplication dimension of basic bonding experiences required in this type of work makes several demands on the empathic capacities of the analyst and calls out a variety of

---

[1]"Replication" was first suggested by Gertrude and Rubin Blanck (1979) to denote transference of preoedipal experience. Later, in response to criticism, they abandoned their use of the term and returned simply to "transference." It is very useful to distinguish this type of "replicating transference" from other forms of transference because it is embedded in preverbal interaction patterns, in contrast to "selfother transference," which specifies a series of ways a person uses the other for self-confirmation and neurotic or oedipal transference based upon the advanced capacities or verbal-symbolic representation of the repressed impulsive life of an oedipal-aged child.

countertransference reactions that can neither be understood as interfering (as in oedipal relatedness issues) nor merely as facilitating (as in selfother relatedness issues). It is for these reasons that I have come to consider countertransference the "royal road" to the analysis of symbiotic (merging and separating) issues. But before considering countertransference as such, I will turn briefly to the subject of analytic empathy.

EMPATHY: A SEQUENCE OF DEVELOPMENTAL FORMS OF RELATEDNESS

Kohut's early work on empathy (1959) held that the data of psychoanalysis have always been provided by introspection, and that the chief mode of analytic observation has become vicarious introspection, which he termed "empathy." As his thoughts evolved, Kohut came to speak of empathy as a faculty as vital to human life as the faculties of sight, hearing, and touch. Harshly critical of those who would view analytic empathy as some sort of "syrupy sweet kindness," Kohut maintained that empathy was to be considered solely as a mode of observation in analysis. A final current of Kohut's thought, however, held that empathic attunement per se often had an enhancing effect. As examples, he spoke of the empathy-less concentration camps that exerted a terrifying, fragmenting, and dehumanizing influence. Conversely, he reminded us of that famed moment when American astronauts, due to a malfunction, were faced with a choice between living a while longer and dying in orbit, or risking a fiery death plunge toward mother earth—a choice that they made without a moment's hesitation. It is better to die in pursuit of the human milieu than to live in cold and empty isolation.

Kohut's emerging thoughts on empathy led him to suggest the need for defining a developmental line of empathy and discovering a corresponding developmentally based line of interpretation. Shortly before his death, Kohut (1981) defined the advance from understanding to interpretation as a progression "from a lower form of empathy to a higher form of empathy." He illustrated the analogous development within the individual by way of the following example:

> . . . a child and a mother were in the park. The child was a young child who clung to the mother. The sun was shining, pigeons were walking around there. All of a sudden, the child felt a new buoyancy and daring and it moved away from the mother toward the pigeons. He goes three or four steps and then he looks back. The general interpretation of that is that he is anxious, he wants to be sure he can come back, to be encased in her arms, cradled, etcetera. That is true, but something more important is true. He wants to see the mother's proud smile; he wants to see her pride at him walking out now, on his own—"isn't that wonderful"—and at this moment, something extremely important had happened: a low form of empathy, a body-close form of empathy expressed in holding and touching . . . is now expressed only in facial expression and perhaps later in words: "I am proud of you, my boy." [Berkeley Conference on Self Psychology, unpublished]

Kohut spoke of the words "I am proud of you, my boy" as a sort of interpretation—or at least a developmental forerunner to what we ordinarily think of as an interpretation.

Kohut then stated that he was certain this would be his last conference. He concluded his remarks on empathy and his brilliant career with a clinical example drawn from a lengthy analysis that he had conducted some fifteen years earlier with an "extremely vulnerable woman."

> She lay down on the couch the first time she came, having interrupted a previous analysis abruptly and she said she felt like she was lying in a coffin and that now the top of the coffin would be closed with a sharp click . . . she was deeply depressed and

at times I thought I would lose her, that she would finally find a
way out of the suffering and kill herself . . . at one time at the
very worst moment of her analysis (after) . . . perhaps a year
and a half, she was so badly off I suddenly had the feeling—"you
know, how would you feel if I let you hold my fingers for awhile
now while you are talking, maybe that would help." A doubtful
manoeuver. I am not recommending it but I was desperate. I was
deeply worried. So I moved up a little bit in my chair and gave
her two fingers. And now I'll tell you what is so nice about that
story. Because an analyst always remains an analyst. I gave her
my two fingers. She took hold of them and I immediately made
a genetic interpretation—not to her of course, but to myself. It
was the toothless gums of a very young child clamping down
on an empty nipple. That is the way it felt. I didn't say
anything . . . but I reacted to it even there as an analyst to
myself. It was never necessary anymore. I wouldn't say that it
turned the tide, but it overcame a very, very difficult impasse at
a given dangerous moment and, gaining time that way, we went
on for many more years with a reasonably substantial success.
[Berkeley Conference on Self Psychology, unpublished]

It is interesting that this incident, so absorbing and crucial
for understanding concrete forms of empathy, was not reported
for fifteen years. Kohut's deathbed legacy points toward a
continuum of empathy from body-close, concrete enactments,
through nonverbal gestures, toward empathy achieved only with
words. Kohut's final case illustration makes clear the close
relationship of empathy to interpretation and the relation of
both empathy and interpretation to the countertransference—"I
thought I would lose her. . . . I was desperate."

SUMMARY AND REVIEW

We are now in a position to integrate the major threads of
this discussion before moving on to clinical illustrations. Chart

8–1 graphically represents the major traditional concerns of psychoanalytic theory as they can be viewed differently within each of the four listening perspectives.

HIDDEN VALUE SYSTEMS IN ANALYSIS

Before further developing my central thesis that countertransference constitutes the "royal road" to merger experience, I would like to make a few comments on unacknowledged value systems that tend to operate silently in psychoanalysis. Kohut (1985) rightly observes that classical technique contains a hidden morality that points toward the achievement of a comfortable relationship to work and a postoedipal, genital, heterosexual orientation in personal relationships. Kohut remarks that these criteria could not possibly be applied to many of the most creative and fulfilling lives in recorded human history. Nor could the Kleinian criterion of cure— postambivalent object relations—be applied. Kohut introduces the criterion of "mature self-to-selfobject resonance" by which to mark analytic progress, but admits that this too represents a hidden system of values that can exercise devious effects over the analytic process. Developmental metaphors likewise can be used to imply a value system that devalues infantile fixations, primitive mental states, undifferentiated object relations, unintegrated affect splitting, and other things such as developmental limitations and arrests. Conversely, positive weightings might be placed on such processes as separation, differentiation, integration, growth, and maturity.

I wish to be explicit in opposing the use of all theoretical or clinical concepts that promote hidden value systems by which to make moral judgments about the process of analysis. However, the adoption of a particular value system by analytic practitioners to guide their own professional experiences may be valuable.

CHART 8–1
LISTENING PERSPECTIVES:
Modes of Psychoanalytic Inquiry

THE PERSONALITY IN ORGANIZATION:
THE SEARCH FOR RELATEDNESS

I. Traditional Diagnosis: Organizing Personality/Psychosis

Developmental Metaphor: ±4 months—focused attention vs. affective withdrawal

Affects: Connecting or disconnecting but often inconsistent or chaotic to an observer

Transference: Connection vs. discontinuity and disjunction

Resistance: To connections and consistent bonds

Listening Mode: Connecting, intercepting, linking

Therapeutic Modality: Focus on withdrawal/destruction of links—connecting as a result of mutual focus

Countertransference: Comforting vs. disruptive, confusing, or non-linking

II. SYMBIOSIS AND SEPARATION:
MUTUALLY DEPENDENT RELATEDNESS

Traditional Diagnosis: Borderline Personality Organization/ Character Disorders

Developmental Metaphor: 4–24 months—symbiosis and separation

Affects: Split "all good" and "all bad"—ambitendent

Transference: Replicated dyadic interactions

Resistance: To assume responsibility for differentiating

Listening Mode: Interaction in replicated scenarios
Therapeutic Modality: Replication and differentiation—reverberation/Confrontation of scenario
Countertransference: Reciprocal mother and infant positions—a "royal road to understanding merger relatedness"

III. THE EMERGENT SELF: UNILATERALLY DEPENDENT RELATEDNESS

Traditional Diagnosis: Narcissistic Personality Organization
Development Metaphor: 24–36 months—rapprochement
Affects: Dependent upon empathy of selfother
Transference: Selfothers (Grandoise, Twin, Idealized)
Resistance: Shame and embarrassment over narcissism
Listening Mode: Engagement with ebb and flow of self-experiences
Therapeutic Modality: Empathic attunement to self-experiences—resonance
Countertransference: Boredom, drowsiness, irritation—facilitating

IV. SELF AND OTHER CONSTANCY: INDEPENDENT RELATEDNESS

Traditional Diagnosis: Neurotic Personality Organization
Developmental Metaphor: 36 + months—(oedipal) Triangulation
Affects: Ambivalence: Overstimulating affects repressed
Transference: Constant, ambivalently held self and others
Resistance: To the return of the repressed
Listening Mode: Evenly hovering attention/free association
Therapeutic Modality: Verbal—symbolic interpretation—reflection
Countertransference: Overstimulating—an impediment

I would place a premium upon the consistent attempt to expand one's listening capacities, specifically upon a deliberate effort to continue developing a wide variety of perspectives from which to listen—in the broadest sense of the word—to the people who come for consultation.

I have defined four broadly based listening perspectives that have evolved in psychoanalysis in the last one hundred years, that define distinctly different aspects of the listening process and that give the practitioner various vantage points from which to receive the words, actions, activities, and interactions brought to analysis (Hedges 1983). Developmental metaphors— for a variety of philosophical and scientific as well as humanistic considerations—are properly used only as descriptions of relatedness modes. The hidden value systems that have worked deviously in the previously employed models of id psychology, object relations, and ego and self psychology need not detract from the descriptive power of developmental metaphors to grasp the wide variety of forms of relatedness that humans are capable of experiencing. Some of life's most beautiful and joyous moments clearly are derived from exercising early forms of organizing and merging experiences and capacities. Conversely, some of the moments of life's greatest suffering and grief are derived from a capacity to appreciate highly differentiated separateness. If there is a value system in the listening perspectives approach, it is in the direction of developing or cultivating greater flexibility in one's relatedness forms, that is, having more possibilities available in individual experience than the narrow or constricted solutions to relatedness issues necessarily developed in infancy and childhood.

PART III

WORKING THE COUNTER-TRANSFERENCE

About These Case Conferences

For over twenty years I have conducted one or two case conferences daily with practicing therapists. One of my goals has been to study countertransference as therapists open their work up for review by colleagues. The groups typically meet with me ninety minutes weekly and have six or seven members. We rotate presenting difficult or puzzling cases. Once a month we devote our time to discussing books and papers that pertain to our work.

I have found the essential ingredient in reviewing cases in this way is for the group to work toward developing a sense of openness and trust so that deeply personal and sensitive material can honestly emerge in a safe environment. Initially, it is necessary for me to intervene to protect the presenting therapist from others who criticize or offer interfering "help." I believe this is important, since most graduate training still proceeds by supervisory admonition and criticism. Students identify with such unhelpful attitudes. An atmosphere is created in which beginning therapists learn to falsify their reports in order to avoid censorship. By fostering an atmosphere of openness and frankness where a therapist's deepest uncertainties can be voiced, therapeutic interactions begin to emerge in which all aspects of the engagement can be scrutinized for transference/countertransference meanings. I never assume that I or any other third-party listener could possibly have a better or more intuitive grasp of the therapeutic interaction than the two participants. We search to see not how the therapy ought to go or might have gone, but rather to notice how the interaction is, in fact, proceeding. We scrutinize every possible nuance of countertransference feeling for the split-off projected parts of self and other that may not have yet become clear, obvious, or articulated in the therapy.

Eight actual transcripts of case conferences follow in which five difficult therapeutic engagements are studied in detail by several different groups. They have been selected to illustrate difficult countertransference dilemmas and how groups of skillful therapists can go about considering them. They are presented verbatim as they occurred, with editing limited to clarification and disguise.

Based upon my experience with case conference/study groups, I now foster many such study groups elsewhere. So much work today with preoedipal issues necessitates extensive use of subjectivity and entails the risks of getting lost in complex scenario replications. The study group has considerable advantage over individual case supervision for this type of work because we can pool the collective relatedness potential of seven or eight people and bring it to bear on complex interactional problems. Although peer supervision groups are no substitute for individual case supervision, the strength of the group process is to focus sharply upon certain transference/countertransference dilemmas that are confounding or blocking the analysis of preoedipal merger scenarios. Periodic case discussion gives the therapist a sense of keeping on track, an occasion for sorting things out, and an opportunity for putting words and images to complex nonverbal processes. I believe all therapists working with preoedipal issues greatly benefit from huddling together in small groups that meet weekly to sort out feelings, to consider work, and to be supported during trying times. In addition, the advantages of seeking out and documenting peer opinion should be immediately obvious in the event ethical or legal questions emerge, as they often do with therapists treating these populations.

I wish to express appreciation to the therapists who have participated in case conference groups over the years as countertransference has emerged as a factor of crucial importance. They are acknowledged at the beginning of this book for their contributions to the development of the ideas presented. I wish also to express my gratitude to therapists and clients, to listeners and speakers, for their kind permission to publish here work that so well illustrates the kinds of dilemmas that arise in this challenging field.

You are about to be engaged in some powerful experiences. I hope you enjoy them and learn from them as much as I have.

9

An Interrupted Life

I find that even as therapists begin to grasp the usefulness of the listening perspective approach, they still retain the positivist, *DSM-III* predilection for defining mythical beasts. "Is this person really a narcissist, a neurotic, or a borderline?" If we are listening for manifestations of self- and other-relatedness, such questions will not arise. In this approach to analytic work we do not attempt to define the nature of the beast as a fixed reality to be studied. Rather, we are aware that our thought tools are a series of perspectives pointing toward an array of self- and other-relatedness possibilities. A century of psychoanalytic research makes clear that our task of consciousness expansion can best be achieved by employing different modes of inquiry and interaction, depending upon the self-and-other-relatedness style currently being represented for us through the analytic engagement.

In the case conference that follows, you will be able to see how the perspective for listening shifted dramatically over a

nine-month period, during which there arose the real threat of
abandonment by the therapist. The use of poetry and dreams to
portray object relations processes is also beautifully illustrated by
this very talented young woman. Note especially how her
earliest life experiences set up a foundation or paradigm upon
which later relatedness modes have been built.

Monique: In terms of the themes we've been talking about, my
work with Lynn will give you all a frame of reference with
respect to some of the things I think about her, and features of
our work that come to mind. Rather than spending a lot of time
with psychosocial history today, I'd like to step right into the
transference and countertransference issues that are evolving.
My fear right now relates to the fact that I am down to the last
three weeks before closing my San Diego practice and being in
full-time practice here, in Orange County. This is a 21-year-old
girl from San Diego who has been seeing me three times weekly
for the past 20 months. There is a lot of acting out. There is a
lot of shutting down. There is a lot of activity centering around
my move. Initially, she was considering moving up here and
applying to UCI or even USC so her therapy could continue
with me. The thought of going to UCI seemed too compliant for
her, like putting herself in my backyard, whereas putting herself
in North Orange County so she could attend USC felt like she
had a little bit more autonomy while continuing to see me. But
these considerations have been off and on, or as Guntrip would
say, "in and out," typical to some of her schizoid nature. So I
continue to feel uncertain and on the edge of my seat as to
whether she is in fact going to continue with her commitment to
our therapy work or whether she's going to break away from the
treatment altogether as I make my move. Increasingly, it feels to
me like she's sabotaging the treatment. She's sabotaging my
being helpful to her, and she's shutting down. She's closing off,
and as Kernberg would say, I feel that I run the risk of her

controlling me, controlling the treatment, of my being a pawn of hers, an extension of her, and thereby less effective.

Larry: All of which we might also consider as an interesting countertransference statement.

Monique: Oh yeah! Where I am right now with Lynn is this: on one hand there's been a lot of effort and energy and a lot of myself, I feel, in working with relatedness aspects that I've given to her. On the other hand, I feel like a battered selfobject of hers. I feel chronically insulted when she says I sound superficial, that I'm not digging deep enough, that I'm being repetitious. Her protest against my ways of working the coun-tertransference has been, "I don't want to hear about what you're feeling, I want to talk about what I'm feeling. I've been coming here three times a week for almost two years and I still don't feel as though I know you. I still don't feel as though I've been here." So, needless to say, sitting on the other side of all of this, it's exasperating. It gets very tiring sometimes. My reaction is to just want to shake her and say, "Will you snap out of it!" We had a very grueling session last Tuesday, a week ago, where there were huge voids of silence. If I don't touch upon that silence, then characteristically what happens is the two of us sit there in fragmented states through the treatment hour and nothing happens outside of just being there with the disjointedness of it all. So I generally go after the silence. I'm very active with it at times. I interpret it. I'll say things like, "You seem to be treating me with indifference so as to make me disappear just as you have felt treated and have disappeared with other people." I at-tempted particularly in recent weeks to interpret her attempt to abandon me before she feels that I'm leaving or abandoning her. I've worked with our relatedness, as Larry well knows, more than with any other patient in my six years in private practice. I've felt obliged to experiment and take risks with her like I have with nobody else. We've sat on the floor. We change positions in the room because sometimes she wants to sit in my chair. She brought a tape recorder with some music one time because she wanted me to hear the kind of music she likes. She brought some poems in, and I did the same with her. At times I've used a Kohutian orientation with her, trying to empathize with what happens to her when she enters the room and finds herself in a one-on-one with me; how she begins to feel such tightness in her throat and begins to feel so fragmented so that she can't feel or seem present. Recently I've been getting a little bit tougher with her and I've been using more of a Kernberg orientation by insisting on some kind of treatment contract and some kind of responsibility that she's willing to take, because otherwise I feel like she's putting the responsibility onto me and living out the wish for me to be the magical therapist who makes the impossible possible with respect to what we can really do and what can really happen in the midst of these huge voids of silence.

Female: How long has she known about your move?

Monique: She was the first patient I informed. I told her eight months ago. So we've had eight months with this.

Larry: Has she actually visited your new office?

Monique: Yes. She came up last week, because I didn't make the hour's drive to San Diego due to holiday traffic. So, yes, this has not been sprung on her suddenly. We've had time to work on many of the issues that my moving raises for her.

Female: What were her presenting complaints?

Monique: At the onset, her presenting complaint was that she doesn't feel like a person. That she looks at other people with

such envy because they seem to be close. They seem to be able
to connect. But in her envy of them she then feels more
separated, more alienated, withdraws and goes more inside, and
then feels awful and miserable. This is a girl who has known for
some time that her inner world has felt quite disturbing to her.
She wrote this at age 14:

Lost forever within my body—
Something indescribable
It just sits there—day in and day out
And controls my life.
I try to push it off like nothing ever
happened—
But it's somehow trapped within me—
Possibly for an eternity.
At times it will disappear and I can
laugh and live again
But it always comes back—
And imprints itself on my mind and soul—
Deeper than ever.
I continue to convince myself that everything
will be okay—
Yet a certain humanism has caged itself deep
inside me—
And even a thousand tears can not drain it
out of me.
For I have cried a thousand tears
And it still sits trapped within me—
        forever.

Female: At 14?

Monique: At 14. This is very bright girl, very introspective.
She's been in a gifted program since the age of 8. She comes

from a fairly psychologically sophisticated family. She was referred to me by a woman whom I was in supervision with. Her father was diagnosed with a bipolar disorder when Lynn was still inside her mother's womb. So we know that at the very beginning, during Mom's pregnancy—Mom has a chronic depression anyway—but during Mom's pregnancy her husband had a break and required months of hospitalization, so Lynn was born in the midst of all of this. And we also know that with everything going on in Mom's life, she hired a nurse who came in to regulate Lynn's feeding. Within three weeks the nurse amazingly had it regulated so we know right from the start that typical with what we expect with schizoid and organizing development, there was really deprivation on an emotional level. And there was a sense of Lynn really missing much needed contact and interaction with her mother.

Larry: Monique, I'd like to orient the others to the way that I've come to see her so far from our individual supervision sessions. When we first started, the more organizing, schizoid aspects were not quite so obvious as they are now becoming.

Monique: Right.

Larry: Lynn was articulate and engaged freely, maybe falsely, but—

Monique: She has certainly demonstrated more of her disturbance over time.

Larry: Right. So early on, when we talked about her, we were working the countertransference. We were doing it the way that we do when we're trying to elucidate symbiotic/borderline structure. We were working on the assumption that she was treating you the way that she's been treated. And in session after session what you did, skillfully, was to pick up on exactly how you were feeling, exactly what you and she seemed to be doing together, how you jointly engage, and you would mirror that back to her. It seemed as though that was very helpful in many ways and appropriate to the aspects of her personality that were in play at that time. Now, in retrospect, we want to evaluate that. This is a question I have not only about this particular woman. We see so many people who, when they arrive for therapy, look much more developed and differentiated than they are. Did we lose time by working the countertransference and trying to deal with the symbiotic structure? Was it pretty much a waste or, at best, relationship building? Or is there also some symbiotic structure that did, in fact, need to be worked on first? As you began to work the countertransference, she was responsive to it. But she's not so responsive now. She's critical of you and your attempts to talk about your relationship. Earlier she was very appreciative of the countertransference work because that was the one point at which she did feel you were being somewhat real. But then she began to present earlier developmental issues and was not interested in countertransference work.

Monique: That was about eight months ago. Well, it really feels like such a struggle every step of the way. I've felt some moments of connectedness. About two months ago, I went to New York to attend a meeting. I knew she was having a difficult weekend so I called her. This is something else that I generally don't do, but it had been a difficult week and I called her. Following that she wrote me a note and expressed her deep appreciation for my having called. That felt, to me, like a moment of contact. In her ability to see my concern and effort and then to respond to that.

Larry: I want to note that whenever we find that we're varying from our normal modus operandi we need to consider the interaction in terms of some form of pull toward replication of the symbiosis. She knows that you went beyond the call of duty to show your wish to be connected to her distress on this occasion, though usually you feel quite unappreciated for your efforts and feel like withdrawing from the ingratitude.

Monique: She has brought things in to me and continues to share with me poems and essays that very poignantly describe her withdrawals into schizoid states. I've felt some connection with her at times like she's really bringing in pieces of her soul. But I bring this here today because I really need some help in surviving the next three weeks, particularly with the "in and out" stuff that is still going on with her commitment. In the midst of it, I see her decompensating. She paged me following our very grueling session last week. I was in a treatment session. I called her 40 minutes later. Her response in answering the phone was, "I've hated myself since I called you 40 minutes ago." I spend about 15 minutes with her on the phone and basically she was unreachable. From her affect and words I found it necessary to assess the suicidality for myself and really express to her my concerns about how far away she felt, and that it felt like I just couldn't reach her and that was really concerning me. Within the past several months, as her upset has increased, she's been willing to see a psychiatrist for a medical consultation. She did see someone here in Orange County that I know. She's been difficult that way too, because she's been very sensitive to the different medications that he put her on. He started her on Klonopin. It made her dizzy and sleepy. She found it difficult to concentrate. Now he has her on Pamelor, the antidepressant. But she's not even up to a therapeutic dose yet. I called him following this disconcerting phone contact with her, really wanting to let him know where things are and how I'm feeling and wondering if medication might play a significant role in this transition period.

Female: What's the plan in terms of three weeks? Then you'll be here full-time: Will she continue seeing you?

Monique: She'll come up twice a week for more lengthy sessions rather than three times a week for 50-minute sessions. We'll do 75-minute sessions twice a week. She's put an application in to USC, but she is tentative about UCI. This is a girl who had been going to Humbolt College, a more laid-back progressive school in northern redwood country. She presents in a very artsy way. She reminds me a little bit of one of the dancers you might see at Juilliard in New York City. She's somewhat frail and kind of hippyish looking. Very serious. In terms of the transference, she has some difficulty with my professional person. She has difficulty with the way I dress. She has difficulty with the car I drive. She has problems with the way I seem to be in the world, too sophisticated, too establishment, not real somehow. She has difficulty with the fact that I wear leather shoes and boots because she's really into animal rights. She says to me, "You are so vain and narcissistic." So all of these criticisms of me and my way of being in the world come up.

Female: And you're moving right into the capital of narcissism and superficiality, Orange County!

Monique: Right! And she's full of protest about that. *You* may want to live here. This may reflect *you*, but this whole environment in no way reflects me.

Female: And of course UCI has to be pretty appalling to her for those same reasons.

Larry: Thinking retrospectively, we were considering the constant barrage of criticism, particularly focusing on your person, your style, your therapeutic technique, and your general way of operating in the world, more as a symbiotic scenario. You attempted valiantly to experience and to find ways of speaking your frustrations, your feeling left out, and your narcissistic injury, all with seemingly good result. But as we begin now to experience more and more the organizing part of her, we have to review our thinking and wonder to what extent all of these criticisms served as a means for her to break contact. Perhaps we need to review some of those earlier hours in light of the organizing modes we are now sensitized to, tracing to see if at the points she attacks you personally, or your style, there was an effort to break, to block some threatening form of contact that was being established.

Monique: It's interesting to consider the concept of envy as a way of breaking contact. Or to consider her criticisms a reaction-formation against tremendous envy and wanting to be exactly like me or to be inside of me, and to be a part of me.

Larry: From that angle we might think of her envying you because she sees you as a real person. She knows that. She knows that you have real relationships. She knows that you're successful, that you're confident in your self—all of these things she feels she is not and fears she can never be.

Female: You're at ease with yourself and she isn't.

Monique: Oh yes. She experiences me as calm. The calmness agitates her. I haven't always known what to do with the envy, how to work with it.

Larry: I recall that when you have attended to it, she opposes you by saying things like, "Of course not. You're just very different from me."

Monique: Yeah. Again, it's an "in and out." There are aspects of myself that I feel she envies me for and then she devalues me for those very qualities. But the countertransference for me is one of feeling put down, insulted, defeated, and at times, less willing to put myself out to take risks with her.

Larry: So you're now in a sort of schizoid withdrawal?

Monique: Oh definitely. I said that to her on Friday when she came up to Orange County, that sometimes my effort to reach out and make contact with her is like touching a hot stove. I feel myself drawing away because it burns.

Larry: This was after the phone call when you were concerned about suicide, about her extreme pain and withdrawal?

Monique: Yes. But I felt the past Friday session was a little better than the one the previous Tuesday in that we had a point of contact around her anger at my leaving and it being just three more weeks before I would be totally out of my San Diego office. And here I am coming down on her with more focus for commitment and some kind of contract so that we could get some understanding of where we are together. "How dare you when you're the one who's leaving. Who are *you* to talk about commitment? You're not committed to me."

Larry: Now is this also the moment she first visits your new office?

Monique: This was the second time. She came down in crisis for an extra session several months ago. (addressing a male member of the group) That's the thing that made me resonate with the case you presented a few weeks ago. On one hand, here is a patient who sees me intensively three times a week for almost two years and is very involved in our process. Yet, on the other hand, I feel totally devalued by her. I feel almost like a nonentity with her. So it's very paradoxical in terms of the mixed message.

Female: I keep seeing the way she's treating you, maybe throughout, but particularly now, as almost a challenge to see if you can respond to Mom any differently than she was able to as an infant when her mother had to be preoccupied with her own depression and her husband's hospitalization. Did I hear you say 2½-year-older sister.

Monique: Yes.

Female: Whatever the child's own needs were or her style of expression was, her mother rejected or devalued them, as illustrated by her having a nurse to regulate feeding. It's like she's being Mom to you in so many different ways. Particularly on the phone call that you described, she wasn't there, she was unreachable, there was no way of making contact. Was she going to suicide perhaps like Mom did by turning her over to a nurse? Thinking about Mom's depression at the time of her birth, isn't that what the baby was faced with? Numerous attempts at trying to reach out to Mom and she wasn't, couldn't be there. So that's what you keep experiencing with her. The Mom that isn't there. The style is one of mutual involvement but with a lack of anything personal. It's as though she's showing you what her life experience was, at least as an infant and maybe throughout eternity—that when she reaches out, nobody is there, or she doesn't know how to take them in. And what keeps formulating in my mind as her question to you is, "Can you handle my scenario differently? Is there a different way to handle a mom who's not there? I'm watching. Show me how to do it."

Monique: Like somehow she's going to leave me before I have a chance to leave her. In this kind of interaction she's been in the place of Mom in so many different ways. But how do you respond to that? How do you make contact with the mom who in the transference isn't there, who has left already?

Larry: How do you hold on, how do you try to get her to be committed to you and committed to relating?

Female: As an infant she didn't have any resources to know how to manage such a dilemma. As an adult you have much more than she ever did.

Larry: I enjoyed the poem because it seemed to capture the content of her distress, her hopelessness.

Monique: I was going to read another one.

Larry: She's so articulate, so expressive. It would be easy to become sucked into the content rather than stay with your process. One of the things we've talked about with organizing level issues is what a mistake it is, whether it's a multiple personality, a psychotic, a schizoid person, or someone better developed, to get sucked into the content of the organizing state. For years therapists have been treating psychosis by attempting to enter the delusional content, with poor results. It's easy to get fascinated, particularly here where we have a bright, creative girl who can continue to produce pictures of an incredible internal world forever. But understanding the organizing in terms of the concrete symbols it offers doesn't at all mean we've got our finger on the pulse of what's important to her. It is all very compelling, but entering the psychotic world never provides an opportunity to study the making and breaking of contacts that might lead to object relations, to the formation of the therapeutic symbiosis. What we're listening for in organizing issues is how she's managing to leave you cut off and abandoned: how she's managing to destroy connections that might lead toward a relationship. Now she threatens to destroy the relatedness once and for all. She may not come to see you in Orange County. Perhaps someone knows a good nurse who can regulate your feeding! (group laughs.)

Monique: Yes. And she articulated the threat again after the grueling session last week.

Larry: So she's holding it over your head. You may die.

Monique: She is.

Female: And if you're devalued, or dead, she hasn't lost anything. Or she re-loses again in the way that she did the first time. But if she does kill off Monique, she's losing her mom again. The fantasy that she killed her mom is alive, I'm sure. You know, why Mom was depressed at her birth. There has to be at least some fantasy life about her having killed Mom off.

Larry: I've noted something interesting in organizing cases or with people who are working at the organizing level and who are deeply involved with it. I hear a number of instances in which people, right in the middle of very intense working processes, simply break off the therapy. It's always at the point at which this early dynamic is being worked on, when the abandoning or devouring mother appears. I have several thoughts so far. We're considering it a transference/countertransference dilemma and we're thinking of it as a working through process. But to the speaker this is *the most real thing* she has ever known. It's as though we've touched her deepest reality. In her mind you are really not there for her, you are not committed to her, you are leaving her, you really do dress funny and talk in peculiar ways. There seems to be a real reliving in some way of that early experience. Ordinary reality appreciation pales in face of such intense internal realities. The only reality at this level relates to how contact was broken off. This is acted out through abruptly breaking off the treatment, with the person retaining an abiding sense of the realness of the abuse the therapist has perpetrated in psychotic transference. Lawsuits are made from the reality sense of the psychotic transference. Freud's ideas about the negative therapeutic reaction relate to his observation that some people, often at the peak of idealizing the analyst, abruptly stop the relationship. Freud speaks of the idealization and extreme devaluation and of moral masochism. There is a sense of a right way to live and the person remains committed to live life in this very miserable way. The psychotic mother, who lives within, forces an angry destruction of all possible relatedness possibilities that suggest that one can live less miserably. The primordial guilt centers around the fantasy that I made her go away because I wasn't good enough. But the primary identity is with the wolf mother who devours and destroys her young. This gets aimed at the therapist and acted out through an abrupt termination.

I don't know if there's going to be an opportunity to interpret such things. I don't know if you're going to be able to save the case. But I've been struck increasingly with the *reality* people experience in the working through of organizing related-ness issues. With the treatment of neurosis, psychoanalysis is a game that we play, a chess game. "I won't tell you anything about me, you tell me everything about you and with these rules we'll go forward." In analyzing neurotic transference constella-tions all of our Freudian cat and mouse games we learned in graduate school really do work, because they tend to bring the repressed out of hiding. With Kohut's formulations of selfobject or narcissistic transferences again, there is partly a sense of the game as we explore the self to selfother resonance. But even so, exploring narcissism seems somewhat more "real" than work with neurosis. With borderline or symbiotic issues there's a lot of interacting and a lot of living out of the engagement issues, replicating the scenario, but still, at times you can count on your patient to be able to game with you for gain, to see what these enmeshed interactions are all about. But when people begin to work through the organizing level, the sense of the game is lost. The sense that we are here to explore something fades into nonimportance along with the blurring of the ordinary reality sense. That there is another reality, that you and I have a working relationship, a therapeutic alliance that we're going to look at, becomes obliterated. Horrible psychotic anxieties that are altogether too real and intense for the patient fill the relationship. "You are really leaving me, how dare you talk to me about commitment?" And it is real. It's not anything to be talked about, to be massaged and understood as transference. I don't know if there is going to be anything that you'll be able to empathetically point out to her. To her this feels like the essence of real life. "You and I are in a struggle to the death and either I am going to die or you are going to die." Who is going to disappear? Who is going to suicide? There is no psychotherapy game here now; this is for keeps. This is for real. There may be an empathic connection that can be achieved by trying to acknowledge to her how real it all seems. I'm mentioning it so that you can look for a possible opening to take up the issue of the loss of the sense of collaboration as she shows you the devouring wolf mother.

Female: How can this be bridged, this distance, this abandonment, this going away? How can she hold on to dead mother or to abandoning mother? Or receive from an available mother in a way that she had never had an opportunity to do before, ever?

Larry: It's very Kafkaesque, as in his incessant search for the castle, for the nipple. The painful search goes on and on. One relationship failure after another.

Female: Has she been in therapy before?

Monique: Never.

Female: So you were her first hope.

Monique: Well, actually she saw a counselor at her first university once a week and it seemed supportive in nature. This is her first deeper therapy experience.

Larry: When she left home to go to college was she beginning to experience some of the fragmentation that she's now experiencing as you're leaving her?

Monique: Definitely.

Larry: So was that previous therapy to try to bridge over a fragmentation that was occurring at the university?

Monique: The object relations that have become internalized for her is Mom's depression, so any experience in terms of object relations of a lost, somber, serious type represents Mom. The superficiality comes from Dad. She really sees Dad as manic and not really stable—very erratic, although he's been tremendously helped by Lithium. And probably the most poignant is her sister, who is 2½ years older. Sister for her is this very controlling, omnipotent, full of talent and leadership abilities object that she constantly feels inferior to.

Female: There's the envy again.

Monique: It's chronic. She hides behind the eight ball. There's no way, there is always somebody prettier, smarter, more talented. She writes me poems. This is the most recent one she's written. You talk about entering into her inner life with respect to primary process. It's called, "Interrupted Life."

words
   snatched from baby's mouth,
sent tumbling
   stolen toys, shattered
somewhere in the
               fall

Who be that monster
stealing the wind as

They all slept,
filling the darkness with fear,
stepping slowly towards baby
    who had not yet a
voice?

Who be that monster
    well-disguised
who hid in the closet
    deathly close to baby's door?
(baby crying for approval, seething
    in self hate, even now
    as she writes these words)

Who existed only for her?
    Knife in hand, strong angry fists
    silently torturing
            baby
Whose voice did indeed begin to grow
    (despite what They,
            the sleepers, will tell you
as patched-over, fist sized holes appeared
    on her own very walls
    (that silent intruder)
But her baby words fell upon
        deaf and
                    mutilated ears,

"I do not know you (or me anymore)
You are not my friend" baby cried,
    despite what They had told her
"But I will be—I will be
    very close—if you just lie there—
still—in your naked baby silence,
    "And do not (you cannot) accuse me, the Wind—

for I have no hands, with bloodstains of your
  everlasting scars,
and your cries will be muted by my
wild roars—
and this, only, They will hear."

Larry: I think as we try to imagine that earliest of interruptions, an impingement into her sense of continuity, we can see it well represented in this poem. But once again how easy it would be to get drawn into the hidden symbolic content rather than to see that she is representing her processes of object relations. Something, the wind, prevented her cry from reaching mother. This issue centers around thwarted connections.

Female: Right. There was presence, but it was a destructive one. One that was monstrous.

Larry: So is that the transference? That you are the monster who makes it impossible for her voice to be heard?

Monique: One of her recurring dreams has been that she's in the back seat of a car. Her mother is driving with a friend. Her mother is chattering, very engaged. This is how she frequently perceives her mother. She is holding on to her favorite doll. The wind blows the doll out of her hands. The doll flies out of the window. She turns to look out the back window of the car, sees flashing lights of police cars, and sees that the doll has become mutilated. Mom continues talking with her friend, not even realizing that her baby doll has gone out the window.

Larry: My interpretation of that dream would be that just as she begins to have a transitional object, something that she can control when she cannot control Mother's comings and goings, no sooner does she begin to have some sense of holding onto a part of Mother, or a teddy bear or a doll because Mother is preoccupied or not available, the wind, this destructive force of psychosis, of the inner fragmentation, sweeps the possibility of safety and soothing out. I thought of that being Father back there on the road, not only because of the association with police, and the superego of the father, but all those flashing red lights, the mania. Whatever shred or whatever hold she might have had on reality, on holding onto mother's body by the transitional object, that too was crushed, taken away by Father's mania.

Female: It's the therapy I keep getting back to. You said at the outset of therapy that it seemed as if there was more of the symbiotic/dyadic structure and that therapy was more of a transitional object for her in the world. Something to hang on to. I think when you figured out in your mind or told her that you were leaving, she felt that abandonment, and that started the regression or the decompensation, or whatever you want to call it. Your sense of preoccupation with yourself, your own needs, replicates the loss represented in the dream and that's why she's so enraged and so lost.

Monique: I feel that too in terms of reaching her.

Female: Do you feel guilty?

Monique: Yeah, I do. But you see, it's mixed. Because I also feel some anger. There's a part of me that feels like my life with her is really ending. She's tough.

Female: Like *why* is she letting go of the doll? Why doesn't she hold on to it?

Larry: I'm thinking that the countertransference may contain the mother's or sister's rage that she won't relate; won't hold on to connections that could help her grow.

Female: When they were maybe more capable of giving.

Larry: Then, because of the internalization of the fragmenting organizing process represented in the dream, she couldn't hold on.

Female: The lapse came from her—her not being able to actualize or utilize what was there. Previous to that nothing was there for her to utilize, but her reaction to that left her unable to take in even when somebody *is* there. You're there, able to give to her, and she can't take that in. The same with Mom and Sister. Maybe at some point they were able to give, but look at what they were met with. I mean parents love their babies, but it's always so wonderful when they start to grow up and you can go back to work and your life becomes more manageable.

Male: There's more there.

Larry: In terms of the dream, the car keeps driving on and she's still in the back seat. But whatever hold she had on internalized object relations has been crushed by Father's mania.

Female: She just let go. It's like what can she do? I think the resolution to that dream is how she can hold on to that doll. Why is she letting the wind take it away? She's got hands. She's got arms she can hold on to that doll with. I mean she's got a window she can roll up.

Monique: But she's also everybody else in the dream. She's angry and violent and wants to destroy the doll, destroy herself, ignore her relatedness needs.

Female: Right. There's a part she has in it now that she didn't have when she was an infant. It's like somehow reclaiming that part. What is she doing so that she could have a new resolution?

Male: I have another thought of the dream being somewhat like experiencing birth itself. Like she is in the car with Mother, in the womb there is a connectedness that she wants to hang onto and keep, and yet the baby part of her is blowing out the window or the womb and is mutilated right away at the beginning. Part of her is in the car, and part of her is out. Simultaneously crushed but trying to keep the connectedness.

Monique: It does seem that outside of the womb she had much more trauma than in. Whatever bonding she may have had may have occurred prenatally.

Male: There is something that she's hanging on to. At least she's in the car with mother.

Female: Right.

Male: Mother is chattering away but she's there. Any connection there is with Mother is interuteral and after that—

Larry: And later in the symbiotic exchange enters Mother's rage that the child won't hold on, the child won't grow and so forth. And then the child's false self tries to conform, to be good. That is, the earlier experience left a deficit in relating that determined the way the symbiotic period became structured.

Monique: That's exactly it. I feel that scenario. There's a part of me . . . how much can you give . . . ?

Female: Without getting bitten.

Monique: Right, that's how I feel.

Larry: The interpretive lines would then be: when you're at the scenario level, she is the mother biting you or burning you or leaving you behind, and you are the one who can't hold on to the doll. You are desperately trying to cling to some object relations but the organizing fragmentation is about to blow it out the window. So at the level of the scenario, there is a certain kind of connection, but it's a connection based on the mother's rage that the child can't hold on, that baby doll gets blown away and crushed. And you're feeling that through the countertransference.

Monique: Yes.

Larry: But at the more organizing level, the dream representation and the countertransference point toward something horrifyingly real. She's being threatened right now by the eruption of a psychotic disorganization. You're trying to control it with medication. You're concerned about possible suicide. And you told us this all began right at the time you were beginning to think of actually leaving her, of moving, nine months ago.

Whenever we have a recurring dream, I feel free to bring those images up in any context, because a recurring dream represents a basic life script theme. People say a dream is recurring, but the dream in its small details is never quite the same. The person may say, "It's just the same old dream I've always had." But it's important to go after all small details. Did mother look the same? Who was she talking to this time, what did the flashing lights and the doll look like? What slight variation is there on the dream theme? With some people who have recurring dreams you can almost track the course of therapy by the variations within the dreams. We are often cautious about bringing up material or dreams from previous sessions into the present, but with recurring dreams or memories that serve as representations of life themes I would not hesitate to bring such images up as metaphors to describe current happenings or to talk about her not being able to hold on to you. Or your not being able to hold on to her. The wind of this fragmentation or this psychosis. To deal with it in terms of the child's inability to hold on and the mysterious forces that interrupt and destroy connections. Which I think I'd want to talk about as chaos in her mind, the propensity to disconnect by confusion and fear. She tells you she has always sensed a craziness, a madness, or in her chaos a wind that made it impossible for Mother to hear her voice. It's impossible for her to reach out to another so that the other person will hear, which is what she is not doing with you. She is not reaching out to you in such a way that you will hear or can hear and respond the way she wants. The wind sweeps up between the two of you. The fragmentation, the criticisms, the scenario. The interpretation may be, "But you do have a choice. You *can* hold on to that baby now. You couldn't before. You are no longer an infant. You can hold on to me."

Female: A resolution.

Larry: Yes. "A new set of possibilities may arise. But if you let go, it will be a re-creation of your entire life. You will let the old madness come up and sweep you away. I want you to hold on to me. And I want to hold on to you." It gives you a ground for something very forceful. A forceful command. "Don't let go of what you have barely started to establish with me. You have touched me. I know you have and you know you have. But in the last eight or nine months it's as though you never made any contact at all. But I know that's not true. And you know that's not true. So I say, Lynn, you must hold on." I speak of this kind of interpretive process (Hedges 1983) as "confronting the scenario."

Male: How long has she had this dream?

Monique: When she first came into treatment she told me about two memorable dreams from childhood. This is one of them.

The other dream is a dream of being in her house. There is a room full of people. There's a party going on. People are interacting. They're nice and sociable. She is little. She wanders through the room and goes into another room where she's alone. Out of the closet comes this man, middle-aged, Middle Eastern, wearing a genie kind of costume with a sword at his waist. He pulls the sword up. He cuts her on her leg. She is terrified. She tries to leave, but feels powerless. She goes into the other room with the people to tell them and show them what's happened to her and they tell her that she's being overly excited. That this is a very nice man, and this is not anybody who would hurt her. So again, she is not heard. That really is a chronic theme. She said that up until the time that she was 16, she was afraid of the closet in that room in her house. It was such a poignant image of that Middle Eastern, middle-aged man with a sword. So those were the two distinctly memorable dreams that she told me about.

Female: The way he has the sword at his waist and cutting her on her legs. I'd say the dangerous, manic, oedipal father. Is he the one who damaged her?

Male: Did she use the term genie when she described the man that was in the closet?

Monique: I think so. Because somehow that's the image that she portrayed to me. That he was wearing a funny costume.

Male: I was just thinking of the wish, you know, the genie that comes out of the closet, the oedipal wish that turns into a sense of injury.

Larry: The first thing we all think about is the possibility of molest.

Monique: Oh, she wishes for that. She wishes that she could put her finger on something that concrete. She wants to be able to say, "This is what happened to me."

Larry: Being a little more Freudian with the dream's possibilities, I think one of the first things Freud suggested to us about racial references in dreams is that they represent a downward displacement of anger, usually from the father. Freud's interpretive hunch is that whenever there's a racial reference, the dream links into a social hierarchy. Within a child's mind are these questions: "Who is up above me and has dominance over me? And can I turn the tables and have dominance over that person?" It's usually the father who is taken and turned into the "inferior" racial person in an effort to try to manage anger. The usual association to touching Aladdin's lamp is to masturbation. So are we talking about a closet in which she retreated to masturbate, and was the retreat because of anger? Anger at the mother or anger at the father? Then when she's thinking about letting the people of the world know that she's felt so very injured by these experiences, of course, once again no one can hear her.

Female: I thought racial reference represents impulse.

Larry: It certainly can be, especially if the accent is on the primitive.

Monique: Where did you get the association about masturbation?

Larry: The Aladdin's lamp theme has often been talked about as a masturbation story. When you rub your lamp, a genie appears granting you whatever you wish. You get to fantasize. Everything comes true. And so I wondered if she's representing childhood masturbation? A retreat to isolation and self soothing that had a damaging effect on her that no one understood.

Monique: Well, it's interesting that you should bring that up because masturbation has been her deepest, darkest secret. She did start masturbating at a very early age and never told anyone.

Larry: She may have started in that closet.

Monique: She felt very ashamed. It was connected with terrible, terrible shame. This girl has one of the most harsh, critical superegos I've ever experienced. If she's talkative, she's not getting to the deep stuff. If she's not talkative, she's avoiding. Every step of the way there's something to be critical of, and she projects that onto me too.

Larry: Before we run out of time today I wanted to think about father material because in both of those dreams we have potential references to the manic father and the early superego.

Female: To transference too. Because she called you superficial at times, and the way you described Dad there were a couple of terms you used that she used when she was picking on you.

Larry: Father crushes the baby. Father damages the little girl. Father criticizes her and she criticizes you. And she makes you angry and expects you to be critical of her. So there are many potential identifications with Father to look at.

Monique: Although recently, she went to a lingerie store and bought some nice underwear for herself.

Female: That's female identification! Isn't it early for that? She's on to you!

Monique: She also bought her first pair of very cute, sexy suede boots that lace up—

Larry: Suede?!

Monique: Right! And she feels terribly guilty for that. She cannot enjoy one minute in those boots, because she begins to think of how vain it is of her to be wearing the skin of an animal.

Larry: I interrupted you when you wanted to read something.

Monique: Well, I don't want this all to be so somber because there have been moments where I feel that there's been some ray of light. This was something she wrote to me, probably about eight months ago:

This is not how I am–
     silent,
          serious,
               slippery
     stone (but never stoned)

do not try to touch me,
     climb on top of me—
or you will fall,
               as I do.

This is not how I am—
     drenched in sadness, aloneness
cannot bring myself to (really)
     smile, laugh

     who poured such cement on me
and left me to harden
                    alone?

I am not quiet or serious or dull—
     my eyes do not want to turn away
          from yours
                    (as they do)

they want to pierce
      deeply   and see

my mouth   wants to spill the truth
that   my eyes   would see

This is not how I am—
      a virgin afraid of touchandwildness,
content and comforted in sleeping alone.

No,   I am wild and free
      and brush slyly against strange men,
      and ask,
                        (in my dreams)
      "do you want to fuck tonite,
                  by any chance?"
and laugh, twirling
      in delight
at my own impish self.

This is not how I am—
      a disgusting lack of words,
creativity,
                  and a magic all my own—
stuck in angry silence
      denying the world
                  (myself)

No—it is all there—
      the lyrical words—

the magic flows from me like rain,
during a long, prolific season of
                  wetness

>   and

>   green,

> and I love

>   (to splash about in)

> the sweet

>   and

>   ticklish

>   smell.

Female: What a lovely gift.

Monique: Isn't it?

Larry: You're saying that it's been downhill from there?

Monique: It kind of has, Larry, as I look back.

Larry: But we don't have to think of that necessarily as bad, but rather a movement back—

Female: A reliving of losses she has experienced as she tries to come to grips with your moving away.

Female: Well, I like your point about having to hang on. You have to let her know how important it is to hang on.

Larry: Earlier, I suggested that for her this is serious. This is real. We're not having any monkey business here. When we're dealing with higher levels of development, we've got lots of room for play, for imagination, for spoofing, for mistakes, for errors, for differences, for stupidities. But not here.

Female: But she achieves a certain lightness and freedom in that poem. There's a component of her that has that capability, at least in some moments in some ways. So it's more than a wish.

I think there's some experience in that place. Even if it is fleeting.

Larry: When we think of the child as developing far enough to be able to hold on to a teddy bear, then we've got a mother who is being represented in her absence by the transitional object, so we have some good connection with Mother. And, given the rest of her good development, I think we have reason to believe that there's a symbiotic self that has developed in certain definite ways.

Male: This is a really good example of a person's primary organizing issues appearing in relation to loss. But other layers of development are clearly there. We even talked about oedipal possibilities.

Female: Right. I'm convinced more and more of the uniqueness of each person's development and how we all represent in our relatedness various developmental stages even though in analysis we study certain central or basic issues. With her the primary issue seems to be a theme of disappearing.

Larry: Our question is this: Is it helpful to listen primarily for organizing breaches? Or is it best to listen for symbiotic or borderline issues as a result of her being able to make partial connection? Holding on to the doll is a partial connection. In the face of potential abandonment she now relies on modes of relatedness that are more foundational because she has to rework to reintegrate the way primary object relations questions were solved.

Male: That raises the question about how much it really matters initially where we put her diagnostically.

Larry: This is one of my main reasons for giving up traditional diagnostic thinking while we're doing analytic work. The listening perspective approach defines four primary ways of listening to four vastly different kinds of human relatedness. Issues from different perspectives come up at different points in therapy. We all have different fixation points at each one of the major watersheds of relatedness development. This seems to be the case with Lynn. So far, the narcissistic material, the Kohut level material, has been experienced mostly by you. That is, narcissistic injury has made its appearance mostly in the countertransference so far, but she may well have a number of selfobject issues to work on. Thank you, Monique, for sharing your work with us.

Monique: Thank you all.

10

The Hershey Bar
Affair: I

Two halves of a giant Hershey bar represent a symbiotic situation shared by a mother and daughter. As the daughter lives out her seductive/destructive need for merged boundaries in the therapeutic relationship, we find the therapist empathically swept up in a merger that leaves him confused, feeling useless, and walking on eggshells, lest he upset her and they have to move back to square zero. We see here, clearly replicated in the therapeutic interaction, the destructive control and compliance that characterizes the early mother-child bond. We also see how a skillful therapist begins maneuvering his way out of the thick of the replication with a series of effective interpretive confrontations of her scenarios.

Frank: This is a woman I have presented three or four times before. I've been struggling through my work with her for almost five years now. My patient's name is Marie.

Larry: We know Marie. She's a part of our group now!

Frank: My life with Marie!

Larry: You're going to have to credit her with your training!

Frank: I think I periodically present her when I'm feeling lost again. I don't know if everyone here now has heard of her. She just had her fifth AA birthday, and that's how I began working with her. She was referred to me by a therapist in northern California. She's 30 years old now, a very, very bright woman. She's a programmer analyst who graduated from a well-known university with a degree in one of the social sciences. Her father is a physician. Her development is soundly symbiotic but at times almost schizoid or autistic in some sense. She's sustained a series of sexual abuses in her life: the first one was when she was about 6 or 7 years old, with a neighborhood teenager. And it wasn't a one-time thing. She was taken down to the basement and fondled. I think there was some penetration too at that point. Then around puberty she was abused by a maternal uncle for a period of a summer when she was staying with him and her aunt. Now the idea of having a romantic involvement is extremely painful for her to entertain. She presents herself, physically, like a waif. She's very petite, and kind of pretty but she doesn't present herself in a sexual way. She looks like a little girl. She's been able to maintain sobriety; that hasn't been an issue. What became an issue, when she adjusted to being sober, was the emergence of what she called "the others." The others were all these voices inside her, usually painfully critical voices. There is a real dissociative component to her. I've always been reluctant and still maintain some reluctance to calling her a multiple personality because the voices don't seem to be distinct characters. One she calls "the screamer." When the screamer screams she's expressing fear and pain. Then there are these two children. One of them cries in a corner, and the other cringes in fear. They seem clearly to be parts of herself that have been split off.

Larry: But she doesn't switch or go into those characters?

Frank: No. We've talked about the others often. There's no development of them over time.

Larry: So it's more that she hears these things. They're head voices.

Frank: Yes, the screamer screams but Marie is not screaming, she hears it in her head. It's very disturbing to her, it distracts her, she cannot concentrate at times. Her basic stance is to be emotionally numb, to be distant from everybody and everything. She has friends, but some don't live locally. She can't tolerate a lot of time with any one person. I spend more time with her than anyone else. At one point we changed to half sessions because a full session was a strain on her, on both of us. I've been doing this for several years and it seems to help. She wanted to feel my presence on a consistent basis, but she couldn't tolerate it for long periods of time. As a matter of fact, looking back, I think that when we met for hour sessions, she would retreat in the session.

Male: How many times during the week do you see her?

Frank: Four times, Monday through Thursday.

Larry: That seems to be a nice pace for you now?

Frank: Yes, she likes it, and it's working out fine for me too. In a social sort of way, she's doing fine; she's managed to buy her own house this year, she has a pretty good paying job and is very respected in her career. I think her career will advance very rapidly because she's extremely bright and dedicated to what she does. She's very lonely, however, and at times she's talked about not even wanting to acknowledge the part of herself that would desire having someone in her life because she believes it's too painful and also because it's not possible. Probably one of the best analogies she's given to help me understand how she feels about relatedness is that she told me one time that she wished she could live in my pocket, go around with me during the day, feeling my presence.

Periodically a man will show interest in her romantically, but she gets extremely frightened by this. This happened again recently, about a month ago. She's learned to tell them that she can't tolerate that. She's frightened because if they say that they still want to be there anyway, she feels inevitably that they're going to intrude upon her, that they're going to make some sort of sexual advance. And she can't tolerate it, it's too painful. She wishes they would go away, rather than wait for the inevitable. Any form of emotional pain is something she can't seem to tolerate, so she'll distance herself in some way.

In recent months, "the others" haven't been there very much. I can remember only one mention of them. I asked a couple of times and they haven't been there, but I'm not sure how to think about that. It's been a more recent change. Her relationship with her mother has always been an antagonistic, painful, irritating, intrusive experience for her. I think of her mother as a bright woman, fairly isolated, a sterotypic doctor's wife. She's now in a lengthy divorce procedure with her husband. I think Marie played an important role in the cohesiveness of her parents' marriage. When she pulled out emotionally, the marriage immediately fell apart. Her parents have been fighting about divorce issues for three years now. It's still not settled. The mother thinks that she deserves to be taken care of financially for the rest of her life. He's fighting it and it's just a mess. From Marie's perspective, her mother is constantly intruding. She wants to be best friends with Marie, and Marie wants to be left alone. An example occurred this last weekend: Last week was Marie's thirtieth birthday and her mother asked her if she wanted to come over to have dinner with her on her birthday. Marie declined. Then mother subtly tried to make Marie feel guilty for rejecting her.

A group of people Marie used to work with had a little party for her, and one of the things they gave her was a ten-pound Hershey bar (they know she likes chocolate). She didn't know what to do with this massive piece of chocolate. She decided to give some of it to her uncle, who had come over to install some mirrored closet doors that her mother had given her for her birthday. He was from out of town and was staying with her mother. That evening the phone started ringing. Marie wouldn't answer it, because she sensed it was her mother calling. Every five or ten minutes the phone would ring again; her mother kept calling and calling until finally Marie picked up the phone because she didn't want to hear it ringing anymore. Her mother immediately wanted to know where she got this chocolate. Marie perceived this as another intrusion; it was none of Mother's business where she got it. Her mother's first question was "Where were you; I've been calling you." Marie said she was with a friend, which wasn't true. Mother's next question was about where she got the chocolate. Marie answered, "Some friends gave it to me." Mother then asked, "Well why did they give it to you?" Marie responded, "Because it was my birthday." This is the sort of interaction that typically goes on between the two of them.

Male: The uncle who did the mirrors is not the abusing uncle?

Frank: No, this is a different uncle. She did disclose to her mother about a year and a half ago that the molest had occurred. Mother confronted the aunt (her sister) and the uncle. As far as

I know there has been no further contact. Marie has never contacted the uncle or the aunt. She has avoided the aunt also because she was present and aware. In fact there were several incidents when she was in bed with the two of them, a threesome.

Male: I would be interested to know her motivation for sending some of the chocolate home with her uncle when she knew her mother would probably call.

Frank: She wasn't sending it to her mom, it was to her aunt and uncle. She didn't know what to do with such a large Hershey bar.

Larry: But they were staying with her mom. She knew mother was going to find out about the chocolate. I think the question is to what extent does she continue to participate in, to provoke the intrusions?

Frank: She feels some sense of loyalty to her mother; she does not like her father's emotional aloofness. He's a schizoid sort of guy. She has a sense of loyalty to her mother for having put up with her father for so many years. She feels sorry for her so there's a tie-in that way. I don't understand it any more distinctly than that.

Male: I'm thinking about the phone situation. It seems like she could get an answering machine.

Frank: She has a machine, but her mother won't talk into the machine. It's like, "I'm not going to play."

Larry: So that's how she knows it's her mother? She hangs up?

Frank: Yes.

Male: It's like she wants her mother to be there. She calls to her through the chocolate but then experiences her response as a molest. There is a yearning, but—

Frank: There's a part of her that wishes her parents weren't there. She periodically says, "I wish I didn't have to be around her at all." But there's another part of her that wants some kind of contact. I don't know what kind. I'm trying to think if she ever initiates contact with her mother. If she does it's very rare. Her mother doesn't let her go very long without a phone call or a weekend visit.

Larry: So sending the chocolate home was clearly initiating contact?

Frank: Yes.

Larry: Is there such an intrusive symbiotic bond that if she "inadvertently" relates to her mother she knows Mother is going to come back with an intrusion?

Frank: Yes. And talking about symbiosis, I experience something in my relationship with her. There's an attachment to me, but I don't feel the attachment fully. I know she needs me, and maybe once in a while she admits it. But it's not like you'd expect even a baby to feel. There's a presence in feeling that baby bonding with you, and I don't feel it fully with her. Something is missing. I just sense it somehow.

Male: I'm free associating about the chocolate being a metaphor, sending half of it to Mother.

Frank: I think that's a good point because it ties into an experience I had yesterday. I feel like I blunder periodically by somehow being stimulated by something she'll bring up. Then I go with it, but soon feel sorry for having done so. Here's what happened yesterday. She arrived in fairly good spirits. She's not the type of person who tends to show a lot of enthusiasm. She started telling me about the new mirrored doors her mother gave her, so I asked her how she liked them. She said she was indifferent to them, because she doesn't really like looking at herself in the mirror. I thought that was pretty interesting so I asked her why. She said that she gets critical of herself. She thinks her nose is too big and things like that. By the way, some of the "others" are very critical in their tones and so are her parents. Her father is a picky sort of negative man. Her mother, on the other hand, says, "You shouldn't feel that way; you should feel the way I feel." Mother lives through Marie; she wants her to be everything that she wasn't. So Marie's perception of looking in the mirror seems illicit. Also, she doesn't want to acknowledge her body. She aroused my curiosity in saying some of these things, so I responded to her with more inquiry. When I did this, she reported getting a pain in her chest and said, "I don't want to talk about this anymore. I don't like the subject." I began to feel badly, because I thought I had blundered again, so I backed off. I let her go to something else and she began talking about the rest of the weekend. When the half hour was over I asked her if the pain was still there. She said, "Yes." In the past when I've made these "blunders" as I call them, she shut off or she stayed in tremendous psychic pain. I can't think if it's ever been somatic like this. Well, she gets headaches, too.

Larry: Has she ever had the chest pain before?

Frank: No, the chest pain is new to my experience of her. I've never heard that before. We can go weeks where I'll be shut out, and I have to find a way of getting back in there again. We go through this periodically. We go back to scratch again, to square zero. I must reestablish myself with her again, until I fuck up the next time.

Larry: The blunders, she experiences them as an intrusion?

Frank: Yes, and it's painful, it hurts. Whatever it is that I'm bringing up is emotionally uncomfortable.

Male: I'm thinking of the countertransference. The blundering that you experience with her is what she experiences in her position in the family. So she's teaching you what she feels, how it is with a blundering family. Is it your feeling or is it that she's teaching you how it was for her in her family—to be shut out emotionally when the wrong subject is brought up?

Frank: I think there's something in the way she relates to me that's helping me to understand that no matter what I do, it's not right. This is a theme of our work together. It reminds me of when I left the country on vacation two and a half years ago. I was gone for three and a half weeks. That was painful for her; she felt abandoned by me. It was very difficult for her to let me know how upset she was about my being gone for that amount of time. She felt wrong for feeling that way, "because you're a nice guy." But still she has to let me know that no matter what I do, I'm eventually going to fuck up.

Larry: (To male:) Did you follow that? Your inferential thinking is right. What we're doing with this countertransference reversal is trying to track her sense of blundering, of always fucking up. I wasn't sure it was going to fit in here 100%.

Frank: It doesn't fit 100%. But it does in the respect that I can anticipate that I'm going to be wrong.

Larry: That's the countertransference feeling.

Frank: I think that's her experience. And I've spoken to that before. So far I don't think it's gone anywhere. I don't think she's at a place where she can deal with this yet.

Larry: My immediate association to the chest pain was nightmares. The history of this word is German, I believe, and the words are basically the same, the sensation of having a horse, a mare, a mother, sitting on my chest and the sensation of suffocation, constriction, and pain. I think that is what's going on between the two of you. You necessarily must intrude. If you show any interest, you're going to be experienced as painfully, crushingly, intrusive. She constricts and gasps for breath. I think for her, the half sessions are nice because you can intrude just a little bit, an amount she seems to be able to tolerate.

Frank: I think so.

Larry: By dosing it you can have a bit of contact and the intrusion is not that awful. If we're going to consider the countertransference reversal, we need to try to get in touch with Frank's feeling that no matter what he does it's going to be experienced as bad, wrong, intrusive. I'm trying to think how we'd understand that with this mother, because it seems the mother is the intrusive one. Would it also have been true for Marie as a child? That had she needed anything or wanted anything from Mother or made a spontaneous gesture, an attempt to be alive for herself, would that have been experienced as a horrible intrusion by Mother?

Frank: Definitely.

Larry: Your message was basically, "I'm a human being in this relationship, and I have a need to feel involved. Therefore I would like to ask you a few questions about mirrors, because it sounds very interesting to me. I would like to know more, to understand you better." It's as though any assertion of your own human curiosity, needs, or interests in the relationship, are immediately experienced as an intrusion. So it's a blunder for you to have any needs, for you to look for any kind of human contact, human exchange, or understanding with her. You would love for her to reveal something to you, but she can't or won't because it's too dangerous. But like with her mother and the Hershey bar, she mentions the mirrors seductively to you. If you ask, though, she will punish you by withdrawing.

Male: Are there any intrusive behaviors on her part toward you, curiosity, or wanting to know about you? Does she do that to you?

Frank: I've had to set some clear boundaries about that from time to time. I mean we've been together long enough now to where she's fairly clear about those limits. But at one point she used to live down the street from me, a couple of years ago.

Larry: She moved there, didn't she?

Frank: Yes. She likes it periodically when I tell her things going on in my life. She loves it when I talk about things that happen to me. She doesn't ask for it, but she likes it. She's told me more than once that she likes it when I do that, but it's just not right for her to have wants. Sometimes I have to squeeze something out of her like, "You do want something, don't you?" I have to beg her to legitimize it for herself.

Male: Do you think she's capable of having any sexual transferences towards you?

Frank: I don't think she's far enough along yet. I think the most sexual she has ever felt toward me is when she says she wants to ride around in my pocket. I think the warm sensation of being held or embraced in some way is where she is sexually, wanting to feel embraced, to snuggle. She likes the word snuggle. In each session, her position on the sofa is to take the pillow like this (covering his chest), take her shoes off, and then she crosses her legs.

Larry: So whatever potential sexual response she might have she keeps hidden behind the pillow?

Frank: Yes. So in today's session with her I'm expecting her to still be in pain. She'll still have the chest pain, or the chest pain will have subsided, but she'll come in and look severe, like it all hurts, and she won't say much today. There will be long periods of silence. I used to have to initiate conversation at every session. That's not true anymore. I'd say at least half the time if I sit there silently she'll start, so that's been a change.

Male: That's an important change!

Frank: Also, in the last couple of months she's talked about things she's never talked about before. She's given me information about her experiences that I haven't heard before. Last week was her thirtieth birthday, so we talked about past birthdays. She talked to me for the first time about how past birthdays have been a real disappointment to her. When she was growing up she didn't like her birthdays because she was allowed to choose what she wanted to have for dinner, but then her father would be busy and her mother would tell her that they had to postpone the celebration until Dad could be there. So they would do it tomorrow or the next day. It was always disappointing. I felt good about the fact that she gave me this information. There have been other situations where she's given me information. That's been the most recent change, a glimmer of light. The material is expanding. I feel there's a responsiveness to me that's beginning to occur. Although in the five years there have always been glimmers of expansion like the one I've just identified, my general sense is that I am always back to square zero somehow. I always feel like I'm fucking up. I've often felt like I'm not good enough, not knowledgeable enough. I feel as though I'm being punished.

One of the more paranoid things I feel in working with her is that there's a part of her that wants to die. We had a little celebration in the office last week for her thirtieth birthday and she told me that she hadn't expected to live this long, that if it wasn't for me she wouldn't have lived this long. Periodically, she talks about not wanting to live. She has many thoughts of killing herself. One of my biggest fears is that her mother would sue me for malpractice. If Marie killed herself, I know for a fact that she would. We've talked about how to stop these suicidal feelings. We've talked about my legal responsibility to her. She says that if she ever decided to commit suicide, she would terminate with me and wait at least six months before she did it. I really don't think she would jeopardize me. I think she feels a sense of loyalty to me.

Larry: The thing that's wonderful about that is that it puts you and her together in opposition to parental intrusion. She knows that you know her parents are disastrous people, that they've done mean and ugly things to her and that they can do those things to you. It seems to me that this understanding is the mutual acknowledgment of this. It creates a sense of togetherness.

Frank: I think I acknowledge how horrible they are much more than she does. I was going to use the word seduce, but I'm not sure if it's a seduction. Maybe it is. Sometimes I think she gets me to speak for her, to articulate the intrusions. I get outraged at her mother's behavior. But even so, I guess the basic dilemma is that I always feel like I am back at ground zero. Five years . . .

Larry: How does that translate to her childhood?

Frank: When I look at her emotional development, she's not far from ground zero, so she's spent thirty years this way. Somehow her parents didn't know how to engage her in a way that would help her move forward. I think they probably got as far as I have in getting attachment directed toward me, but not a full bonding. She's telling me, "I can't let you experience fully all my wants and needs."

Larry: That's the transference. So we might infer that if she were to reach out to her parents, her mother, there might well be some sense that there was a person there but the other would be experienced as distracted or unavailable for contact and she would fall back to square zero. In the symbiotic period it is crucial for the parental auxiliary ego to be present while various ego functions are being learned. We are aware that nascent ego functions are available when Mother is present and absent when Mother is absent. Over a period of time, with Mother there in a reliable way, the child learns the skill. It sounds as though every time Marie was on the verge of learning a new skill, of reaching out in some effective way, Mother would vanish somehow. And the ego function to be learned or solidified would go back to ground zero. That would be my guess. I think that's how you felt when you got all this mirror information. You reached out to her, feeling that you really wanted to find out about her experience with the mirror, to touch her emotionally. Now you're anticipating that when she comes in today you will be back at square zero. In some way or another she will not be there in a way that allows you to feel fully connected, and good or safe about your connection. It reminds me of the nature of the symbiosis, as Mahler's research shows (Mahler 1968). The child would be trying a new skill. In Mother's mind, growth was apparently seen as the threat of the child growing up and leaving Mother. The child would be trying the skill, the mother would pull her attention away, and the child would collapse in failure. Mahler filmed many vivid pictures of the mother withdrawing support at a critical moment so that the child would collapse and remain dependent. Masterson bases his entire therapeutic approach to the borderline on the observation of what he calls "abandonment depression" (Masterson 1972). This is what it sounds like Marie is teaching you, by showing it to you in the countertransference. Just when you feel like you have something good to hold on to, to make life together meaningful, she shows you that it's a blunder to have any needs or wants for contact exchange or even for a sense of feeling personally validated or alive within the relationship.

Frank: I felt strongly that I was wrong for having brought it up.

Larry: That "wrong" feeling is something you want to pay attention to because that may be how she feels. If she tries to do something, Mother leaves, and it's as if she's done something wrong. However she tries to express herself, her needs for contact, her right to be acknowledged as an important person in the relationship, it's going to be wrong.

Male: She denies you the whole experience. She doesn't let you feel the satisfaction of growth, her change, her feeling better about herself. Her half and your half make a whole life—the Hershey bar affair—but she doesn't see your whole and her whole. The two can't mutually consider each other.

Frank: The question that keeps running through my head is, "How do I help her move from this ground zero?" How do I speak this to her? She'll really have to strain to hear me. Then she'll let go and the blockade will come down. It seems that there can never be a full acknowledgment.

Larry: Maybe that's what needs to be spoken first, that if you show your feelings and concerns for her, you worry about being abandoned, blockaded by her. You might say it even if you have the sense that she may not be ready at this point to respond to you in any way about it. So much of confronting scenarios depends on frontloading, on planting seeds that can later develop. The point is not about her mistreating you, but rather that she's showing you the way it was for her, the frustration that her mother would not give her any reassuring or validating response. If she wanted something from her mother, her mother was not going to give her any acknowledgment or let her feel valued, validated, or reassured. She didn't get the chance to feel fully human. Whether you use the Hershey bar affair or some other example, I'm sure that you'll have plenty of opportunities. So that may be the next step of the interpreting process, to show her that even if she does grasp the idea, there is still not any attempt to relate. She's not able to emotionally resonate with you about what's going on between you. And that seems very much to the point.

Frank: There's something else that we're getting into now. When I talk about these issues here, it helps me revive myself in terms of the energy of my own thought processes. When I'm in that situation with her, I begin to deaden inside to the point to where I can't even generate thoughts. I slow down inside.

Larry: You need to tell her that too. The deadening is of course what's happened to her.

Frank: I'll have to go through great pain to tell her these things, but also to let her know that it's not her fault. The first thing she'll say is, "I'm wrong again. I shouldn't have told you I had this pain in my chest yesterday." I'll respond with, "No, that's not it at all. It's perfectly fine. I'm glad that you told me." I'll really have to stress that.

Male: I see a common thread here. When she's intruded upon by the environment there's nothing left to give. When guys are intruding on her, I wonder if this might be a cue that she's not going to be available for you. My fantasy is that when she's doing okay she can be there and deal with your intrusions somewhat. But if someone intrudes there's nothing left to relate to you.

Frank: That might be a hint to the sort of deadening that I feel inside, that there's nothing left, the well has gone dry.

Larry: I think there might be a way to let her know that you belong to a small consultation group.

Frank: She knows.

Larry: And then to tell her just what you told us. That from time to time you feel deadened and you're aware that you need something fresh. When she was a little girl there weren't any outside resources for her to consult with and to feel better about herself.

Frank: Yes. In fact, when we did some of this, this is where the second instance of her being abused came up.

Larry: I think this can be brought up to her. It might be said that you realize when you talk about her to your colleagues, somehow you feel you know what's going on, you feel revitalized. You then have a better idea of what she's showing you, and how good that feels to you. Then you begin to feel that her experiences were not validated for her. When she reached out no one was there for her or else when she reached out she got abused. She has no auxiliary resource, and there again, she's giving you her mother by restricting your spontaneity, by not letting you connect and not following through in reinforcing the connection—leaving you feeling deadened and depleted of energy and capacity for thought. She's showing you the way she must have been mothered. You're feeling the helplessness that she feels, and has always felt. You at least have some help; she didn't have any. The help she could find might have made her feel a little bit better but fundamentally it was abusive and disruptive.

Frank: I feel periodically that I have to inject her with life. I feel like I'm breathing life into her. I feel it's coming again. Our rhythm has been established; she lets me know when I need to respond. It's going to take a lot of energy when I go back to her and tell her everything I now see as a result of talking about her here. I think there's a part of her that wants life. Then she becomes deadened again and that's my cue to breathe life back into her.

Larry: Does that correspond to our way of thinking about the countertransference? The reversal?

Frank: Of course. It's exactly what I'm doing.

Larry: Did she ever do that to her mother?

Frank: To breathe life back into her? She's the only daughter. She has three brothers. I think her mother has always viewed her as the person that she (the mother) couldn't be. She wants to live all her fantasies through Marie, to feel alive through being in contact with Marie's sense of life.

Larry: So she's needed Marie to live her own life through, particularly now that she's going through this difficult divorce. Here's Marie feeling sorry for her; her mother is in trouble. Mother calls and calls, and Marie feels like she has to answer the phone and breathe a little life back into her depleted mother. Mother is frantic. She's bored and lonely, and she wants to know who Marie is giving her chocolate to, who else is taking life from Marie. Marie has to restore her mother from deadness.

Male: How do you understand her alcohol and drug usage through all of this?

Frank: She's thirty years old and she was an alcoholic from about age 16 through 25. She was also into cocaine and a little marijuana, but primarily alcohol. I think about it mainly in the sense that it reinforced distance from her own emotional pain; it protected her.

Male: When you said that you needed to inject her with life I thought maybe that's how she used cocaine.

Frank: Yes, but the alcohol served more as an anesthetic to numb her.

Male: Why does Marie think her mother gave birth to her?

Frank: She doesn't think like that. Her mother would say, "I wanted all of you kids a lot, I'm a good mother."

Male: No specific identity was there? She just belonged to all of them; she wasn't a special child?

Frank: I think that her only specialness was that she was a girl and her mother wanted this ally against the boys.

Male: But it sounds like there's no happiness. It's so hard for her to get happy about anything. That's why I asked the question. No spirit, no inspiration.

Frank: I get angry with her once in a while about the fact that she won't enjoy anything.

Larry: In time, you may be able to get angry with her about her refusal to enjoy you. You enjoy her. You might say, "I see you four times a week, and there's always something new."

Frank: I think I can say to her, "And I'm not even permitted to say that to you because you'll misinterpret what I'm telling you to mean that it was your fault or that you were bad, or wrong, so I really can't even say that to you."

Larry: I'm impressed with how you've worked with her over the years and I'm very impressed with how far the work has proceeded. You've reported major shifts in the past six months.

Frank: Technically, each time I present her, I know that, but experientially I never feel like that.

Larry: Are you aware that you talked differently about her today? When we first heard about her you were tied up in knots. I don't feel that today. I feel you're tracking her. You're frustrated, but you're coping with that. There isn't the sense that this is a totally defeating case that you don't know what to do with. There isn't the former sense of helplessness. You have confidence that your work together is moving forward, despite frustration, depletion, and setbacks. I don't think you used to have that.

Frank: I do feel more confident.

Male: Also, before, I had a sense while you were talking that you felt drained. There's much less of that today, more hope. You feel the sense of being drained and you can look at it with more of a sense of humor and understanding than before.

Larry: The words I would like to put on both instances are that I think we hear the posture, the form, the mode of the symbiosis. You already know what today's session will be like. She knows what you're going to say and she knows that she will have to shut you up. So the whole replication of the early bonding experience is coming to light. You're working on finding various ways to stand against this scenario, to confront this way of being because it's so limiting. It limits both of you.

But you don't really have any way to confront it until the two of you are doing it together, until the replicating transference is being lived in your relationship. I had the fantasy that maybe this afternoon won't be the way you think it will be. When she comes in with her injury, you will be in a better position to confront it. You might say, "You know this morning I was thinking about what it would be like today, and I thought maybe the pain wouldn't be gone. I knew that in some way or another my being interested in you yesterday was something I wasn't supposed to be doing, and that you hurt as a result of my showing an interest. In some way or another it will probably be important for you to still be hurting today." Now that's bound to produce a different reaction! I'm sure your words would be different and better than mine. You call the shots and show that you understand them. Somewhere in the background is the implicit question to her, "I wonder if you will ever be able to give up this self-limiting, self-destructive pattern?" You may or may not choose to say that, but the implication is there. You might say, "This is a very strong pattern. Your mother is still holding you in her grip. Sooner or later you'll probably let me show some interest in you. You may feel the intrusion or the pain, but you may also feel some resource inside of you to let me be interested in you without it being so painful, so abusive, so deadening, so draining on your resources. Some day you may be able to take pleasure in my interest." Again, you may not actually need to say it, but that's the background atmosphere for whatever you do say. "Sooner or later I think we'll find a way out of this pit that you've been in for thirty years." But at the present time it's important for you to show her that you see the pit. You know what's coming, and maybe at the beginning you might introduce some humor about it. "I was trying to think if there was any way you could come here today and be in good shape?"

Frank: How about, "I'm ready for you today!"? My sense is that her body message will be, "I don't know if I can really hear that." I'll have to repeat it again and again.

Larry: As you anticipate her reaction, you might even start off with, "You know I've tried to imagine what it would be like today. I know there are some things I would like to tell you, but I also know that if I do, you will experience me as intruding. Furthermore, I feel sure that the things I would like to say today are things that either you won't want or will not be able to hear from me."

Frank: ". . . and then I am going to intrude some more and then you will feel the pain of that and it will be harder for you to hear it."

Larry: ". . . and I anticipate that this is how our session will go today. I feel I'm getting to know you pretty well and I think I can now appreciate how very difficult it is to let these interactions occur. It seems you have been very successful in your task here of showing me how things are for you."

Male: Then she'll say what?

Frank: No, it'll be silence.

Larry: Did everyone follow that? When we do think we're on top of the symbiotic scenario, we are always aware of how it is *not* going to be received, how it cannot be received because our interpretive confrontation violates some basic sense of reality expectation of the person. So you can begin your comments with that as well! We are not trying to trick, manipulate, "heal," or "cure" anybody. We are simply trying the best we know how to mirror what is given to us. When we anticipate problems in the communication of what we think we are seeing or feeling, then we must begin by addressing this non-verbal, interactional problem—this is the "I can't, you must" resistance that all of us hurl at our elders. So, Frank, do you think you're ready for her today?

Frank: I'm expecting to be rolling around in here for quite a while!

Male: You say she's been at ground zero for thirty years. You'd go through this agonizing process too if you had such a major change to accomplish!

Larry: I think it's starting to pick up. What she's been telling you in the last five or six months is very important.

Frank: There's another thing I'm doing, and I don't know if it's really helping. She tapes our sessions. If I say something I think is important for her to hear, once she walks out the door it's gone. My voice and my thoughts don't exist any more. So I mentioned taping a couple of times, to try it and see what happens. So for the last few months she records the sessions, and listens to them the following morning before she comes in the next day.

Larry: She does?

Frank: Sometimes she hears it, and sometimes not. Sometimes she gets distracted.

Larry: I think the interpretation you might make there is, "I've suggested this tape recording so that I can beat my messages into your head. Now I feel like 'My God, your mother never heard shit.' When you were growing up she never got any messages, she just blanked out." You picked up the "blanking out" disease from her!

There's something else I'm beginning to see. Here's an example. She's beginning to identify with her mother's position. The way I share this with patients is, "There's something here that's a total fraud. As an infant you were able to understand your mother and the way she turned away, blanked out, was distracted. You had to build up a model of her in your mind, like all babies do in order to understand their mothers. Because your mother could not hear and was not available, you built up this model inside, this primary identification in order to understand her. But as you built up this mental model it also became you. In a way then, you're living sort of a fraud, this not hearing, this blanking out, this distractibility, this not knowing what I've said, this not being able to get messages from me, not being able to enjoy me, or let me enjoy you. You block it off. I don't think all this blankness is you. I think it's your mother living inside of you, and it's a lie! It's not the way Marie wants to live!"

Frank: That's right! I believe Marie wants to live with full and resonant relatedness.

Larry: Yes. We must try to figure out, how an infant understands Mother. Our best guess is that there has to be some kind of mental model. As an infant finds Mother and understands who Mother is, mimicry is the main form of relating, primitive identificatory thinking as we studied in Alice Balint's paper (1943). All the child can do is to become that which the traumatizing mother is experienced as being. Mother is not noticed as separate until she fails in some way. At that earliest age the mimicking or identificatory thought is a global body process. The infant models his or her body according to mimicry in an attempt to understand the mother's failures, which is why studying the countertransference is so important and gives us so much information. That early mother is living inside and Marie gives her mother to you. Your problem, Frank, is this: You, as an adult, can think about her in a particular emotional way but you can then also let go of it. I mean you have a lot of other ways of understanding the world. But the mental processes that an infant has from the first year of life are so limited that mimicry, imitation, monkey-see-monkey-do is all the infant can achieve. So the primary bonding relationship is based upon what Mother can give in the way of relating. When I tell people I think something fraudulent is going on, it startles them. "It sounds like everything you've just said to me is somehow a lie." They react, "What!?" They are startled that I would charge them with such crimes. Here they are trying their best to be themselves, to tell me what they're thinking, and I'm saying it's a big fraud! Of course, I only do that if I can show them that this is not the way they want to live, that this is not their true self, not who they want to be. I might say, "I know you very well. You are not this way. This is all baloney! This is the kind of abuse you were subjected to and now you're doing it to me and others who are close to you." It's harsh and strong, but when you know the person well enough to feel somewhat certain, it's illuminating. The person begins to realize that he or she is living with an alien being inside that they hate. The question is, "How are we going to understand this?" I usually suggest that it happens between us or with a spouse or someone else close. I use the "symbiotic we." "We will study it together. We will find a better way. We will devise some way out of all of this." I hope to hear more soon on Marie. Thanks, Frank.

Frank: This was helpful. Wish me luck!

Group: Good luck this afternoon!

11

The Hershey Bar Affair: II (one-year follow-up)

Frank: This is an old friend of ours, Marie. I brought my notes here today because I wasn't quite sure what I wanted to present. I've been seeing Marie now for a little over six years. Her parents have divorced since I last presented her here. I've experienced a profound sense of disconnectedness with her over the years, but I feel like I have some grip on where we are now and I feel positive about what's happening. I feel like she's developing some insight into what's going on with her. Two main themes, I think, have been developed in the last year. One is her increased tolerance to being in the sessions and not tuning out. There's been a lot of focus on that. The other one is talking about the theme of disconnectedness versus connectedness in our relationship. That's getting explored in the therapeutic relationship not only more thoroughly, but clearly and regularly. So I feel really good about that. My notes are mainly for me to maintain continuity so that they're not process notes. But in going over some of the material I wanted to present today, I was wishing that they were process notes because the material is getting richer. I'm going to read to you some things that have happened and maybe they'll provide an opportunity for us to discuss and to develop some of the themes. Last May she started talking about her mother more. She made the comment that she's like a turtle in a shell dealing with her mother. When she returned from a visit to her mother she seemed less distant in sessions than she had previously been after such visits. Before, after she had some contact with her mother, she went into a protracted state that she calls numbness—not feeling, being very distant and sometimes even having a blank stare. If you remember, I was seeing her four days a week for half sessions for the last few years at Larry's recommendation.

Larry: You're still not able to see her for whole sessions?

Frank: I am now. Earlier, she couldn't tolerate whole sessions. She's extremely bright. She's a Phi Beta Kappa. Finally, now, insight is starting to unfold. After this trip to visit her mother, she mentioned that having her mother as a mother has been like having an overwhelmingly demanding infant without room for her own needs or wants. Whenever she gets in contact with her own needs, wants, or wishes, she feels wrong. I thought that was a pretty significant breakthrough.

As she began to shut people out less and there was less distance, she began to recognize that there were more predicaments for her that were beginning to arise in terms of the need to set limits with people. But accompanying her need to set limits is the fear that she'll become selfish. Another fear is that she'll be found wrong if she sets limits with people. People will disagree with her and find her to be wrong. She talks quite a lot now about being wrong. If she expresses her own needs or wishes to somebody, she's wrong. So there's lots of self-doubt. Almost ten months ago the "others" started screaming one day. But that's another change or shift that's been happening. The "others" don't seem to be surfacing so much. They don't seem to be coming out as often.

Female: Those are her internal voices?

Frank: These are people inside her that are not well developed or distinct from one another. She talks about "the screamer" a lot. The screamer is this woman who at the top of her lungs is just ranting and screaming. Sometimes she seems to be very angry but often she's an expression of fear. And then one of the other others is this little girl who's curled up in kind of a fetal position and is very quiet and withdrawn. She expressed fear long ago that if she allowed them to be discussed more they would come out more. She was afraid that they would take over, take control. But the most I've experienced with her is her talking about them screaming inside or cowering inside. No more than that.

Larry: Did you ever explore with her if she was afraid to have them come out, or if you would be okay with them? Were they ever invited to be present in the room?

Frank: Yes. I encouraged her to talk about them and to allow them to be with us.

Larry: So if she needed to live some of those characters in the hour, she has the sense that it would be okay with you?

Frank: Yes. There's one incident where the screamer came out ten months ago. As she was continuing to contend with intrusions from other people, both in the work setting and socially, she was feeling more vulnerable to intrusions because she was doing less distancing. She was anticipating a visit with her mother on the Fourth of July. She said she wanted to get numb. I asked her if my time with her was an intrusion. In our sessions she was becoming more focused and less distracted from her internal processes and I was encouraging that. She didn't respond at the time, but a week later she said that she didn't see my "keeping her from oblivion," those were her words, as an intrusion. She wanted me to intrude in order to establish some kind of connection with me. Again, those were her words. But she didn't want me to intrude by eliciting uncomfortable feeling states in her.

Larry: Can we review that?

Frank: Yes.

Larry: What I heard was if she goes into head voices she goes into oblivion. She would rather be in contact with you?

Frank: Yes.

Larry: Being in contact is not intrusive because she feels rescued from oblivion. But it would be intrusive if you ask her about her feelings. If you ask her about her feelings, the head voices start up again to take her into oblivion?

Frank: Yes. If I ask her to be with me in feeling states that are uncomfortable or painful for her, than she'll end up numbing or distancing. That's an intrusion and she doesn't want that.

Larry: Am I making a leap that isn't correct? If she didn't numb you off would that mean she would go back into the voices? I'm assuming the voices are representations of unpleasant states.

Frank: Yes. They would occur if she's not numb.

Larry: Okay. So she prefers the contact with you over the abandonment to the voices.

Frank: Yes.

Larry: If you want to relate to her on the feeling level, there's the risk that you'll force her into the voices. She would rather relate to you, but not on a level of unpleasant feelings.

Frank: Uncomfortable feelings. The next session she seemed very disconnected. She said, "I have the image of you coming over here and slapping me to get out of it." By the way, part of what was happening was that I was getting ready to leave on vacation. That's always been difficult for both of us. I've learned to prepare for my vacations well ahead of time.

Larry: How do you do that?

Frank: We start talking about it usually a month to two months ahead and I give her phone numbers where I'm going to be. She's the only person I ever do this with. And I usually call her when I'm on vacation, usually once if it's a week or maybe a couple of times if it's more than a week.

Larry: How did you handle the three-week China trip several years ago? You were seeing her then.

Frank: Oh, that was awful. It was months of disconnection after that, literally. There was no emotional contact in sessions for at least three or four months after that. Last summer I gave her phone numbers where I would be on my two-week vacation. When I returned she had stomach pains. She told me she was going to be tested for a possible ulcer. But she was less distant than I expected her to be. There was less numbness than in the past when I've been gone. The following week, for the very first time, she raised the issue of having a child. She just made mention of it; she didn't really develop the theme very much, but she came back to it later. I thought that was very important.

She started talking more about not being able to set limits with people without disengaging them. About three weeks later she brought up that she thought her mother may have been sexually abused also. That scared her. She was afraid of being sucked in by her mother. They would have something in common that would give her mother an "in" to be intrusive again with her. The following day, I brought up a countertransference reaction of anger toward her for feeling discounted by her distancing behavior. This was the end of August, so I had been back maybe four weeks. I'm trying to recall what that was all about. I'm not really clear except during that period of time after my return there was a low-grade distancing from me, a numbness, and a lot of effort on my part to develop the theme of connecting with her. I felt pushed away and frustrated with that and so I spoke my anger and frustration to her. The following session she became more responsive.

Larry: In the countertransference interpretation were you able to touch any of the dynamics that perhaps you were feeling, or what she was feeling with her mother?

Frank: I've talked about that quite often. She said that usually if somebody is angry with her she sees it as her fault and that she felt stressed by my confrontation. She then talked about her mother's intrusiveness. It can't be confronted because she ends up feeling little and "losing it." By losing it, she means that she can't remember what it is she wants to say when she tries to confront her mother about how intrusive she is. Losing it means that she can't be with her own internal state enough to be able to verbalize to her mother what she's experiencing. She was raised by her mother to believe that women manipulate men for what they want and that men are to be catered to in order to manipulate them effectively.

Female: This how you deal with men?

Frank: Yes. She also said when she was talking about her mother that she didn't learn right from wrong or ethics from her mother, but rather from her peers, because her mother does whatever she wants to get what she wants. So she sees her mother as amoral. Gradually there's more clarity, more pieces being put together. She also began talking about feeling pressured to perform for me rather than just being with me in session. She feels the connection and sharing her perceptions will end up with her feeling like she's foolish or wrong. We related this to her erratic connection with her mother and how it wasn't permissible for her to be herself with her mother without feeling as though she was wrong because she had to accommodate Mother's scenario.

Larry: In your relationship with her, has that been brought out in the reverse, how much you've had to accommodate Marie?

Frank: Yes.

Larry: For four weeks after your vacation you had to accommodate her disconnection. There you are, struggling, trying to relate, until you finally just get angry with her and tell her so. But it seemed to be a useful interpretation.

Frank: Yes. In October she said that she wanted to cut off thoughts of babies. When I encouraged her not to do this she was initially okay until she became hopeless about the desire to have a companion that she believes she can't have. Occasionally she'll bring up that she will never be able to have a lover or a mate, that she can't tolerate that kind of closeness. Initially, when she talked about her desire for a baby, we considered the possibility of artificial insemination. But later, having a baby became related to having a mate and somehow it became hopeless. "I can't relate."

Larry: Has she talked about the babies as representations of her self?

Frank: When babies came up I felt initially that she was representing the connection she wished to have, was having with me.

Larry: That she was being born as a result of the connection?

Frank: Yes. In the next session we talked about that more specifically. The wish to have a baby was a wish for a human relationship and a purpose for living. The only way she might be able to have such a relationship is to have it with a baby. She couldn't have this kind of connection with an adult and sustain it. She was able to express some sadness in not always being able to feel connected to me. She said she was least likely to experience connectedness when she feels the most needy. That's when she's most likely to withdraw. She expects not to be responded to, so she distances. She expressed some relief and joy after spending a weekend with her mother. Her mother is beginning to develop a social network outside the family and this allows Marie more room to exist, rather than always having to protect herself by disconnecting.

Larry: This is all startlingly different from how she's been before!

Frank: Yes, it's very different. It's very different in that there's much less disconnection. She's beginning to trust some of her internal states.

Larry: Before, you were having to pull everything out of her.

Frank: Yes. It's very different in that respect. Another big issue came up in November. She was employed for a period of about two and a half years by a large corporation, which also happens to be where my wife Joyce works. My wife had been responsible for getting her the interview there because the headhunter she was working with wasn't able to get her an interview. So as a result of going to work there, she developed a friendship with

Joyce, and they would have lunch together every three or four weeks.

Larry: Joyce is aware of your connection with her?

Frank: Yes. Last November was Joyce's fortieth birthday. I gave a birthday party at my house. I thought about what I was going to do because there were a couple of other people from Joyce's work who I felt it was important to invite. But I didn't want to deal with the idea of Marie being there. What ended up happening is that I did something rather unlike me. I ignored the problem. I had the party, did not invite Marie, and did not process it with her. I tried to slide it by her. And it didn't work.

Larry: Well, "the screamer" is about to appear, I'm sure. And all this just after you'd established a connection.

Frank: Right. Well, obviously she got numb, for about a week after the party. You know, she became distanced and numb.

Larry: But not saying anything to you?

Frank: Not saying anything. So I brought it up.

Female: Boy, guilt!

Male: You chicken you!

Frank: My guilt got to me!

Larry: You had plenty of reason to feel that she would hear about the party because of who else was invited?

Frank: Yes. At some level I knew that was going to happen. I was hoping somehow I wouldn't have to deal with it. But I needed to deal with it. It was becoming painfully obvious to me that this was why she was numb and distanced, and so I brought it up. She admitted to feeing very angry at me for not being included in the party. That was toward the end of the session. By the way, last September she had told me she felt ready to come for whole sessions. She can only afford to pay for Tuesday and Thursday as full sessions but Monday remains a half session and we skip Wednesday now. She's been able to tolerate the whole sessions for the first time. That's been going on now for about six months. So at the time we're processing this we're having full sessions. I brought up that I felt like what I had done was much like what her mother had done with her, which was to discount her and her feelings in order to avoid feeling her own discomfort. For Mother to get what she wanted at the cost of ignoring what was happening to Marie. She listened very carefully to that. She didn't respond too much until the next day. She told me she felt very positive about our last session and that she was glad I had spoken with her, though she had some feelings of being overwhelmed by my interpretation. The power of the countertransference and the relationship was a little overwhelming to her and she felt pushed way back as a result.

Larry: But still, she felt very good about it?

Frank: Yes, she felt really good. She knew what had happened was important but still she could feel herself pushing back. I thought it was positive that she was able to verbalize what was happening for her and to be there enough to be able to speak that to me.

Larry: Anything about why she didn't bring it up herself?

Frank: The only comment was that somehow she was wrong for being angry. So that passed. She seemed to be there. The episode led us into talking about being able to set limits with people again. She wants a relationship. But she also wants to deny the wish to have a relationship in order to avoid the pain of not being able to tolerate intimacy. "I want to cry," she said. "Relating is right here, but I can't." The following session she said she had been asked out on a date and that she had told the man why she didn't date at this point in her life. This was a difficult step for her, because she was afraid that by verbalizing what her reasons were for not dating, the reasons weren't good enough. She told this man that she doesn't date because she can't tolerate sexual intimacy, that she had been sexually abused, and that she hadn't worked through that yet.

Male: I'm impressed by that disclosure.

Larry: I was thinking it was a little strong.

Female: It seems unnecessary. He only asked her for a date.

Larry: How did that go? How did he handle that?

Frank: He backed off.

Male: Very quickly! "Okay, see you later. I understand!"

Frank: She talked the next time about recognizing a part of herself that's sexual and that wants a connected relationship but she feels hopeless about the ability to ever tolerate it. She expressed a desire to work on this somehow. In the past she's been so hopeless when she gets in touch with this sort of thing that she's become suicidal. I've had to have suicide pacts with her before because when she starts getting in touch with her loneliness and despair she seriously starts contemplating how she's going to kill herself.

Larry: So this is remarkably different, the fact that it came up so quickly. She told this man, "I can't have a date with you because

I'm afraid of sexual contact." Then she stayed with her feelings somehow and didn't go suicidal on you.

Frank: Yes, right. There was no mention of any kind of suicide. She was able to stay with the feelings of hopelessness about ever being able to tolerate a relationship.

Larry: But meanwhile, she remains able to tolerate a relationship with you rather well.

Frank: Yes. Her holidays went better than they had in the past. She felt more freed up to be herself with her mother. She felt like she could hold on to her own life. She took a new job at the beginning of this year. My stance has been to try to be neutral about that. I don't encourage her to date; I don't encourage her not to date. She's opted not to. It comes up every few months. Some man will approach her again. She's cute, sort of pixie-like.

Larry: Does she want your help with dating?

Frank: She wants a relationship. So yeah, she wants help with that.

Larry: Someday you might be able to ask her what she needs from you in that regard. You've wanted just to be there for her in whatever way she needs you and you haven't particularly encouraged or discouraged her, but perhaps she needs something else? Is there someplace that she would like you to be when she talks about the topic of a man or friends? Is she wanting something from you but she doesn't know how to ask for it?

Frank: I think that may be true.

Male: Frank, has she had any friends at work besides Joyce?

Frank: She's very well-liked, and very well-respected. She changes jobs about every two or three years, which in part is because of her own difficulty tolerating stress. She feels she takes on more stress as she gets to know somebody because she feels that to be herself with somebody else means that she's wrong, or that she's going to disappoint the other person, so she'll change jobs. But also in the kind of work she does it's common for people to change jobs. Actually, this last job was the longest she's been in any one place, two and a half years. That's analogous to her situation growing up. Her parents moved fairly often because her father would move from university to university teaching, and so she learned not to develop attachments. But there's always a longing for a sustained attachment. I think I need to place more focus on this whole issue of the dating because it seems to be coming up more.

Larry: Traditional technique demands neutrality in treating neurosis, but we always have to reevaluate the usefulness of strict adherence to the frame when dealing with preneurotic issues. You might simply tell her that you're not sure of where you need to be with it. It sounds to me as though she views her defect as not knowing how to relate. The best causal explanation she's got is that she was molested as a child, which doesn't tell us a great deal. Certainly the molest was an important event, but we have a sense that the difficulties with her relationships date from the symbiosis. She was forbidden pleasure for herself, forbidden any relatedness with anyone but Mother. She's starting to have some ideas about dating but she doesn't know what to do about it. Where does she want you to help her with it? Does she want you to keep quiet? Does she want you, maybe, to ask questions or to urge her to explore more with men? I mean, "What do you want from me? Should I keep my nose out of it? Should I bring it up? Should we talk about your fears about being with men? Should I encourage you to go out on a few dates so we can see how they go and try to understand them? Maybe you're concerned that I, like Mother, may not approve of your efforts to enjoy relating to other people, to men." I think she sees her defect as not being able to develop and sustain a relationship. I also think she may need more direct intervention on your part, perhaps even so an intrusive replication can form.

Frank: Yes. That she can't tolerate relationships.

Male: A real danger, of course, is that initiating talk about men and relating is inviting the intrusion. I think what you've been able to do with her so far is not to collude with her numbing, her distancing scenario, by not intruding.

Larry: For you not to have invited her to the party was a way for her to build independent self-structure, because you didn't invite the intrusion. I think the sexuality is going to be a difficult dance because she doesn't know how to relate without you two intruding on each other. That's her scenario, her perversion. "How can I get you to love me by intruding?" I think that the problem in the sexuality issue is how to help her build independent and pleasuring self-structure while not allowing her to become a victim of your intrusion, and without your feeling abused by her intrusions.

Frank: Right now she's in the Far East on vacation. She's making another job switch when she gets back. She took a job in January and found out that this was not a good place for her to be in so she found another job and then left for vacation.

Female: Vacationing in the Far East? And she has financial limitations?

Frank: The last couple of months there's this man who's a corporate executive where Marie worked. Upon her leaving, he took her out to lunch and said, "You know I'm really sad to see you leave. I respect you and your work a lot." This man is divorced and she feels herself turned on to him. She talked about that with me. The screamer was coming out because she was afraid of getting involved with this man. She wanted to, but she's afraid of it. There's this real sadness for her in not being able to have a relationship with him. He asked her at lunch why she wasn't dating and so she told him, but she did it in a softer way. What was significant about this situation was that she was able to identify and to be with her internal state very quickly. It wasn't like the event had occurred and it took a week or so to get in touch with it. She was able to talk about it the following day. Since that time, occasionally, she's talked about this man. She started looking for another job and she contacted him with the idea that she wanted to use him as a reference, but I think she also wanted to make contact with him. He asked her if she would be interested in having dinner when she got back. She said, "Yes." She told me, "I guess that was easy for me to do because I know I'm going to be out of the country for several weeks, but I'm scared to death about having to deal with relating to him when I get back."

Larry: The baby is on the way! I'm thinking, Frank, that this gives you a perfect opportunity to take up what I was talking about. Not to wait for her to bring it up, but to say, "You know I had you in mind the whole time you've been gone. I remember we have a drama working here. On one hand, I know this is an important issue for you and I would like to be with you and be able to encourage you in relating. But on the other hand, I know how easy it is for you to feel invaded. You've been intruded on enough in your life, so I don't know if I should ask about your friend or not. I'll be happy to let it go. Or we can maybe really get into the thick of how relating to a man feels to you. It sounds like he's a good person and that your thinking about him may be an opportunity for us to explore relating." And you let her change the subject. Or not. I'm thinking she's needing help here, not in encouraging her to get dates so as to build her ego, to strengthen her capacity to socialize, but rather for exploring with you this area where her flaw seems so painful for her. Such an intervention, if she is able to make use of you, would constitute a powerful interpretive confrontation of her blockade scenario. Some sort of full-blown dissociation might appear if she ever actually lets herself be in contact with a man. The screamer already appeared while she was talking with him. As she feels better about herself, as she's able to connect more, to trust that she has you, I wonder what will be the nature of the future therapeutic disruptions? These voices may take on more importance, more substance. If the voices serve more like an imaginary companion, we know we don't usually have to talk with imaginary companions. They tend to gradually disappear as the need for them wanes. But we also tend to think of imaginary companions as a formation of the oedipal or immediate preoedipal phase when the child is feeling estranged from the loved persons for reasons of oedipal inhibition. The child forms fantasy objects. The parents never hear much about imaginary companions. They may not even know they're there. When the oedipal trauma gets worked out, the imaginary companions generally disappear or remain in sort of vestigial form. Recall that wonderful Disney movie, *Pete's Dragon*. Have you all seen that? Be sure to the next time it's around. It's a masterpiece on imaginary companions. In the end, when Pete finds a foster mother and father and finds love, Elliott, the dragon, says, "I must leave now. You don't need me anymore." Everybody in the theater cries as Elliott flies off. But it seems to me that her voices function more as a process of dissociation, probably not from the molest, but from prior to that time. They're more akin to what we might see in a multiple personality formation. Whether they need to come into more direct representation as personages or whether she simply needs to know that when she's talking with someone the screamer may well begin, I don't know. But I would certainly be prepared to follow her through whatever she needs in this regard. I think she needs your help on the issue of men because if she feels you're watching her and following her through whatever disruptions she needs to experience, then I believe she's going to be able to do whatever is necessary to define and to know her inner self more thoroughly, but all the time with you continuing to say, "I don't want to be intrusive, that's happened too much already, but. . . ."

Male: Would her dissociations be a way for her to coalesce herself, like some people do around a rejecting object? The rejecting object is the mother who was never there for her.

Larry: Her mother intruded. Her mother's intrusions molested her as an infant. You could formulate in terms of her coalescing around rejecting objects but I prefer to think more simply in terms of her being habituated symbiotically to an intrusive other that she must numb herself against to feel safe. There's her alcoholism in a nutshell.

Male: So in developing some sort of self-structure she had to create these private fantasies or head voices.

Larry: Very likely.

Male: If he's connecting with her though, and he's a good internal object for her, maybe those might subside for her.

Larry: I'm not so sure. I think that they may need to be interpretively constructed and worked through. That's why I'm contrasting the later oedipal constellation of imaginary companions, which dissolve when there's no longer need for them, with the earlier dissociative mechanisms that seem operative here.

Male: That must be extensively represented before the split-off parts can be reintegrated. So that's your reason for almost promoting her regression? Because I think he should be there for her when that happens.

Larry: Right.

Male: Okay, that makes sense to me.

Larry: Whether she's going to experience the screamer in the transference or whether she's going to experience it outside the transference, in the so-called parallel transference with her man, I don't know. It won't matter. She can do the work either way. Since Frank is her only significant relationship, she may fear endangering her relatedness with him and choose to have the disruptions in relationship to someone else.

Female: Would you use the words organizing and containing for these voices? Is it a way that she organizes herself?

Larry: I don't think we know yet what they are. My general formulation on the multiple personality is based on Glover's (1932) paper discussing ego nuclei. He talks about how the ego begins to form in the earliest months of life. We can now extend his formulation into the intrauterine environment. Kernberg (1975) develops the notion further. He talks about a representation of self, a representation of other, and an affect that links them as primary ego states that are the building blocks of personality. All babies have twenty-five nascent personalities and you can watch them emerge and disappear during the course of a day—one when they're happy, one when they're sad, one when they're hungry, one when they're watching the kitty and so forth. All of these different personalities appear while Mother keeps addressing the central personality. It is she who reduces all of them into, "Now you're feeing this way, now you're feeling that way, now you're feeling some other way." In multiple personality we have a sense that those separate selves never came together under the aegis of an organizing maternal care. Or that a psychic trauma caused a regression to the point where these had not yet come together. Most so-called multiple personalities initially present as borderline until the therapeutic regression begins. Research has shown that it takes an average of six-and-a-half years of clinical contact to be able to make the diagnosis of multiple personality disorder because the borderline look was there until the regression to the organizing stage finally began. I'm thinking that Marie may need to explore some early affect states that are being represented as these voices. The avenue will likely be either the transference with Frank or the parallel transference with some friend, perhaps a boyfriend. Because she needs you so much, she may need to use a parallel transference for regressive exploration. I don't have a problem with that. I think we're seeing more and more, when earlier developmental states are being worked on, that the transference can be experienced outside of the therapeutic relationship in a way that's quite workable. When we're working with a neurosis, we generally don't want transference outside the analytic relationship. We call it acting out. With someone who's well developed, who has an integrating and symbolic capacity that's very well developed, and she's developing a boyfriend outside, we continue to say, "Yes, I know you feel that way about him, but I think you also feel that way about me." That is, we always bring the experience into the here and now transference. With earlier-developed people and earlier-developed issues, the parallel transference is frequently the preferred way things get worked out if for no other reason than these people have such a hard time finding satisfying relationships that they don't want to jeopardize the analytic partnership. You can say, "You're telling me that this is a very difficult area for you, and I want to let you know that I'm available to talk about it, to work on it. But I worry that if I begin to bring it up I'll be intruding." This tack is usually more relevant to preoedipal replicating transferences, I think that can be your theme song for the next year. That statement would seem to be a kind of transference interpretation that's going to get you to the way that she felt with her mother. She feels her mother is a big baby who has to be taken care of and she's constantly worried about intruding on her mother's space. Although it appears as though it's the uncle and the mother who are the intruders, within her subjective space she worries that *she* is the intruder. In a relationship, she's worried that she'll express herself or she'll say the wrong thing. The screamer will begin. I think what she's saying is what it was like with Mother, that she'll intrude on Mother's space with aggressive and sensual demands.

Frank: Exactly.

Male: So you see it as the most fruitful area for regression?

Larry: Yes. And because she's doing so well I think she's almost ready. People can't go into these very frightening things unless they're feeling like they're standing on solid ground in the analytic relationship. None of us can. Freud's genius in pointing to the Oedipus stage was that he understood that what integrates us within human culture is the symbolic level. That's the point at which we become mythic beings ourselves, by virtue of being seen and symbolized by a third party. Through the symbiosis we learn how to live in a world with another human being, but it's not until the third party—the language, the culture, the symbolization, the mythology of the human race—enters that we become fully human. So at the oedipal/neurotic level the experience of instincts and psychic conflict can be symbolized, repression can occur, and transference can be interpreted by means of words. But in preoedipal transferences, interactions and affects hold the key to how early experiences can be remembered and interpreted. These can be explored in many ways other than symbolically projecting repressed experiences onto the therapist. But, we're getting away from Marie.

Frank: One of the things I could anticipate coming up is that she may want to invite me to intrude by making decisions for her about what she should do with this man she's interested in.

Larry: Yes, but in order to think about how that may happen can we go back to how it is you intruded by arranging a job for her. Is that relevant here?

Frank: Sure.

Larry: You sort of skipped over the story.

Male: I was enticed.

Larry: Looks like I'm the only one brave enough to ask you what happened.

Female: I've had one or two worse ones if it makes you feel any better!

Frank: I'm amazed that I've done some of this stuff. Well, the way it came up was that she talked about needing to get another job. She was working for a company that was bought out by a larger corporation. She was given an option to remain employed with them but she would have to move out of state. She said, "Either you'll have to move with me, or I have to get another job."

Male: Good blackmail! I wonder if that's how the molest occurred. I wonder if it was blackmail. It would be interesting to find out.

Frank: I could see her mother blackmailing her.

Larry: So you're blackmailed. She's either going to leave you or you have to provide for her.

Frank: Right. So she started looking for a job. She used to live in our neighborhood and so knew from neighborhood picnics where Joyce worked. Her headhunter knew that there were positions available there but the headhunter couldn't get her an interview because they were looking for someone with more experience than she had, though she's very competent. That led me to ask Joyce what could be done in personnel to get her the interview.

Larry: How did that go with Marie? Did you just volunteer this; did she ask you?

Frank: I volunteered it. I think I said, "You know, I probably could ask Joyce to talk to somebody in personnel and that way we may be able to get an interview for you if you like."

Larry: "This will feel good, Marie." I think it's important to pay attention to that, because there's the blackmail theme, there's the penetration theme, and there's the molest theme, and they're going to come back in various forms. You've already noticed the additional countertransference tendency, which is to pay attention to your needs and not to bring up whatever problem she may be having. I'm thinking it would be very easy to let the blackmail and the rape themes slip through your fingers and not bring them back up.

Frank: I'm sure you're right.

Larry: What I'm saying is you've intruded in a way that was supposedly "good" for her, which is usually the rationalization of the molester. It's always, "She liked it; she wanted it." You need to keep that in the back of your mind, so as to be able to say to her, "Well you know, I did after all go right in there and make you feel good. And you did like it. But it sounds as though my action had a destructive element to it too. I don't know how we'll come to understand the destruction involved, the loss of self that my intrusion entailed for you."

Male: I think that's so powerful. That enticing object with her. How she wants you to do to her the exact thing that deprives her of growth, of independant living apart from you. That's her mother again.

Female: Yes. But she hasn't acknowledged that yet.

Male: That is the meat of the case.

Larry: It may be a while before that can be spoken, but I'm saying you need to keep it in the back of your mind, particularly because you've already seen that there is a tendency in the countertransference not to deal with difficult emotional issues.

Frank: This came up too when she changed jobs, because I charge her a very nominal fee above what the insurance pays. With my seeing her multiple times a week, the insurance of course runs out very quickly within any calendar year, so the rest of the year I see her for what she pays out of pocket. When she decided to change jobs, what was interesting was that she didn't ask at the place she was taking the job what the insurance was going to be. I got angry about that and I confronted her about it—that she had ignored me in that.

Larry: And now the trip to the Far East rears its ugly head! She can afford that but—

Frank: Actually this was before that. She had planned this trip about nine months ago, so that had been going on for a long time.

Larry: But have you talked with her about the low fee she's paying in relation to her expensive vacation? I think we're always in a bind there because we know the people we're working with need various things and have a certain lifestyle to maintain. But if you agree to a very reduced fee, her taking a trip to the Far East seems a bit extravagant, and at your expense!

Frank: I'm wanting to protect her, to defend her now.

Larry: Okay, defend her.

Frank: It's not like she's taking trips on a regular basis. This is the first big trip.

Larry: So you think it's a very important thing for her to do?

Frank: Yes.

Larry: Okay, so . . .

Frank: I don't see it as an abuse.

Larry: It may be important to try to talk about it, not so much as an abuse but in terms of the implications for the relationship. To be able to show her that you support her and that you know how important a vacation is. But at the same time, there may be some interesting implications for the relationship. Again, it may be a while before it's time to bring that up because she's relating to you better than ever. On the one hand we're happy to see that she's doing things she's never done before. Yet on the other hand, is she squeezing, manipulating the relationship?

Male: I'd like to see you stretch her.

Larry: Financially?

Male: Yeah. I think you need to feel better about your work with her.

Larry: As soon as she gets stabilized in the job to let her know that you want to be taken better care of.

Male: Yeah, because you're doing super work with her.

Frank: I made one increase about a year ago.

Larry: I think the thing that's being suggested here is that it may be time, once she gets stabilized in her new job, to put a bit of pressure on her and say, "When you went to the Far East I was very glad you did that. I know you needed it. Yet I was aware I wasn't getting paid my customary fee. That money could have gone to me. I didn't want to spoil the fun by saying anything, but I think our relationship is of enough value now that I would like to see you in a bit of a squeeze to get me the best fee you possibly can." Too early to do that? Go easy, then. It's going well, Frank. Don't let us press you prematurely. A scenario of deprivation and need has to be confronted here in time but there's no rush. Until you can stand up for your needs in the relationship, her own willingness to capitulate to demands of the other will remain uninterpreted.

Male: What did she do when you raised it last year? How did that go?

Frank: If I had not brought it up it never would have happened. But when I did bring it up she said, "I knew you deserved more."

Larry: Since she's relating to you better, I think it's very good to try to put that out as a slight pressure in the arena for her to do the best that she can for you, whatever that might be.

Frank: There's another potential molest coming up that I want to add.

Larry: Go for it.

Frank: The molest is, now that she's taken on another job, her insurance will change. There's a preexisting clause that says the insurance will not come into effect for one year. So there's this whole issue that we've left until after vacation about what we're going to do in the meantime. The hint that she laid before she left was, "I can mow lawns, I can do this and that." So there's an invitation for another intrusion.

Larry: I'm thinking that it might be important to say to her, "Well, how much do you make on lawns?" You know, joking, but let her know that she's relating to you well, that she's doing better than she's ever done. She knows that therapy is important to her and you'd like to see her do the very best that she can to insure reciprocity. There's another background reason. I think in the next year she'll probably be ready to move into a regression to begin representing the voices in many forms. I think she needs to know you're going to be there, that you're feeling good about the relationship and that you're properly taken care of. If she feels you're doing her too big a favor, how can she lay all this on you? I think gentle pressure is in order. Are you worried the fee is going to be low for a while? Is that the way it looks?

Frank: I think I need to process it with her again. I don't think we finished with that whole issue of her making the assumption that my needs could be ignored. I think that has to be processed more.

Larry: Speaking of your needs, we only have five more minutes. What can we attend to of your needs?

Frank: I see a lot of good self-structure being built.

Larry: Definitely.

Frank: The feeling I'm having is being unclear, and I think this is her experience. I'm unclear about how much I can press my own needs, how much I can speak them to her. How much can she, as Mother, tolerate my needs?

Larry: There's one way to find out. Ask her. Say just what you said here. "You've been so pressed upon. Your mother was so needy. Your uncle was so needy. People have pressed their needs upon you and it has to bring up nightmares. But you want to develop relationships. In order for you to develop relationships you've got to find some way of tolerating other people's needs without distorting yourself or feeling raped. I want to press my needs on you a bit more, because I think you're better able to deal with them now than ever. Yet I want to be very respectful of what you're caught with. I need your guidance here."

Female: That's a really respectful way to say it.

Male: Yes, I like that.

Female: That's lovely.

Larry: Tell her you don't know what to do.

Frank: Yeah.

Male: Because I think the fee issue is that she's stretching you like her mother does. I mean I'd like to see you stretch her and take better care of yourself.

Larry: I think she's needed to know how well Frank is willing to take care of her. Would he see and be responsive to her needs? And he has. He's done very well. I think it's an important time for him to say, "All right, you're in better shape than ever. I know you're not going to have insurance this year, but I really need you to pay me as much as you can. And when the insurance kicks in next year I would like the insurance money in addition to what we've already agreed upon." It might be that you're going to have to wait a year, but at least you'll get a fat raise when you get it. I would try to structure it that way.

Female: Where does her money go? I mean she makes a decent salary doesn't she?

(Discussion of finances follows; group believes she could be paying more than she is.)

Female: You're working hard! You've done beautiful, beautiful work with her. She's not going anyplace. She may holler and kick and scream at the cost, but she's not going anyplace.

Larry: And now, she's in a place where she's articulating, she's verbal. You're going to be able to say to her, "I want a raise. I want the most you can give me. Let's talk about it." You heard the consensus here. Everybody felt that she could be doing more for you than she is. But we also understood why you've left it the way it's been. But you're going to have to pluck up the courage to say to her, "You're doing so well. Now it is time for you to figure out what you can do for me." The bottom line is, "Write me a check, now!" But what may come up in confronting the fee issue is the manipulations of Mother in the symbiosis.

Some time ago, I remember her compulsion to share everything with Mother and how she provoked her mother into a demanding intrusion by not sharing her large Hershey bar with her. So in tampering with fees you may run into chocolate fever! Just remember, Frank, you like chocolate! You deserve your fair share and there's no need to let guilt from the replicating transference/countertransference prevent you from asserting your needs! Hoorah for Hershey bars! (Group laughs.)

Female: Thank you, Frank.

Larry: Yes, it's always nice to hear about people who are able to make such good use of a therapeutic experience. Congratulations on your patience and persistence.

Frank: Thanks. I'll remember I like chocolate. I need chocolate! You're right. The fear of intrusion is her perversion, not mine!

12

The Birthmark: I

Nathaniel Hawthorne's "The Birthmark" (1967) is a moving love story of a woman with a facial blemish on her cheek. Her beloved husband, a physician, searches for a way to remove the blemish. But even as he succeeds, she dies. She is so identified with the flaw she cannot tolerate its removal.

Hawthorne's story stands as a powerful metaphor to represent one of the most profound problems involved in psychoanalytic transformation. Can the damaged, deformed, or limited self, developed during the symbiotic period, ever be relinquished? And if so, at what price? It is not uncommon for deep and disturbed grieving to follow in the wake of analytic change, frequently accompanied by alternating fantasies of suicide (death of an old self) and birth (of a new self). People often know intuitively how disruptive the change is likely to be and fear going forward.

In this moving account of a woman with a facial deformity from birth, we see how the birthmark has come to represent her damaged self. The damage is repeatedly replicated in the transference/countertransference engagement as the woman becomes increasingly afraid of her private madness. She uses her lifelong knowledge that she is deformed and her mother's refusal to acknowledge the profound impact of that damage, thus creating further damage, to support the fear that she is crazy.

As she and her therapist move toward the critical countertransference interpretation work they both become frightened that she will damage or kill herself in an effort to represent the early trauma in transference action.

Fred: Sally has had a facial disfigurement from birth. I think all of you are familiar with Sally. I've been seeing her for almost five years, twice a week, and have been presenting her here fairly regularly. There's a series of events and experiences that have occurred between us in the last two months, but I'm not sure how they're related or exactly what they mean.

The first one was my telling her, only two weeks in advance, that I was going away for a week's vacation.

Larry: Why did you tell her just two weeks before?

Fred: I'm not sure. Well, I am sure. It's just hard for me to say, I guess. Because I anticipated what happened.

Larry: I just wanted to know.

Male: "I don't want to deal with this. I know what's coming."

Fred: Yes and no. It's transference I began to become aware of that I want to talk about and make sense of. I think I understand some of it, but not all of it. The second event is my return from vacation and the processing of that. Third is a dream she had about a woman who was about 44 and a girl with long shiny hair who is 16. The faces were not very distinct. The 16 year old is saying goodbye to the mother. She's saying she has gotten some things from her and she needs to go, live her own life, do her own thing, and move on. I immediately became aware that for about two years Sally has painted a vivid picture for me of herself as a little girl with a disfigured face and long shiny hair who's running carefree through the breeze with her hair flowing back. I had this sense that it's some aspect of her true self. While she at first thought the dream referred to her daughter and her, we later discovered it's also her and her mother and a few other things.

Male: Could you give me the picture again?

Fred: She's between ages 2 and 4 when she wasn't disguising her face yet, because now she wears heavy makeup. Now she has short blonde hair and is somewhat overweight. The image is of her with the side of her face disfigured running toward someone and the wind blowing in her hair. It's kind of like in a field somewhere in the Midwest.

Larry: At a time before she became self conscious?

Fred: A time before she became self conscious. We now know when the deepest pain began. It was when she was 10, when she had a series of surgeries she thought were going to take away the disfigurement forever. She felt abandoned. Her mother wasn't very supportive of the whole process. She just dropped her off. We can go through her devastation that the mark remained later if we need to. But that's the dream. And so when she started talking about the dream, she said it was her daughter who is much older than that and is working through more separation issues. I immediately thought of her.

The final item for discussion is a fear that first emerged three years ago, very briefly, but recently has become more prominent, more intense. She is afraid and literally believes her car is going to get her into an accident and kill her. The fear is curtailing her activities.

Larry: Her car is going to get her into an accident?

Fred: Exactly. Last session I asked her what's happening with the fear we've been trying to figure out for almost six weeks now. "I know, I have this sense that the car will kill me." It's as if she has no control of this car. She's going down the road and she wants to go straight and the car wants to pull over or not stop when a car pulls in front of her. At first when she talked about it, it was more like *she* was doing it, but now it's become the car.

Male: You.

Fred: Me?

Male: Yes. You. You are doing it.

Larry: Forces beyond her control.

Male: Yes, transference is the car I think. You.

Larry: It sounds like transference from the organizing level, a transference from inanimate forces that cannot be controlled.

Male: What's getting stirred up in your relationship will kill her.

Larry: Whenever we hear references to movement, inanimate intention, we are looking at the earliest aspects of life. Those of you who have studied the Rorschach test know a particular determinant scoring category . . .

Male: . . . called "little m."

Larry: "Little m" is scored where inanimate movement gets projected onto the blots. It's not a usual or expected response. What is highly expected is that animal movement will get projected onto the blots, and with well-developed people we see human movement projected onto blots. But inanimate movement is not considered usual. I don't know if you know that wonderful study conducted by a psychologist in the Royal Canadian Navy, a brilliant capturing of the moment. He was on the high seas in the middle of a major storm on a ship about to capsize. In the midst of the panic he drags sailors off the deck and gives them the Rorschach ink blots! The protocols are full of little m's. The world is moving terrifyingly around them. Hyperactive children have lots of little m's. The inanimate movement response is presumed to be related to the sense that the world moves around me and does things to me beyond my control, as in earliest infancy. So when we begin to hear inanimate movement in her material we can see that she's touching an organizing taproot.

After nearly five years of therapy we might well expect the therapeutic regression to be dealing with very deep levels. We might speculate about how her parents might have felt about a child being born with such a disfiguring deformity. What sort of activity was going on around her that she was not in control of?

Female: And felt really disconnected from. No one was in rhythm with her.

Larry: Searles (1960) points out that in psychotic states there is a predominance of nonhuman imagery in therapeutic representation. But with ordinary people we don't expect it so much unless they're showing us their earliest experiences.

Fred: When I first presented her, I was thinking that perhaps she was an organizing personality and then we discovered that basically she wasn't. She might have various organizing issues but basically she had reached a borderline level. She appeared organizing because she was talking about frequently feeling, even as a little girl, like she didn't belong here, like she was an alien from some other planet and that she really belonged in some other world. As therapy has progressed she's been able to articulate that feeling more clearly.

Larry: Are we going to hear more about that dangerous car?

Fred: Yes.

Larry: Be very alert because at times maybe you shouldn't let her drive off by herself. You may have to ask her to take a cab home and come back for her car later. Little (1981) reports having to take someone's car keys away because she was endangering herself.

Fred: That was a concern I was beginning to have. There are times when she's the last person I see, and when I leave the office as much as half an hour later she is sometimes still sitting in the parking lot.

Larry: So she's processing the disturbance of her session?

Fred: Once I was thinking about going over and saying something. Then I thought, "No, that would be an intrusion somehow." I left it alone and drove by later to find her car was gone.

Larry: When we deal with primitive parts of people, we may not need to be quite so worried about intrusions as we do when we're dealing with better-developed parts of people. Primitive parts often respond best to a little bit of touch, concern, a little care. I'm worried about the woman's safety. If she's experiencing this fear right now, I think you ought to be sure to go with that fear.

Does she have somebody who can bring her back and forth to therapy for awhile?

Fred: Not really.

Larry: Okay, well just keep an ear open for it and tell her you're concerned about this fear of hers and that we're going to explore what the fear is. Meanwhile she needs to be very careful that none of the fear gets realized. If at any point she's unduly worried, she needs to stop her car and get out, catch a bus home, and go back to get her car later, or whatever she needs to do. Warn her that while this fear is active she needs to be very careful with herself.

Male: With my organizing lady, she'll sit in the parking lot sometimes dozing afterwards for four hours. When I leave, I tap on the window and she lets me know that everything is okay. That's the way that she's got to coalesce herself. When we make contact during sessions she's disturbed and then she has to deal with that. So I intrude. I say, "I think you should stay out here as long as you need to."

Larry: It's like dealing with a child who is momentarily caught in some form of helplessness and a helping hand comes along and says, is everything okay? Is there anything I can do to help? You know, just lightly, gently, letting her know that you're there. You're concerned. This is not traditional technique but these are not people who can be analyzed with traditional technique.

Fred: As you were saying that, I thought that her response would be one of alarm rather than being soothed, because she'll say, "Oh you mean this is really something to worry about?"

Larry: Well, talk to her about it first then. Talk to her about it in a session. Say to her that you've been concerned several times. Say, "Everything may just be fine, maybe there's nothing at all to worry about, but I know you're dealing with some fears now and fear can be overwhelming. I hate for you to be uncomfortable and I would not want you in an accident."

Fred: I guess the point is that if she gets alarmed . . . well, "Yes, there may be reason to be alarmed," and "Yes, we are going to talk it through."

Larry: You might also say, "Look, when people get into deep and unique parts of themselves there's sometimes reasons to be concerned about safety. When we begin to get in touch with our infant body, we have no business running around in this world that's designed for adults." I don't allow people to leave this room if I feel that they've been jolted, or entranced, or depressed without stopping them and saying, "Are you okay, or would you like to sit somewhere else in the building for a while? Do you need a cup of tea?" It's crazy to let someone leave dazed from a psychotherapy session and try to drive in that concrete jungle out there! I also think we could be held liable for inducing an altered state without warning the person of danger.

Fred: Well, that I've done. Because there have been times when she's had some very difficult sessions, particularly connected with thoughts of her grandfather.

Larry: Well, talk it over with her ahead of time and tell her that you don't know if there's reason to be concerned, but that you don't want her to be doing anything that's unsafe. Another thing I sometimes will do is to say, "Look, put your family on notice that this is going to be a rough period of your therapy and that sometimes people need to be fragile, irritable, or explosive. Tell people in your family that you may fly off the handle at them or be feeling particularly needy on occasion because of the therapy work. They need to be aware of what you're doing in therapy and cut you a little slack for a while." Sometimes supervisors at work need to be informed when a person is going through a difficult period. But in this case, "Tell your husband that you're a little worried about your safety, that you don't feel as safe as you ordinarily do, and that you and I have talked about it and we feel it's a phase you're going through in your therapy. Ask if he can take you to the store or help you shop, drive you around; this won't go on forever, but while it's here and you're feeling a little wobbly, be very careful." People have horrible accidents when they're in these phases of their therapy.

Fred: Well, it's interesting because she's related several real close calls in her car.

Larry: I would not hesitate to show alarm and to let her know there's danger. Have we talked about this before? Have I given you my grim stories? The one about the wine glass? The first time I saw this frightening kind of danger was some years ago with a man I was seeing three times a week. He would pass the dentist's office on the way to my office when I was in a medical building. He wanted to know if I knew that dentist and I said as a matter of fact I go to him. He began to go in and make friends with this dentist. He hadn't been able to have a dentist look in his mouth for twenty years and his teeth were rotten with all kinds of painful things happening, but he was terrified. The dentist was wonderful. He could quickly see what was going on. First he only talked to him in his office. Then came the day of the initial mouth opening, but no fingers, no tools, just lights and looking. On later visits the examination became more complex until the day came when a root canal was scheduled. The dentist said, "Look, I'm going to charge you whether you're here or not, because that will give you the freedom not to come and you won't have to worry about me." The man was wealthy and I thought this was a very sensitive thing to do on the part of this dentist. The night before my man got into a fight with his girlfriend. He got drunk. He hadn't been drinking for six months. He pitched his wine glass across the living room into a brick wall. It shattered all over the couch. He staggered over and collapsed, puncturing his jaw badly with the broken glass. My supervisor at the time said, "The longer I'm in this business, the more terrified I am of accidents happening when people are deeply involved in therapy."

I heard recently of a woman who has been victim to accidents involving her feet and ankles all of her life. Her mother had gone into a terminal illness when she was about 14 months old. Mother was in isolation in her bedroom for six months where the child could hear her mother, but she couldn't be in the same room. Couldn't touch her, or be with her. Of course, that was the time when walking was being learned. Just when the function of being on her feet was developing, there was the falling, the collapse, because the relationship upon which the walking function first depended was disturbed when her mother disappeared and later died. Her therapist begged her to be very careful but nevertheless, during significant periods of her therapy, she sustained several bad falls. They were understood as body memories of her legs collapsing when she felt loss.

I tell you these things to alarm you and to let your people know to be very careful when we're exploring deeply disturbing things. When we begin to explore early ego functions, we're talking about balance, movement, coordination, alertness, vision, orientation in space and time, sound, and all of the perceptual-motor coordination and judgment skills. We never know what we're going to be getting into. The development of all ego functions is originally dependent upon and organized around the structure of the symbiosis. People who failed to develop a reliable symbiosis display erratic and unreliable ego structures. When the symbiosis begins to get disturbed by the therapy, the functions associated with the symbiosis during the specific relevant phases of development become disturbed as well. And so for a period of time people can be in great danger. There are plenty of reasons to be cautious and to alert your people to danger. There's reason to say, "While we're going through this period I want to let you know that I'm concerned." "Does it mean I'm sick? Does it mean I'm crazy?" "No. It means our therapy is working. It means you're doing what you came here to do. But as a result of its working, you're not quite yourself just now. You can't quite depend on your body working in the way that it ordinarily does. Everything will come back, and when it comes back it will be better than it ever was before. But for right now, let's be very careful." Who knows what your woman's fear might be about, but we certainly don't need accidents.

Fred: Well, I do know that they were using abrasive things, sandpaper techniques on her face.

Larry: All the way from birth?

Fred: She remembers when she was a little older, but they may have even been doing it when she was in the first year. I mean literally sandpaper.

Male: God, can you imagine that?

Female: Wow!

Fred: I've never seen her deformity, but she tells me that it covers the entire side of her forehead.

Female: You've never seen it?

Fred: No, she keeps it covered with heavy makeup. Interestingly, the treatments are beginning to have more of an effect than ever before. I wanted to share with her the Hawthorne story you gave me, "The Birthmark," but I've been reluctant to do it at this point. I've decided to hold off. It's a wonderful story. I read it and I appreciate your sharing it with me. Sometime we will probably watch *The Elephant Man* together too—when she feels brave enough.

Female: I wonder if she's becoming more open and that's why the laser treatments are becoming more effective. I wonder what happened in utero to this child.

Fred: Well, something might have happened, of course. No one knows how these kinds of deformities are created. (The nature of the deformity has been altered for purposes of discretion.)

Female: Most of them I've seen are extraordinarily disfiguring, particularly on men, who don't wear heavy makeup. I just ran into a guy about a month ago at the tire place. He turned around and looked at me full face and I kind of sucked in my breath. I had trouble staying in contact with him. I mean I really needed to look away.

Fred: Well, going through that experience after starting to see her helped me understand the feeling that you have that I've gotten in touch with, but never really felt and experienced at the same depth before.

Female: It's powerful. Really disturbing.

Fred: It really is. You realize that the fear of being looked at in horror is not merely a fantasy.

Larry: No, it's almost an instinct. Most mammals shrink away from defective ones. Herd creatures even leave defective ones to die. There is something about deformity and defectiveness that's like a genetic shrinking away and we have to work hard to do something other than that, so she's absolutely right.

Fred: And of course, shrinking away has come to be the form of the symbiosis, of interpersonal bonding, and the connection with others for this woman.

Larry: Thinking about her car doing something to her—does that represent the cruelty of children, or parents saying that something is wrong with the baby? What on earth is she telling us that happened during that early time?

Fred: At first I thought the car fear was a suicidal kind of thing because she was talking about it in terms of herself. She even wondered whether her thoughts were suicidal. But she said, "I don't really feel like I want to die; I don't want to die."

Larry: I think I might want to say to her, "I thought a lot about your fear that your car is going to do something to you. I don't yet have any idea what that means. I think it's going to take us a while to unravel it. But I was trying to think of something that seems like it's a part of you, but is actually outside your body that might endanger you. That's the way infants experience the world. Things and events outside have power over me: the power to feed me, the power to deprive me. But I don't have the sense of agency or authorship here. The agency is possessed by forces outside myself."

Fred: Which of course is the way she's always felt. She's talked a lot about that.

Larry: I think I might relate it back to infancy and try to see if you and she can develop any fantasies or reconstructions of what it might be like to be a baby born into her family. Knowing her mother, knowing her father, knowing her older siblings. What might that have been like?

Female: I was thinking of the first time Mother saw her. Right after she was born Mother saw her. What must Mother have felt?

Fred: Yes. I've often wondered about that.

Female: Maybe Mother felt like dying at that moment.

Fred: Well, Sally has the feeling that she was supposed to be dead. She wasn't supposed to be there.

Larry: Go ahead and tell us what else you want to tell us. We have so many ideas about your case, Fred!

Fred: I want to go back to the issue of my vacation and my not discussing it until two weeks before. What happened was that she became very upset. I think I knew intuitively that this was what would happen, and why I so carelessly waited until two weeks before to discuss it. It's interesting because I've been going away every three months to attend conferences at my son's boarding school, and she knew that. She needed to know exactly when my trips were scheduled. We would talk about them and she'd been working through a lot. So for the last couple of trips it had been much less difficult. And yet this was very painful for her. She said, "You know, I really can't take all this abuse. I just can't take this. You promised me you weren't going to leave for another six months, and here it is three months later and you're going away again." I had told her that I hadn't intended to take a vacation until August but that for family reasons, I had to change it to June. She became very angry. Then she said, "Well, how do I know that in August you're not going to go away again?" I said, "Oh you're right, I'm going to go away for a week in August too." Then I realized what I had said when I saw the look on her face.

Larry: You were being facetious when you said that?

Fred: Well, yeah, I was being facetious, but I also later realized that at some level I was being deliberately cruel. And I had done it once before. So I began thinking about the countertransference. The feeling at that moment was, "God damn it little girl, grow up! Get off my back! God damn it, I deserve a vacation, leave me alone. Fuck off!" Of course, I didn't say those things but she usually reads me pretty well.

Larry: How did she handle it?

Fred: At first she was really angry. No, at first she was very hurt. "It's happening all over again. Maybe I have to leave because I can't do this anymore. I mean every time, in every relationship, there's abuse, and now you've done it again and you've done it so many times. You're way off the wall." Then she listed all the abuses she had to experience in the course of our relationship and work through. But then she got angry. She told me what a shit I was, and what an abusive bastard I was. Then she got terrified again because I was leaving. She then remembered a dream she once had, of a plane flying over Dodger Stadium. She knows I'm a great Dodger fan and that I go to Dodger games. The plane explodes. I'm in the stadium, and I'm blown to smithereens. As she was relating the dream to me she was trying to act as if she was really sorry about it, but she appeared to be really glad. I commented to her that it was a really angry dream, that she really did want to have me blown up. She said, "No, no, I couldn't bear it." For the next two weeks we dealt with this issue of her being angry, and wanting to tell me. I supported her in struggling to express her anger and also in the anxiety over its expression. At the same time she was terrified of my going away. She had to keep reminding herself, or be reminded by me, that I was going away on a planned vacation, that I wasn't going away because she was angry at me. She had another fantasy that I was going to New York to find a job there so I could finally be rid of her, because "after all that's what I said to her." In her fantasy I had told her to get out of my life. I wanted her to leave therapy, and so she'd better leave now.

When I returned, I found myself really looking forward to seeing her. I was really anxious to see her, to say hello, to be with her, and to do some more work with her. I felt like there had been some things that we hadn't been able to finish, and I wanted to. I heard the door open, and I went and opened the inside door. She was there and I said "Oh hi! It's great to see you, how are you?" There was icy, cold silence and I knew she was angry. This has happened frequently when she's angry and is unable or too frightened to express it. It seems that underneath the anger is a longing, a dependent feeling, a feeling of being out of control. It was difficult to be alone without me. But she proceeded as if nothing was wrong, everything was fine. She told me newsy superficial stories.

I kept trying to get her to talk about the anger for the concerns she had. "What's the point, you know, you want to get rid of me anyhow." I said, "But I came back." "Yeah, you came back because you have to come back—so what? I'm just another patient and once again you've just proven to me that I'm not special and I'm not important because you put your family ahead of me and go off on a vacation. You tease me and make fun of me when I'm afraid. And when I feel bad you make jokes about going away for even longer periods of time. What's the point? You want to get rid of me anyhow, so I may as well just get rid of you." I said, "That's not true, I'm here." Then I shared with her what I had felt, that I had genuinely looked forward to seeing her, that she really was very special to me. I valued her for many things but especially for her willingness to look at herself and to struggle with issues that were very difficult and painful. Our going through all kinds of experiences together for four and a half years has built a relationship for us that I really value. I really was very glad to have her back, and to be spending time with her again.

Larry: It sounds like her whole experience is organized around feeling devalued and being angry about it.

Fred: People are cruel to her. She tries to reach out and people are cruel and want to push her away. I said I was really happy to see her, being fully aware that my attitude is a confrontation of her scenario. We started talking about the connection, about her being really angry before I left. We talked about her fear that something might happen to me, that her anger might destroy me. But it didn't because I'm here, and I want to be with her. She's important to me. Right after that she became afraid that her car was going to destroy her. It's almost as though she's only able to deal with the injury, the humiliation, the cruelty, the aggression, in projected form.

Larry: "It's you, my symbiotic mother, who are mean and cruel to me." Through projective identification she's managed to have that replicated in your relationship repeatedly. But you've confronted that. You said, "I am here, no matter what you might think, no matter how badly you might want me gone or how badly you may want to destroy me. I am here and I want to be here." Then, she goes into the inanimate force. I have the feeling that the transference has dropped a level, to a deeper level, before Mother was known as a separate person, when her very life was endangered by an out-of-control mother.

Fred: I said all that to her. She really experienced it and it took her breath away. She just sat there in a stupor. In fact I offered some time in the waiting room, because I did have someone else I needed to see. She didn't like that very much, because she wanted to stay in my room. I said, "I understand you would rather stay here with me. But we have an agreement, you know that." So she went out and stayed in her car for a while. When she came back the next week, she wanted to clarify with me what in fact I had said, and was it in fact, true.

Larry: That you were going to stay with her?

Fred: That I'm there. I also talked about the possibility that in the past, the way it was safe to relate was based on cruelty, pain, and abuse, and that I felt like we were at a crossroads where we could stop doing that. We needed to work to the point where she could see the possibility of relationships that are based on non-pain, even on pleasure, and begin experiencing them.

Larry: You're also attending to her belief that relationships are impossible, that you are cruel to her, that there is no point of going on, and that it's impossible for you to join her. That's her belief, that's what she's living with. You confronted the scenario by saying, "I am not that way, I am not leaving you, I am here for you." But you need to add "I know there is no way for you to believe at this time that safe relating is possible. Given your whole history and everything you know about the world, you are certain that I, too, will throw you away, will reject you, that it's not possible for me to be with you. I know that's the only thing you can believe at present."

Fred: I did manage to say something of that sort.

Larry: Okay. It's so important to acknowledge that given their experience, people don't believe that analytic transformation is possible.

Fred: The following session she said to me that she had some dreams she couldn't remember, that she had been feeling very stirred up and very upset, that she had thought many times about calling me, that she couldn't get out of the house. It was the car fear. She told me she believed what I had said to her, that I would be there for her, that things could be different.

Larry: Did you believe her?

Fred: No.

Larry: Okay. Because I think so often when we've made this kind of confrontation of a scenario, what we get in the wake is a false self. "I know there must be another way." "Don't give me that. According to everything you know, there isn't. I'm telling you that there is, and I'm telling you that we're going to find it, but don't tell me that you believe for one minute that there is, because I know you don't."

Fred: Well, that definitely fits.

Larry: When we've made our confrontation with the basic symbiotic pattern or mode, we can expect somewhat of a false self attempt to say, "Well yes, I know that you're right." At that point, we need to communicate somehow, "You don't have to say that for me. Are you trying to make me feel better? I don't feel better. I'm not leaving. But you don't have any way of knowing that. All you've known is cruel humiliations and abandonments, and so far you've experienced plenty from me. It's impossible for you to believe that our relationship could ever be transformed into anything else, so don't try to tell me otherwise. I'm telling you I'm going to stay here until it is. You don't have to believe that. You just keep coming."

Female: In my way of thinking she can't feel him. She doesn't know what he means when he's saying "I'm here." She can't tell he's there.

Larry: That's right. And so for her to say she can is strictly a false-self conformity.

Female: And you would confront that?

Larry: I would confront it. I mean why promote a lie? She's lying. She's saying, "I know it's true, I know that there's going to be another way." I say, "Wait a minute. You have no such knowledge. You're saying that for somebody. Is it for me? Is it for your mother? I mean all your life you've been saying you think things are going to be better, like Little Mary Sunshine. I don't think you believe a word of it." Perhaps we need to distinguish between the hope that change might be there, and the fact that she has no basis for really believing things will ever be different.

Fred: That's good. I like that because that's a good way of talking about it with her. She does have that hope. I haven't been distinguishing between her hope and her actually believing it. I like the way you put that.

Larry: In years gone by, with a couple of people at this kind of critical juncture, I've had to say to them that I'm not leaving no matter what, that they had to continue whether they wanted to or not! "You know, I don't care what you say, I don't care if you try to leave and get out of this, I will pursue you, I will call you, I will track you down, drag you back in here, because I have too much invested in this. I want to know how this is going to turn out. I'm not letting you off the hook. We are going to go forward. You've gotten away from everybody in your whole life, because there's something inside of you that makes you disconnect, makes you believe that relationships are never possible and that things will never change. I don't believe that. You're not getting rid of me." Several times I've had to be very tough until the person could say, "Well, okay, I'll keep coming, but I don't believe anything." And then you're in business again. Because that's an honest statement. "I don't believe anything is going to change." And you say, "Well, how could you? It's never been any different. You've always been an alien. What on earth reason would you have to believe that things could ever be different? I believe we're going to make things somehow work. I don't know how, but somehow, we're going to find something that's different." This may be the turning point in your work with her. I say that because immediately after that she gets to the deeper level of transference manifest in the car fear.

Fred: Yes.

Larry: The world is trying to do me in. Impersonal forces. The wall of the uterus, scraping against my face, rupturing the vessels, is going to destroy me.

Fred: Her license plate is "SALS TOY."

Female: I've been thinking about what she has controlling her, because a car is different from something that's from the outside world. It's something she has control over. She brings it to the mechanic. She changes the oil. And—

Fred: But she doesn't, and that's the point. That's what she's telling me. Or told me the last session that we now need to talk about today.

Larry: She doesn't feel in control of it.

Fred: She's no longer in charge of the car. She's terrified. She sees the car in front of her and is sure that it's going to stop and her car is going to go right into it. And she's not taking it to the mechanic. She's not in charge of it anymore. It's as if there are forces, me and the world—

Larry: You may have to ask her if she needs to find a way not to drive very often for a while. She's not in a padded womb, she's in a steel and concrete jungle. And when she was in a padded womb we think it bruised her face. We don't want her bruising her face again.

Fred: It's putting chills through my spine.

Larry: It should. "When you were in the womb you were damaged. I do not want you damaged again. I think you are needing to reexperience that moment of damage, but we don't want you damaged in the car. We want to reexperience it here in my office where it's safe." What we are concerned with here is damage. She's a damaged woman. The question she's exploring is *what* damaged her. We want to make sure she doesn't act it out.

Fred: Yes. She's experiencing the damage to herself on a new, deeper level. That's what it is.

Male: Unconscious processes.

Larry: It's absolutely terrifying what happens to people when they're working on these early layers. I heard a terrifying case of a man who was very self-damaging and getting sicker and sicker. Doctors couldn't diagnose his illness and he was going downhill rapidly. His therapist started seeing him seven days a week. She finally got up the nerve to say, "I am terrified that you're dying." He responded, "Oh, well, you know I died when I was born, didn't I tell you?" Five years into treatment! "No, you didn't tell me." He was born legally dead and in the treatment regression he was re-creating that death!

Female: Oh, my goodness!

Larry: Here we have bad facial damage. Think of all the things that face means. Face is our person, face is our being. Face is our pride. Face, face, face. So if she has to reexperience or redamage whatever face means, we want to make certain that she doesn't hurt herself. I'm feeling that we need to talk about her again next week, because you seem to be in a crucial nexus now, in a turning point in her therapy and in her life.

Fred: That would be great! I would love to be able to do that.

Larry: Take very good notes of your sessions this week. We need to stay right with you through the turning point here. Talk to her about its being an important turning point. We've got to reexperience this damage, but we don't want to be unsafe.

Male: You may want to try to pull her in more for a while.

Larry: Yes. You may want to try to see her some extra time during the next few weeks just to stay close and to let her know that this is important. "We've worked a long time to get here, and it's very important that we stay right with it."

Male: You won't be sorry. When I had this one lady get to that point, it made me feel a whole lot better to see her four or five times a week until things got sorted out. It doesn't go on forever.

Larry: Even if you have to touch base with her on the telephone. Just touch base to let her know that you know she's going through a lot right now and that you want to be there for her.

Fred: That's interesting. I've had the impulse to call her in between sessions recently. I should use that as a cue next time.

Larry: Don't let her make a big deal about it, like she's going crazy or something like that. "That's not it. We are finally where we need to be. I want you to feel supported by me. I know that when you begin to let these unsettling things come up they can be very scary. I want to let you know that I'm right here with you." Thanks, Fred, have a good week. We'll be looking forward to a report!

Fred: Thank you all.

13

The Birthmark: II
(one-week follow-up)

Fred: I saw Sally the afternoon of our consultation group. (reading from notes) We went into the room and she said, "You have a pad and a pen. You must have something serious on your mind." I smiled and sat down. She said, "Well, you're on time, that's really very nice. I like that." Recently, because of where I have to drive from, its been difficult getting there on time. She started talking about the situation with her daughter. I made a conscious decision at that point. I could have continued with what I wanted to talk about. My sense has been that it's always been a disaster with her. I have to let her do what she needs to do, and then wait for the time to do what I want to do. And that's what I did. Her daughter is 21 years old, has been living for several years with a chemically dependent young man who had a job he recently lost. They're going to have to move from their apartment. At times, Sally has tended to be very co-dependent, symbiotic with her daughter, sometimes feeling as if she ought to rescue her but not really wanting to and resenting the fact that she has to. Approximately three quarters through what was basically a kind of report about what had happened, she said, "I feel like you looked at the clock for the second or third time." She said, "I feel like you haven't been listening to me. Like you have some agenda you want to talk about, and you're not interested in what I have to say." I said, "I do, but I also don't want to intrude into what you need to talk about. That's what's most important." And there was a silence.

Male: A technical question here. Definitely he's got an agenda. Should he wait until she's done with her agenda?

Female: Well, personally, I would have wanted to get it out of the way, to find out what the note pad was about.

Male: She's obviously sensing there's something up. Right away she noticed you had pen and paper.

Fred: Well, actually I had left it on the table at that point, but she's very sensitive and she reads me.

Male: And you're also on time for a change. So from a technical standpoint, if you do have an agenda should you simply start with, "I have some reactions from the last session"?

Larry: You certainly could. We try to leave our agendas aside when possible, as Fred did, but this one is so obvious to her that waiting or not at least announcing that you have some things you want to bring up sometime today leaves her in an awkward place.

Fred: In retrospect I think I should have.

Larry: She knows you have something on your mind. Is she using the pen and paper, your showing up on time, and your apparent preoccupation as ways of not connecting to you?

Fred: That may be. I think it's clear, from what she says later on, that she knows exactly what the agenda is. She knew exactly what I was concerned about, and she probably knew it before I did, her having out-of-control fantasies, and getting hurt in her car. But I was frightened and unwilling to verbalize them until I came to group and we processed them. I got some help with defining what I needed to do. When there's something on the table, so to speak, typically she'll bring up some crisis of the week. And it's quite interesting that when there isn't something hanging there she really doesn't bring up anything that urgent, in terms of a fire that needs to be put out. So I sometimes think that it's a way of . . . it's not really resistance, it's more . . .

Female: . . . Control?

Fred: Control, yes, I feel like it's control. Trying to control and avoid, and trying to stay in control. Because she feels that she's going completely out of control, that she really is going crazy. So she's desperately trying to hang on to anything she possibly can. I tried to stay with the process. I wasn't sure whether to go with my thoughts or wait for her to go where she needed. But she caught my distraction, my impatience.

Larry: When we're concerned about someone's safety, I think that has a certain priority in terms of intervention mainly because people are not usually aware of the power of psychological processes. But within a session there may be no rush to speak what we need to.

Fred: (continuing notes) There was a silence. I said, "I've been wondering if you had any thoughts or reactions to our last session." She said, "You know that if it's important, I'm not going to remember it." She smiled and laughed. I said, "You had said that you were afraid of the car killing you." She said, "Yeah, well, it's the same as usual, it's just the same way it's been before." I said, "No, not exactly. Before, you had expressed it as getting killed in the car, or getting in an accident. Last week you talked about the fear that the car was going to kill you." She started twisting and jiggling and pushing the table. Silence. Then she said, "You know I can't talk about these things until I know it's safe." I said, "I've been very concerned about you this week. And I've been thinking about your safety and what the fear of the car might be about." "Yeah," she said, "it's okay, it's nothing much." And she looked evasive. I told her, "I've been worried that you might have an accident, that you might get hurt, and that you wouldn't feel you have any control over this." She said, "Well, I'm very careful, but I almost got it twice coming here." But she began to laugh and she was very light about it. I said, "Are you frightened about my concern and my worry? Does that make it more real?" She said "Yes!" So then I said, "Well, I am concerned about your safety. I am very worried about your having an accident, not meaning to, and not wanting to perhaps, but nevertheless having an accident. While we're talking here about this fear, there may be times when it's very difficult for you to drive. You may have to stop and wait until you collect yourself before you drive. I've noticed a couple of times when I came out that you were still in the car waiting." She said, "Well, I don't remember."

Larry: It's so much more frightening when denial is operating, isn't it?

Female: It is. Yes.

Larry: If she were more worried, we would be breathing a little easier.

Fred: Yes, it's true. I said, "Well, I think that while we're trying to figure out what this is all about, talking about things might be quite upsetting. You might not be able to keep your mind on driving at times. She said, "Should I stop driving?" I said, "Not necessarily. That's not what I'm talking about. But wherever you are, if you feel that you shouldn't be driving I want you to stop and call me, call your husband, call someone and have them come and get you or talk with you until you feel that you're ready to get back into the car and drive." She then said, "Yeah, well, there have been times when I thought I wasn't going to make it home. I thought about stopping and calling Joe." That's her husband. I said, "Good. If you need to do that, do it. And if you want me to talk with him in advance, I will. But we need to be very concerned about this." She said, "You're scaring me." I said, "I'm scared also. I don't want anything to happen to you. I want to be able to understand this and work it through with you, but I want to be able to do it here, or in your dreams, not on the road."

Male: Boy, very good!

Fred: And I laughed, and she laughed.

Male: That's a perfect delivery! A "10"!

Fred: Then I said, "I also want to share some other thoughts I've had since our last session. I'm very excited about where we are in our work together right now. The appearance of fear, I feel, marks a turning point in our work. It's something we've been working toward for five and a half years. We've finally gotten here, and we need to stay with this until we understand it completely. Not avoid the fear." She said, "That's comforting. Do you know what all this means?" I said, "No, not entirely. Do you remember how we've been trying to pull together your reactions to my leaving and returning from vacations, the dream about the little girl and the mother, and this fear? I wonder if the fear is that you now have the hope that there is a world or a way of being that's not based on pain and torture? But you don't believe it. You want to give up old ways of being, and are not sure what to replace them with or even how to go about it, and that's terrifying." She said, "I hadn't considered that." Then there was silence.

Larry: Are we to understand from the way you're reporting it, that by this time, she's kind of wide-eyed and aware that you're saying very important things to her?

Fred: Yes, she's listening very intently. And she's really with me, not moving.

Larry: She's knows that you're speaking truth?

Fred: Yes, and she's listening to me.

Larry: You had to break through the denial.

Fred: Yes, because she was in denial for a while. But at this point, she's right there with me. Yeah, we're very much together.

Larry: Okay.

Fred: There was silence. Then I said, "Perhaps you're trying to reexperience or rediscover a part of your life that's been hidden." There was more silence. She was clearly thinking. I said, "The car killing you, damaging you, how does that relate to the past?" "Well, I am damaged," she said.

Larry: She's picking right up on it.

Fred: I said, "And perhaps you're trying to back up and understand how you became damaged." More silence, then tears and more silence. I waited and then asked her what she was thinking about. She said, and this blew me away when she said it—and it was the end of the session—she tearfully said, "I'm wondering what my mother's first thoughts were."

Male: Oh my God!

Female: That's what we talked about last time!

Fred: That's exactly what we talked about.

Larry: Did she say any more, or was it only "I'm wondering what my mother's first thoughts were?"

Female: And what Mother's first feelings were, when she saw her.

Fred: She feels, I think, that although we have her picture of a little girl who felt free and unselfconscious without makeup, that the world always saw her as damaged, and was always appalled.

Larry: I think the image is her own. That she was not aware of the damage. But the world always was.

Male: How was the session for you, Fred?

Fred: In wanting to talk about my fears and in being very concerned about her safety, I found after leaving our group session that it was very difficult for me to concentrate until our next session. I had this urge to call her on the telephone to tell her to be very careful when she drove. I left here at 1:30 and I saw her at 5:00. Being here and talking about it gave me permission to feel what I had been vaguely sensing a long time, but had repressed and not allowed myself to really feel. I was somewhat overwhelmed. "My patient is in danger; I am alarmed." I tried to focus that for myself and then to talk with her. She felt I wasn't listening to what she had to say. I think under the circumstances perhaps it would have been better to just go ahead and say what I had to say, knowing that she was going to sense my preoccupations anyhow.

Larry: What I liked about the way you handled the hour is that sometimes when we've tuned into something, the patient has simultaneously tuned into it. For the patient to structure the hour and bring up the concern always seems so much better than for us to structure it.

Fred: That was my hope.

Larry: She felt damaged the minute she entered the room.

Fred: Because I wasn't listening?

Larry: The note pad. She knew you were going to take notes. The pen and the paper were on the table, and you were watching the clock, preoccupied, like her mother was preoccupied with giving birth to a damaged child. So we saw the scenario come alive before our very eyes.

Fred: That's a good point.

Larry: That was a beautiful session. Do you have another one?

Fred: Yes.

Larry: Wonderful! Is there any discussion? There are times I think we simply feel an obligation to intervene. We always feel a little uncomfortable about it, because we're trained to wait and let the person run the hour. But when we fear people's lives, health, or safety are in danger, it's very important that we do exactly what you did. It may be difficult for us and for the person. But as you can tell, as soon as she could see that you were there with a serious agenda, she felt quite understood. Toward the end of the hour I thought she was crying because *she was aware that you were seeing her damage. You were not looking away from it.* You took the opportunity to tell her that you feel we're doing what we must do, and that you're concerned that she'll hurt herself in the process. "I don't want you to do that." Very moving.

Female: Yes.

Male: I think the sense of urgency I was experiencing in your wanting to talk with her about your preoccupation is that the original psychological damage came from Mother not having spoken the truth—her fears and feelings about damage. I saw you as wanting to somehow acknowledge that damage, or prevent further damage. It appears that the worst damage was caused by Mother pretending there was no damage, that everything was okay when it clearly wasn't.

Larry: Exactly.

Male: That's the emotional damage.

Fred: It's the emotional damage because one of her agendas from day one has been: "Are you going to listen to me, I mean really listen where there is no other thought in your mind, where you are constantly looking at me, and it's just you, me, and that's it, and the less between us the better?"

Larry: And, "You know I am damaged, you can see and feel it."

Fred: Yes. But it took me a while to get to that.

Larry: I think that's what she realized when she said "I wonder what my mother's first thought was." We can extrapolate that Mother's first thought was a denial, "This child *isn't* damaged."

Fred: Yes.

Larry: "This isn't happening to me." What she wants from you is no denial.

Female: Mother didn't look at her.

Larry: And you are looking at her. You're looking at her and saying, "You are damaged," and furthermore, "You are on the verge of hurting yourself more, and I don't want you to do it. I won't let you use your relationship with me to damage yourself further." That's a confrontation of a scenario. Her mother wasn't able to do that.

Fred: Once I spoke what we both had been afraid of, it was a tremendous relief. "This is something really serious." I wasn't able to include it in the notes, but she did indicate to me a couple of times how reassuring it is for her to know that she really isn't going crazy, that this is not something she's making up, that it's not some craziness she's developing, but rather that it's an actual process of remembering she has to go through. That it's a reliving of an early traumatic experience.

Larry: She's being taken seriously.

Fred: Yes.

Larry: "Nobody's trying to say 'this is just a fiction, this damage is fictitious. You really aren't all that damaged, just put some makeup on darling.'" Nobody is minimizing who she is. Somebody is taking her seriously.

Fred: Right.

Male: She's existing.

Fred: Her mother always said, "Be happy that you have two legs, two arms, and a whole face." There happened to be a little crippled boy in the neighborhood. She was always compared to that child.

Male: If that was going on, it's another way of holding on to Mother too, to continue denying.

Fred: Yes.

Larry: By your refusing to deny it with her, you're confronting the whole mother scenario. You're saying, "Something serious has gone wrong. You are damaged. Everyone wants to look away. I want to see you, to know your damaged self."

Male: It seems to me that Mom was not available for Sally to borrow from Mom's ego in order to develop. Basically, the only way she learned how to cope in the world was to use her mom's unconscious ego. My sense is she's more aware of other people's unconscious than she is of herself, of her own ego processes.

Larry: That must be true. The moment Fred enters the room she knows he has an agenda. He tells us how sensitively she reads him.

Fred: My experience of her has been that it's like being with someone for two hours each week for four years, with nothing on, including my skin. I don't have skin, I don't have clothing, I don't have anything. It's like sitting there with everything exposed. But that's also her experience. She wants there to be nothing between us.

Larry: Yes, she wants you to know how uncomfortable it is to have someone staring at your damaged self. She busts you for every flaw, every flinch.

Fred: In the second session we initially had to deal with something about her going to a four-day work week. She worries her therapy appointment times are going to get messed up. I said, "Well, I'm sure there'll be a way to work our time out." She finally figured out how our schedule was going to work. She got all this settled at the beginning of the session. Several months ago she was a data processor. There's been an overhaul in the job descriptions, the ratings, salaries, and titles. She's at the top of where she can be in terms of her salary, but she thought she was going to have a title that was different than the one she got. She felt that as quite damaging to her. She had wanted a certain title, and she didn't get it. They had told her at the time that what she needed to do for thirty days was to improve her accuracy. Then they would give it to her. We talked about that a lot. She confuses someone saying that her work is not 100% accurate with her belief that she's damaged.

Larry: The other option is that in order to sustain the fantasy of being damaged she maintains imperfection in her work. You might be able to turn that around to see if there's some self-concept of damage that she acts out in terms of inaccuracy.

Fred: I hadn't seen that twist. She confronted the supervisor who had made the promise to her. She thought he had tried to weasel out of giving her the title, and not keep his promise. She was basically asking him to do what he had said he would do. The message she got was, "You know, your accuracy is not quite where it ought to be; in fact, it's going down." She said that was because they took a smaller work sample. She said, "You're asking me to be perfect." He said, "Now that's being nit-picky." That's basically where it was. She felt good about it because she had never gone in and followed up on anything that had been promised her. She stood her ground with him. She still felt uncomfortable and angry, because she feels they're not hearing her, not understanding her, and wanting her to be perfect.

Female: It's interesting in that Hawthorne story when the doctor removed the flaw, she died. She so identified with the damage that she couldn't let herself be perfect.

Fred: She said, "I'm not going to be invested in this company anymore. Because I can't be perfect I'll never get the title. That's OK, I got the money, and that's what the bottom line is anyhow. It's money, so screw them all."

Male: I've been thinking about you and her all week and my fantasy is that as she gets closer to you she's going to get more suicidal. That is, if she has an undamaged connection in the world, she will be objectless. Her only objects have been based upon damaged connections.

Female: No identity.

Larry: That certainly is the danger. But when she confronts her boss, she's saying, "I do not want to be considered damaged." She finally had the courage to say it.

Fred: In this session she talked about the idea of giving up the old but that then there's nothing to hold on to. She then said her daughter is moving out. "I feel like I don't feel anything, numb sort of." She's referring to her daughter, Mona. In the past, this would have upset her terribly. She would not have been able to sleep at night. She'd be very worried about it and feel very badly about her. But she's now saying that she doesn't feel any of that. She said, "Is it protecting, or taking care of myself?" I said, "That's a good question." There was a silence, then she said, "She can take care of herself." And then another silence. Then, "Am I being selfish? Can she really take care of herself? Do I not have to feel anything? Is it okay not to feel anything? Or am I just a rotten parent?"

Larry: A lot of the general discussion we're having is related to the question: "Is she willing to let go of the scenario of being a damaged child, and therefore the mother that's connected with that scenario." I think she's saying, "I couldn't do this with my mother. At that time I couldn't numb it out. I had to partake of my mother's scenario. I had to read my mother's subconscious." I think she's set on doing something different now. "It's painful to have my daughter grow up. It's painful to have her leave. But I numb out. Am I supposed to be concerned about her? Or perhaps I'm only taking care of myself." Is she creating another defensive structure that replicates her early childhood or is she doing something new?

Fred: Well, when she framed it that way, instinctively I knew that she was worried, much more than I was, that it was taking care of herself. That's what's forbidden.

Larry: When we look at symbiotic constructions, we see in them some form or another of denial, avoidance, or of not dealing with reality. But we also created ourselves in this way. She seems to be asking, "Is this what I was doing as an infant—just taking care of myself? In developing this whole damaged scenario, maybe that was the only thing I could do to take care of myself then. I see I have options now."

Fred: There was silence, and then rather emphatically, Sally said, "I don't have time to be concerned about her. I've been thinking and involved with me. A car is going to kill me. I'm afraid I'm going to get killed in the car." There was another silence.

Larry: The car fear is paired with separation. She's talking about separating from her daughter as an important step in her therapy. We're talking about her separating from the damaged symbiotic scenario, and her having a whole undamaged relationship with you.

Fred: More silence, then she says, "Maybe when I care about others, I don't have to give up caring about me." That's the first time she ever said something like that.

Larry: It's a breakthrough.

Fred: She's beginning to put it all together. Sally says, "I always do that. I make others feel good, make sure everyone else feels good, then I'm okay."

Larry: Going back to the damaged scenario, "If I take on my mother's scenario, learn to see myself as damaged, I'm okay that way. But if I give up the damaged fantasy I have nothing else to hold on to." Now she goes further and says, "Possibly it doesn't have to be one or the other."

Fred: So it's not others versus her.

Larry: Yes.

Fred: Gee, I wish I had—

Larry: That's okay, it'll come up again. She's working very well. You just have to be there, be quiet, and she'll keep working. You can't stop her now.

Fred: I said, "Perhaps this is because you've experienced yourself and others as the same?" "Yeah," she said. "I always need others to give me justification for being here. I didn't believe I belonged." Now that's interesting, because it's put in the past tense, rather than in the present tense. She's always said, "I don't belong" rather than "I didn't believe I belonged." "I'm letting go of the old, but there's nothing to grab onto."

Larry: I can't tell you how often this comes up when people are letting go of symbiotic scenarios. Whether they're borderline people, or more advanced people, it doesn't matter. When the "Mommy and me" interaction is relinquished, it's as if the foundations of reality are shaken. There's not an awareness of how else the person might be. At this point we so often hear suicide fantasies. The suicide fantasies are correctly interpreted as, "But, you are dying, your old self *is* dying. The only self you've ever known, the only mother you ever knew is dying, and I think that's being represented now in your suicide fantasies."

Male: This lady's made a real leap in the transference.

Larry: There's no question about it. A new kind of connection.

Male: Yes. A new and different object.

Larry: A person who sees, "I am damaged," and wants to continue relating.

Fred: I said, "Now, how does that fear fit in with the car killing you?" There was silence. Then she said, "I felt good last time, knowing I'm not crazy. That it will pass, but that I have to go through this. I'm not sure where I'm going—I've been talking to Joe and explaining about the fear. Since then he hasn't bitched once about driving." She's now asked him to drive all the time for a while. She won't drive on the weekends. I've encouraged her in that. I've said that it makes sense, that it's okay, and that she's going to be fine when we get through this, when we understand it, and have worked it through. She said, "At work, I told a little bit of it to Elizabeth." Elizabeth is the new person in the area that she was transferred to recently. She's had an off and on love–hate relationship with her. She feels at times she can come up and talk with her, tell her things, but at other times, she feels like Elizabeth's not there for her. Sally said, "She told me that she'll come get me. In fact, she said 'You better call me if you need help, and I'll come get you.' " She said it just like that, and she was smiling and laughing. She said, "Isn't that great?" This is the first time she has experienced people in her world as responding to her.

Female: The first time she's reached out in a positive way for a response.

Larry: She's reaching out and saying, "There's something wrong with me right now, and I need your help." Others have responded.

Fred: She called her sister. They have lunch every Wednesday together. Sally has tried to talk with her from time to time about things that she's experiencing, feeling, and remembering from when she was a child. But whatever Sally is feeling, her sister has already had it, and she's had it even more intensely. So if she's angry at her mother about something, then her sister is three times as pissed about it. She told me, "We were going to lunch and she wanted me to drive. I said, 'No, you drive.' Then I told her some of what was going on, and she said it had happened to her. 'But it must not be as bad, or anywhere as near as scary as what you're going through now.' Imagine, imagine."

Larry: She broke through being damaged by her sister.

Fred: It's an empathic response by her sister.

Larry: Right, but in the relationship with her sister, she conveyed it so that she was not damaged by the sister's response.

She presented herself in such a way that her sister had to take her seriously for the first time. She's having breakthroughs everywhere in her life.

Male: It's not coincidence.

Larry: No, of course not. She related to her sister in a way that she had never related before. She told her something that her sister took seriously, and didn't try to take away from her. Paradoxically, in discussing her damage she refuses to be further damaged. "Something is wrong with me, I can't drive. I'm going crazy in therapy," or whatever she said. But however she said it her sister does not repeat the damage that she always does to Sally by minimizing her. I think it might be important to point that out to her.

Fred: Sally continues: "Imagine, she didn't have to have it worse than me. She's always had to have that. It's so reassuring knowing I'm not crazy and can tell others. I don't have to hide everything."

Larry: That's come up four times, Fred. "I am not crazy." I think that's going to be important to investigate. At one level I think we understand it perfectly well. Everybody has always said, "You're crazy. This or that damage isn't important." I think the fact that everyone has always minimized her is an important part of the scenario. "You are not really damaged." But she knows she is. Somehow that comes across in, "You must be crazy when you think there's something wrong because there isn't." "Well, Fred says something is wrong, so I feel validated. Fred sees I'm damaged. My sister now sees I'm damaged." She is feeling seen. Her husband says, "I'll drive." And so she's letting everyone know that there's something that she's been dealing with for a long time that is wrong. "I don't know what it is, but it's very important. I am not crazy. I thought I was crazy, but I *was* damaged."

Fred: Let me see if I hear what you're saying. You're saying that for her the craziness was to know that she was damaged and yet to accept her mother's saying that she wasn't.

Male: Yes. The truth is being spoken. What a relief!

Larry: Tell us how it ends, Fred.

Fred: This is the end. "I don't have to hide everything." And as she was saying that I had the image of the makeup, of course. "I don't have to be perfect." I said, "We have to stop in a few minutes. But it's interesting how we started the session with your boss demanding for you to be perfect in what you do. And we're ending with you realizing that you can begin to take off some of the mask and show your imperfection."

Larry: Bravo!

Fred: She said, "Well, I don't know whether I'm ready for that yet, but I'm getting there."

Larry: But you said the right thing.

Fred: Yeah. Well, I said, "It's time to stop now." She said, "Okay. I'll leave now." She got up and left. It's usually hard for her to leave.

Larry: How are you feeling, Fred?

Fred: Excited. I'm feeling really good.

Male: Show up on time!

Larry: Or if you decide not to show up on time, at least every time you're late you need to talk about how damaging that is to her. Thanks, Fred.

Fred: Thanks again, to all of you. I feel like we're in a whole difference place now. We've made a quantum leap. Now we have to work it through and grieve the loss.

14

The Holiday Hug

Every therapist has experienced working with someone who reminds him or her of a well-known person from his or her intimate personal life, past or present. Under such circumstances the therapist frequently has to do a double take to be sure what is coming from the speaker in therapy and what residue of personal experience might be coloring the therapist's perceptions.

The young man to be discussed here is an adept at entertaining his female therapist and indeed reminds her of an old boyfriend. On the one hand, she finds herself needing to go along with the good-natured and apparently innocent seductions in order to understand the nature of the symbiosis. But on the other hand, she worries about remaining objective, not confusing him, and not replicating a harsh rejecting character from his childhood.

Another significant feature to be illuminated here is the telescoped quality of a 4-month-old affective "koochie

koochie coo" resonance, with a 3-year-old twinship transference in which, through humor, the speaker is highly invested in demanding affective mirroring.

Elise: There's a part of me that comes into this room today feeling a bit vulnerable. If this man is going to be helped, it's really going to come through the analysis of the transference and what's going on with us. In bringing this case into the room there are parts of me that I'm going to be exposing and talking about. In some ways I feel a little less objective about this case, so I want your help where I may appear fuzzy or confused, even though that's part of the process too. I'm going to present today a 38-year-old physician, whom I will call Dr. J., because a very big part of his identity has been constructed as a physician and his commitment and dedication to medicine and all that that means to him. I presented him early on when I began working with him about nine months ago. I presented him initially with these concerns: here is a really bright, smart, ambitious guy coming in to a psychoanalytic, psychodynamically oriented therapy. He had never really had this kind of experience and he was coming because he was in crisis. Was I going to be able to hold on to him and find a way to offer him some meaningful therapeutic experience? Or, when the crisis blew over was he going to somehow drift away? I was also somewhat concerned at that time about some possible erotic transference, which has become somewhat of a consistent theme in his treatment. I continue to be somewhat concerned about it for a couple of reasons. On a personal level, and this is really uncanny, I don't know if any of you have ever had the experience of sitting in a room with a person who reminds you a lot of an ex-boyfriend or girlfriend. He's close to my age. His physical appearance and his style of being witty and funny and his way of engaging by making me laugh remind me of an old high school boyfriend I had. Fortunately, this old boyfriend and I still interact and are on good terms, so there's no residue with regard to what I might unconsciously be carrying. But there are parts of him that really remind me of somebody from my past. So specifically, I want to take a look at what's going on in the transference and what's going on in the countertransference for me.

To give you a picture of Dr. J.: he is a 38-year-old physician whose specialty often keeps him involved in intensive and emergency care. His professional identity is extremely important. I've been working with him for nine months, two times weekly, and as his treatment has proceeded, he's come increasingly to feel empty gaps inside himself. He's come to see how much he defends against that emptiness, how he wards it off, by projecting jokes and by an engaging style aimed at making me laugh, entertaining me. He's come to see the degree to which his empty status really constitutes a lack of self and he's been very fearful about what that means. One of the ways he's referenced himself is like a "burnt out matchstick inside," at his core. He's been a very good patient to work with through the treatment process. I like him. I like working with him. Developmentally, he's further along than many of the people we've been talking about here. His issues range from trying to establish a symbiotic tie with me to his using me as a selfobject. In terms of relatedness he'll try to pull me into a common affect with him around a common agenda or a common area of concern or will use me as a selfobject to have a common affect with him.

Larry: More like a twinship transference?

Elise: Right.

Female: And if he doesn't get the common affect, if you don't experience that with him, what does he do?

Elise: Good question. I really want to talk about that because one of my dilemmas with him in making use of the transference has been that I've felt guilty because he's an entertainer by nature. He's bright, he's verbal, and he's witty. His mind works very fast. And at times he entertains me. Sometimes I sit back and say, "What's going on here? Is this therapy? I feel entertained." I've been curious about watching more *Comedy Store* skits on T.V. just to compare his style. He's pretty good. There's a part of me that responds to that in the course of being with him and wanting to develop a therapeutic alliance with him. And there's another part of me, that's pulled back at times so as to try to put a little more of a frame on what we're doing. But for the most part I've gone with the former rather than the latter. Now there are a lot of double binds that show up with him. For example, if I laugh and respond to something he's saying—and generally his jokes are similar to *Comedy Store*—he makes use of the room, the Kleenex box, the clock, a book that's there. He uses very here-and-now sorts of things and creates a whole skit out of them. Or a certain way I might ask a question and he'll kind of do a skit with it. So there's a part of him, and he's been able to acknowledge this, that goes after my smile. We've been able to trace that genetically to the sense that, at times, I feel like Dad to him. Dad is the figure who knows all and expects a lot from him and he feels like the helpless, stupid little kid who really can't measure up to what's being asked of him. His way of defending against that is to entertain Dad so as to break the void with a smile. So we've been able to trace that, such that he'll immediately go after a smile from me. But if I smile too much and let myself go too much, if I really genuinely show pleasure or enjoyment with what he's saying, he'll say to me, "Whoa! You're supposed to be an objective observer. What are you doing laughing so hard?" So there's a real double bind that gets presented in the transference. If I don't laugh I'm this castrating, rejecting dad who sees anything and everything he does as inadequate, but if I do laugh and engage, to the point where he feels that maybe there is a closeness, maybe there is a connectedness, he wards that off as well by putting me in my place.

Larry: How does he do that?

Elise: For example, he'll say to me, "You're not supposed to be laughing like this. You're supposed to be an observer. Now if you laugh, I feel like I can manipulate you. I feel like I can right now take charge of this hour. If you give me an inch I'm going to take a mile, because if I can see that I've really got you in the palm of my hand, man, I've got some good skits I can practice with you." And he'll just take off that way.

Larry: And how do you respond to that?

Elise: I say something along the lines of, "Well J., how else am I really going to understand you and be with you unless I can totally climb into what you bring into this room and what you bring into our interaction? If I set myself apart from that I may be missing something."

Larry: And then?

Elise: He likes that. Although there've been times when it seems, in retrospect, like he's testing boundaries. I don't think he would still be with me after nine months, twice weekly, if there wasn't the engagement that I think we've been able to create, because he's very busy and his practice is very busy and he really has to carve the time out to come and see me.

Larry: When you say he tests you or tests the boundaries. . . .

Elise: He tests the boundaries in different ways. That's an example of one way. An example of another way—and I don't know if I would view this as a therapeutic error or not—I think it was a therapeutic error, but I think we were able to use it as grist for the mill—there was a session in December, where I felt he was peeling away some of his need for omnipotent control by his grandiose self. In the process he was touching on the emptiness he feels inside. It was a particularly tender and touching session where I felt that there was less of a need on his part to make me laugh or to entertain me. The mode felt different, more serious and sincere than usual. We weren't going to be seeing each other for ten days. It was Christmas break and he was going off somewhere and I was going off. At the end of the hour he asked me for a hug. Now, the way I've been trained to think about that is if the patient spontaneously goes over to hug you, then be responsive, but if someone asks, then you really want to use that for interpretive material to see what it means and what's going on with it. The scenario of the session, the mood, the tone, was such that I didn't want to spoil it, particularly at the end, by saying to him, "What does a hug mean to you? I think we have to talk about it." So I responded to it. But in responding he didn't just give me an AA-type hug, he took my elbows and pulled me to him and gave me a more seductive kind of hug and then broke it off somewhat abruptly.

Larry: He did?

Elise: Yes. And then he said, "Goodbye." He called me the next day and said, "You know, I think I need to talk about that hug. I swam an extra hundred laps trying to figure out what it meant and what it was about. (He's a swimmer.) I wondered why you did that. I've never been in this sort of process before, and I'm not really sure what's supposed to happen between therapists and their patients, but I just haven't been able to stop thinking about this. What I'm afraid of is that I'm going to come to these sessions and try to get more of this from you, which is going to jeopardize my getting out of these sessions what I really need to get out of them." Well of course I was very empathic. I was very supportive and indicated to him that his feelings certainly needed to be looked at and respected. It seemed to me that yesterday was a particularly moving session and I felt that a lot of his guard had been down. He knew that it was going to be some time before he would be coming back again. In that time and place it was as though saying goodbye with a hug seemed appropriate, but now it seemed to me, in hearing how he was feeling and what he was left with, that perhaps it was something that the two of us really need to set very strong limits with, with the understanding that this is not something that's going to happen again. He introjected, "Well, I don't want to feel that this is never going to happen again, but I guess I'm feeling that I need to feel a little bit more safe with it." I felt very uncomfortable with the way he pulled me in to hug me, but at the same time, at the moment, given the tone and given the sense of closeness, I felt that it would be so cold to say, "We'll talk about that when you come back in ten days." So in retrospect, I think we were able to make use of it. However, this is a man who tests me continually and double binds me. That's another example similar to my laughing and being spontaneous.

Female: Right. How much can he seduce you?

Male: He's seducing the hell out of you is what he's doing.

Elise: Yes.

Female: What was the crisis that brought him into therapy?

Elise: His core issues revolve around his sense of impairment in being able to have and to sustain an intimate relationship. At 38 he's had two committed relationships. Both relationships lasted a minimum of five years, so it's not as though they're really short. But because of medical school there was little doubt where his interest and his investment were. In analyzing the transference into dyads, what we've been able to label relative to us is that in one dyad he experiences me as the omnipotent dad who is all-knowing and all-expecting of him with his split off self being the helpless, inadequate, stupid little boy who really doesn't know how much he can do to win the affirmation that he needs from Dad. Another dyad that occurs with us is that I remind him, in part, of a previous girlfriend.

Larry: Number one or two?

Elise: Two. So this is interesting too. We'll call her Brenda. He met her working at a swank nightclub in Miami. He was a bartender; she was a cocktail waitress. He feels a continued attachment to Brenda. But he also has a lot of guilt about her. He feels that he was a real asshole, that basically he didn't treat her well. She deserved more. He abandoned her. They're still in contact. It seems that she's still interested and he toys with the idea of their getting back together. What brings him into treatment is that he yearns for a loving relationship, but he doesn't feel that he can sustain it. He doesn't blame the woman for not being attractive enough, not good enough, or whatever. He really blames himself. He persecutes himself for his immaturity, for his just not having his act together enough to be able to give these women what they want and need from him. One of the core themes I see with him is this need to comply. It's almost the twinship; he does to you what he wants you to do to him. He'll try to read what you may want from him so that he can comply with it. But when he finds himself in a situation where that really doesn't work for him, he avoids. He abandons. That's what happened in the last relationship. He complied with her up to a certain point. When he felt he could no longer comply, he left Miami and moved here.

Larry: I wanted to return to the theme of the engagement where he gets you to laugh and you do laugh and then he expresses that he's afraid he will take charge and control you. I was thinking, "What is that about?" The way you handled it was very nice. I had a quick fantasy of saying, "Well I suppose I will just have to let you control me until . . . what?" Like, "Why should I attempt to limit my laughter if you come here and want to entertain and control me? Why do I need to limit it? Why can't I just enjoy you? Where will we go?" I was feeling there was some fear behind it, but I didn't have an idea about what the fear might be. One way of playing it would be to challenge him and see where the fear leads. But when you told us about the hug, we saw a bit more. He takes charge; he hugs and then he's worried. He says he's worried that he's gone too far. But what is it that worries him? "Well, suppose you hugged me whenever you wanted to in whatever way you wanted, what then?" There's some fear lurking. It doesn't seem that he's simply afraid he's going to take charge and manipulate you. Or that he'll give the whole hour up to trying to seduce you. What's active here is not a seduction. It's more profound. He may be seducing you, but that doesn't seem to be to be the point. There is fear.

Elise: I agree with that and I feel that.

Larry: I think the fear is loss of self. What he's worried about is that if he begins to engage you, like with the second girlfriend, and begins to play to you, it will only be a matter of time before he has no self, before he's playing strictly to you. That relates to playing to Father, playing to Mother, playing to the second girlfriend, but I think it's a fear of the collapse of self, the total loss of personal identity.

Elise: I think what you're saying is right. He wards off painful affects by making a joke of them. For example, he'll come in and he'll do this whole skit around, "God, here I thought I was this young adult professional physician and now I'm questioning whether I'm even an embryo, a zygote, oh my God!" And he'll start talking about fragments of himself feeling so minute and small.

Larry: That's no joke.

Elise: Absolutely not.

Larry: I think the only way he knows he's alive is if he has the other in the palm of his hand.

Elise: There's a hypomanic style to him. He'll say to me, "Sometimes after these sessions I leave and I can't be with my girlfriend or with anyone for the first couple of hours because they tell me I'm too manic, because I get so wound up being here for fifty minutes."

Larry: I think he gets wound up defending against the horrible feelings of emptiness and depression that he becomes painfully aware of the minute he comes into your office. It's as though that tiny little embryonic self isn't a self. We don't know yet the best words to convey how empty, blank, undeveloped, frightened, and depressed that self is. He's terrified of it himself and terrified of the pain. What engages right away are the manic defenses, the jocular activity. I believe he fears that "if you engage with me at the level of the manic defense, then neither one of us will ever see me." If he were ever to go into an embryonic thing like that again I think I might laugh and enjoy it and then I would stop him and look him square in the eye and say, "We're laughing, yet this may be the most profound thing you've ever told me. I believe you're telling me that there's a tiny little undeveloped self that no one has ever been able to see that's you. Nobody can see it, nobody can relate to it. You bring it to me with the same fear that, like your father, I won't see it, that like your mother, I won't see it. I think you're afraid that if we get too much into laughing, once again you will have been overlooked. There will have been no relationship, just like with your two women.

Elise: I like that.

Larry: "And yet I think it's going to feel really awful for us to take a good square look at it. I don't know whether it's going to be depression, fear, terror, emptiness, deadness, or whatever. I don't know how to consider this little embryonic self, but I believe it's our job to identify and define the essential you. I want to let you know that I love your laughter and I love your entertainment. I know you love for us to laugh together as well. But the serious part of our interaction is getting to the small, fragile, empty self." I would be willing to put a lot of different and tentative words on it. I wouldn't be willing to commit myself to any particular words saying, "I don't think we know the exact qualities of that self yet. Maybe you have some inclinations, maybe from your dreams or thoughts you have some sense of what it may be like, but basically we don't know too much about the nature or the character of this embryonic self yet."

Male: It feels like the erotic transference is almost a way of throwing you off the scent.

Larry: It certainly functions in the service of the manic defense to avoid difficult feeling states.

Elise: I like that because there's something every time. He'll notice when I'm wearing a new pair of earrings and comment on it. He'll notice when I'm wearing a different pair of shoes. "I haven't seen those shoes before." But he goes so fast with it that when I try to back up to zero in on whether that has any meaning, he'll experience me as the persecuting mom and say, "I wasn't hitting on you," and then just skate into something else.

Larry: But you see, I think he's right. He wasn't hitting on you and it didn't have meaning in the ordinary sense of the word. When we look at the manic defense and try to understand the so-called meaning of it, meaning collapses. The only meaning we can say is that there's a frantic effort to get away from feeling small, lonely, empty, and sad. If he thinks you're trying to introduce meaning, like hitting on you, then you're not seeing him and so he says, "I'm not." The manic defense functions to ward off affects and their meanings.

Elise: He assumes that hitting on me is what I'm thinking.

Larry: No doubt because that's what others think. He does all these wonderful entertaining things for women and they feel right away he's hitting on them. I mean they get sexually excited because they think this is a sexual come-on and it's not. He's trying to find somebody who can see and respond to the tiny, frightened little boy inside.

Male: In the session where he hugs you before the holiday break, he feels the void, the collapse of the self. He then calls you up and begins pointing out the defense of seduction, trying to keep the focus on the defense rather than on the despairing feelings themselves.

Larry: Yes. Rather than saying, "I was aware that we have a Christmas break, that there are depressive feelings present. I'm discouraged about where I'm going to be and maybe you're discouraged too. We won't be able to talk for a while." Instead of trying to deal with whatever those feelings might be about the season or the break, he moves right into this rather pressuring manic defense, but then is worried that they'll get swept up in the seductive coverup.

Elise: Yes, he is. He's worried that I'm going to get swept up in it.

Larry: At that point you won't see the sad, lonely, frightened self. You've described it as the twinship transference and I think that may be the upper or later level of his development. I'm wondering what the earlier level is? I think it's something at about the fourth month. I'm thinking of Mommy and baby laughing together, touching noses, and putting their fingers into each other's mouths—two laughing and playing together with a rich affective resonance. This early way of relating has been called transitivism, where two do things to each other, mimicking with matching efforts.

Elise: Oh, he demands that the affects match.

Larry: When we talk about the twinship transference modeled on a 3-year-old level, we're talking about something more cognitive. But matching affects characterizes the early symbiosis where we have to be together to be safe. We have to resonate with each other at this level. We affectively play off each other. I think he strives to recreate that early "Mommy and me" resonance in his comedy act. It would seem that the comedy or cartoon act functions not merely as a manic defense, but is also an attempt to represent a 4-month, maybe 6-month-old kid and mother in a "koochie koochie coo" routine playing off each other's smiles and laughter.

Male: I need some help with this. The hug scenario is confusing to me based on what you're saying. I was looking at it in terms of a dance of control and optimal distance, of going in and then undoing. What I think I'm hearing from you is that it's a developmentally earlier experience.

Larry: I think it may have many meanings because this man has a development that spans a number of different years, so we have to consider various layerings of emotional experience and the many aspects of himself he's simultaneously representing in his engagements. But the part I want to highlight, and it remains to be seen how it's going to evolve in the therapy, is that he's uneasy if she becomes caught up in his seduction. He knows he's seductive, he knows everybody falls in love with him, loves to laugh with him.

Elise: He is funny.

Larry: He's terrified that if he engages Elise at that level only and at the level of being seduced, she's going to miss him because there's a him that hasn't yet been seen. She's even saying in the countertransference, "Sure enough, he reminds me of somebody else I loved." I think he's showing you not merely the manic defense quality but also the most primitive "Mommy and me" relationship where we just play together. Like somehow that part of his development went well. With his early mother, the affective resonance worked well for him and he tries to recreate it. But when it's recreated he experiences the painful loss of not being experienced in his own right.

Elise: I would love to get at that fear but he's so defended. The session moves so fast that it's hard to find a time to analyze the transference or work my countertransference.

Larry: I'm sure that in some of the laughter there are opportunities to begin making comments like, "This is so funny my stomach just hurts from laughing, but there's something really frightening about it. Like somewhere underneath this kind of humor there's also something kind of sad." Or, "We're full of joy but it feels like there's also an underlying emptiness." Even within the quickness of the hour you can begin to let him know "I see this part and this is the part that's wonderful, but there's more than meets the eye and I don't know quite what it is." Not expecting him necessarily to respond right away or be able to dialogue about it, but more registering your awareness and marking important moments.

Female: You haven't mentioned his mother.

Elise: Okay. He idealizes his mom. He sees his mom as a wonderful lady. She was a real cookie-baking type. He'll say to me, even though sometimes he feels like a child with my being his parent, that somehow I don't seem like the cookie-baking type of mom. So it's more of the dad that gets transferred onto me, who seems to know more.

Female: A cookie-baking type—that's kind of the opposite of the cocktail-waitress type. She was home.

Elise: She was home. She was nurturing. He felt very safe and secure with her. Dad was the one who was feared. Dad was the one who did the discipline. Dad was the one he used humor with to break through what he felt like a wall. But climbing into his world of experiencing Mom, it's like he basked in Mom's affection. "I feel like I was really an enjoyed baby and my mother, by the time she had me, was very versed in the tasks of mothering." Mom is almost a *Leave It To Beaver* mom. When I asked him to describe Dad, he spent a considerable amount of time talking about Dad's hands. "Dad has big hands." J's hands are also very important to him because of the meticulous kinds of medical work he does. But the image that was conveyed to me of Dad is I just see this big hand. Dad just seems so competent that he could fix anything and do anything.

Male: You're saying that Mom is idealized. I wonder how you see him idealizing you? Because that's the way he could see you as Mother, through the idealization.

Elise: He idealizes me a lot. Sometimes, in my countertransference, I ward it off, because it imbues me with so much power that I'm not comfortable. But I've learned to tolerate it as long as it doesn't really interfere, recognizing that he has a certain need to do that. By and large, he views my words as golden. I make an interpretation and he's right on the edge of his seat, all ears.

Larry: The countertransference here is really rich because it seems to represent one aspect of the way he was responded to as a child. He tells you about being a loved and enjoyed child with a cookie-baking mom. But what's coming through to me is that with all of this mutual attentiveness, neither mother nor child could be honest and genuine with each other. Mother idealized her baby somehow and in idealizing the baby, everything that the baby did was wonderful. But the small, fragile, depressed, frightened baby had no place. The authentic, real self with bad feelings didn't have a place, only the idealized baby. I'm thinking too, of how when he entertains you, he worries that if you really were to let yourself go, something awful might happen. There again, you can't be authentic in the room. I think he was not allowed to be authentic. His mother may have been very depressed when he was born. She may have needed to idealize this baby because who knows what was going on in her life. She needed to be entertained, lifted, brought up by this baby. Perhaps she felt good when being a dutiful and cheerful mother. But however it might have been, he seems afraid that the two of you are going to get into mutually seductive enjoyment, idealizing each other, thinking wonderful things about each other, having a wonderful time with each other. Once again he'll be lost.

Elise: That would be easy. But a difficulty for me arises when I do try to identify a defense that might be operating. He experiences it as almost persecutory.

Larry: You've only seen him twice a week for nine months. It's very early for him to be able to move comfortably with depth interpretation even though he may be very insightful at a verbal level. He can say many things because he's bright and because he's been with many verbal people. But the much truer and deeper affects and defenses I don't think he's ready for. Who would be in nine months? About all you can say now is, "This was a wonderful joke but there was something almost macabre in it." Or "We're really having a great time but I have a sense that there's something else happening here." Or, "That hug was really great but there's something that concerns me about it." He knows there's something else. He knows his true self has to be seen and responded to. But he doesn't know exactly what the something more is. I think he's terrified to let the manic defense of the joviality drop off for fear of what will happen then.

Elise: Absolutely. He's even said to me, "You know, I feel very defensive about your taking this away from me and even introducing me to a way of feeling vulnerable or a way of grieving my losses, because I can't do my job feeling vulnerable or grieving losses. I need this compulsivity. I need this hypomanic style in order to be a physician. Otherwise I'm just not going to be effective."

Larry: I would say, "Bullshit." We know that what he's saying can't be right, because what he's saying is "I can function best with a constricted, isolated, split-off part self." Ultimately that simply can't be true. His concern about losing familiar habits is certainly a valid one. We know that as people begin to open themselves up and begin to integrate the deeper parts of themselves, there are bound to be some disruptions, some grieving periods. He may have to turn a piece of complicated work over to a colleague one week. Most people starting analysis say, "I can't possibly get into my deeper stuff because of blah, blah, blah." That is, "I believe a partial self is better than a whole self." The therapist has to be prepared to say, "That can't possibly be true. The deep, the sad, the empty, the grieving parts of you represent wells of inner resource and potential power and creativity that you had to cut off as an infant. I can't believe that a whole self is going to be less effective than a part self. I can believe that while you're studying yourself there may be disruptions. While you're reintegrating lost parts you may have to find ways of making sure that you've got adequate backup if you feel your hands are shaky one day. That being potentially the case, you need to let your superiors know that you're working on some disorganizing things in therapy and that the time may come when you'll need to call on outside help to get through a tough situation. This potential for disrupted functioning is a regular aspect of analytic therapy and needs to be dealt with realistically, regardless of the person's daily occupation. Times come when a person in depth therapy simply cannot engage in daily activities as efficiently as usual. And if some sort of danger is involved, like work with machines, driving cars, and so forth, then we need to alert our people to the dangers they may be facing. People don't usually notice, for example, that their reflexes are slowed down when they're acutely depressed. We do know this and I believe it's our responsibility to warn people that they may not be quite themselves today and to take care to be safe while going through these changes. You might sit down with him and say, "Okay, let's look at it realistically. What do you need to do to feel safe when you're having a bad day or a bad week? If you need backup support then let's think how you can arrange it. As long as you think you're the only person in the world who can do the work, that you're the center of your mother's love, that she's going to die if you don't keep her happy, then you're living in a world of infantile delusion. You can indeed turn to others for help in order to make sure that the things you do are safe and sane." There are hundreds of physicians who are a beeper away and three minutes from the emergency room if he needs backup. But as long as he believes he's the only one who can take care of Mother's survival needs, he will not be able to develop a true sense of himself.

Elise: I hear what you're saying and I agree. Are you also saying that he hasn't addressed that primitive, inauthentic sense of himself?

Larry: The depressed empty self that didn't have a mother that could respond to him?

Female: Right.

Larry: Yes. But now let's shift for a moment to the counter-transference you're enjoying.

Elise: At times I feel maternal toward him. But I also feel at other times like a seductive object.

Larry: Which for him represents Mother. Mother and he seduced each other with excitement, joy, cookies, and cream!

Elise: I feel the maternal and I feel the erotic.

Larry: For him I suspect they're the same in that he has never moved to a place where he can have an erotic relationship with a woman apart from the maternal.

Elise: It's interesting the way you're seeing and interpreting this because where he still is in his own view and understanding is that, "Mom and Dad have a wonderful relationship. In fact, last Christmas Mom crocheted a jock strap for Dad to keep his balls warm." He thought that was so cute. And so he'll talk about "Gee, what a wonderful relationship they still seem to have after all these years."

Larry: And perhaps they do. But what we want to respond to is despite the fact that he basically had good parents and they basically have a good relationship, there was a need of his that was unresponded to. A need to experience and to learn to represent loneliness, injury, sadness, emptiness, fear, and other bad feelings. There is some part of him that went unresponded to because of his mother's need to have everything happy. Naturally he fears beginning to explore the unknown, split off depressive and negative affects.

Tony: I wanted to say something because my child now is 4 months old. As you (Larry) portrayed this person in a 4-month-old frame of mind, I'm now seeing this in my daughter, because the primary way most people are connecting with Darlene is through laughter. They try every way to get her to smile and laugh, even when she's not feeling like it. I'm really trying to be responsive to the part of her that doesn't want to laugh. Everyone is saying, "We have to smile. Get the tissue or the squeaky toy and make her smile."

Larry: That's the point at which Mother does something like bake cookies or crochet a jock strap and then says, "Isn't this a darling baby."

Male: Right, and fends off the part that may be tired, irritated, or whatever. Are you saying it's too early for her to address the countertransference issues?

Larry: Not necessarily. But I am saying she's in a place where she can see considerably beyond what this man is ready to deal with directly. She's naturally feeling somewhat impatient to get to the deeper material. I'm saying "Look, he's only been in therapy nine months. He's a very busy man. . . ."

Elise: But he's intense, Larry, and he does think fast. If somebody does the therapy in five years, he's going to do it in two.

Larry: Fine. We'll see how fast he can drop into a fragmenting depression. (Group laughs.) We know that takes time and hard work.

Female: He's been in a competitive, achieving mode his entire life, but he's always paid a price for it.

Larry: The price is not knowing about his depressive feelings.

Female: I'm always suspicious of these really happy families where everything is so idealized. What was their need and what is his need to deny the other side of life?

Larry: There are many fine people and many fine families and relationships that are basically solid and happy. There's nothing wrong with that. Except, Tony, what you're saying with your little Darlene is that right now you can see that if someone isn't responding to the part of her that either needs to withdraw or that doesn't want to laugh, if someone doesn't see the sad, frightened, rejected, or lonely child, they're not responding to her. You see now at the fourth month she's developing well and she's beginning to experience depression because she's aware that she's not in control of Mother's body. Depressive feelings are essential to her mental development at this point.

Male: Right.

Larry: Melanie Klein teaches that this is the time when the depressive position appears. If everybody is busy trying to have a happy baby, the depressive position can't fall into place. It seems that it didn't with this man. But shifting slightly, I'm thinking in the countertransference that you can be a little more devilish, Elise.

Elise: Okay, give me some input.

Larry: I'm going back to the first example you gave where he had you in stitches. You're really enjoying him. You love this man. He reminds you of an old boyfriend. You have a good time with him. As you're talking about him we can see that you think he's wonderful and you've got this happy baby who's entertaining Mom and it's beautiful. So we now have this Madonna and child halo around this happy, happy, happy child and mother combination.

Elise: I'm feeling guilty that this is too good to be true.

Larry: But this is not your therapy. It's his. He's a great guy. Why shouldn't you enjoy him? He's got to be the one who begins to show you what's wrong with the enjoyment. He says, "If you laugh and laugh or if we hug, don't you think you'd better control yourself? Shouldn't you be more objective? Shouldn't you be a little more of a therapist?" A rib tickling answer might be "Why? Why can't I enjoy you? Why can't I just have fun? Why can't we hug forever? What's the problem here? You're very funny. You're a very nice man. You're intelligent. You tickle my fancy. I enjoy you. What's the problem?" All this, done in such a way as to put the responsibility back on him. He knows you enjoy him; it's plain to see. But if you begin to say out of guilt, "Well, maybe I should be more objective. Maybe I need to be a better therapist. Maybe I shouldn't enjoy him so much. Maybe my own neurotic countertransference is getting out of hand and I need to control it more, not be so seduced, and so on." Then you're taking responsibility for the evolution of his material. And that is not your job, it's his. We understand that all of those various considerations are important and valid as considerations. But in some way or another you've got to be able, with a twinkle in your eye, to say, "This is just fabulous. I think we could laugh and go on enjoying ourselves forever, but there's something that's not present in the room. There's something that you're not telling me yet. A piece of you is missing here. While we're having all this fun there is something else going on and you haven't been able to tell me what that is yet." But the twinkle in the eye is meant to say, "I know there's a you in there that you're not showing me yet and I'm waiting. Meanwhile I'll laugh myself silly. It's your job to show me what else is there. I can't do it for you." I think you understand what I'm saying. You have to put the responsibility for the therapy back on him in such a way as to say that you know there is more here. "You believe you can't let a sad, depressed, or angry self come out because you won't be able to do your work. I say that's ridiculous. You can arrange backup support, take a little time off, or whatever else you may need to do to take care of yourself. Your soul is what's important here."

Elise: He resists that.

Larry: Well, that's fine, but from your standpoint you've got to say, "This is a defense, just like any other defense. And it's a fantasy that says 'If I'm not there taking care of Mother's body, she'll die.' That's what you've had to do your whole life. You've had to take care of Mother's heart, you've had to massage it, and keep it happy. What about you?"

Male: Is he ready to hear that?

Elise: He wouldn't be willing to hear about taking time off.

Larry: Fine. But you hear the point behind it that he has to be challenged on his belief that he's the guardian of everybody's well-being and happiness.

Elise: Yeah, well I think he feels that.

Larry: Of course he does. And what you've got to communicate is, "That's your delusion. You're not the guardian of everybody's well-being. What about your self?"

Elise: That's been a core theme. There's a real compliancy there.

Female: Don't you think it's his fear, also? I mean I don't think he would really decompensate if he got in touch with more of his emptiness and his self.

Larry: No, that's his fear.

Female: It's his fear. It's a delusion.

Larry: Yes. But I think it is important to acknowledge a truism, that when we get into disruptive or regressive places in our therapy, we're not our best selves for a few days or weeks. Analytic therapy is specifically designed to destroy certain crippling or limiting ego configurations and body constrictions. When those configurations and constrictions are attached to daily skills, the daily skills are disrupted for a period of time until they can be reintegrated. I think we have to address that aspect realistically.

Elise: I'd lose him at that point. That's my fantasy.

Male: You'd lose him at what point?

Elise: If he has to get depressed.

Larry: Now, let's think countertransference. You're in the infant position saying, "If my mother is ever allowed to fall into a bit of depression, or to be anything other than a happy, jovial, well functioning, cookie-baking mother, I will lose her."

Elise: Hmm, well maybe.

Male: Can't you speak that to him?

Larry: We've got all of these ideas, but we're a long way ahead of this man.

Male: Yes, but I mean to speak something about the fear of losing him.

Elise: Oh, yes, I've done that. There have been times over the nine months where he's gotten busy, and he hasn't come in twice a week, or we've missed a week or two. I definitely speak my concern about losing him. And then he'll come back, and it's like he wants to protect me, so he'll say, "I need you more than you know." It's like he'll really give back to me.

Larry: Now, that sounds like a cookie-baking mother.

Elise: Well, that does, as I hear myself saying it. And he does give that.

Larry: He tries to calm you down, so that you're not afraid of losing him.

Elise: That's his comeback.

Larry: But what about your deep fears, what about your depression? What about the real self that's inside? He doesn't know how to attend to that. Now, way down the road, that may have some interesting implications for some transference concerns. That is, he has to be able to sense your realness as a person with fears and depressive feelings if he's going to relate to you. Ordinarily, we don't think about the speaker needing to know about our frailties and vulnerable feelings. But if what he's got to do is to break through falseness and joviality and to realize that he has depressive aspects to himself, and that you do too, he may need to delve a little more deeply into who you are and the things that bother you, disrupt you, or leave you feeling fragmented or despairing. The replicated symbiotic transference has to be worked through in both the passive and active dimensions. Ordinarily, we don't think that the speaker has to be responsive to our depressive parts. But since there's a scenario here, that neither he nor his mom ever responded to each other's depressive parts, part of breaking the scenario may include such responsiveness. Imagine coming in on a certain day, say maybe you're a little off, and maybe you know something has happened. He'll read it right away. He'll know something's wrong.

Elise: Oh, he'll know. This guy would know.

Larry: Okay, suppose either you or he is pretending that it's not there. He's busy trying to entertain you or something. I think there's an opportunity to confront the scenario by saying, "You can see that there's something wrong with me today, that I'm not quite my usual self. And you've shown indication that you can sense when that's so. But you're not going to go after it. You're ignoring an aspect of our reality here. What's the matter? I'm not here for you in the way that I ordinarily am. You can plainly see that. How does that affect you? What does that bring up for you?"

Female: Does he go after it when he sees you're off?

Elise: Well, not yet. He'll just try to entertain me more.

Larry: Right. Rather than saying, "It looks as though you're off." Sometimes this is a problem that gets discussed as disclosures. If we're disclosing for the sake of disclosing, I say, "Tell it to someone who cares." (Group laughs.) But when we're trying to confront a scenario, and in this case the scenario is the refusal to see the true self in its depressive aspects, disclosures could be essential. If he's trying to entertain you, because you're clearly in a bad place on that day, and he can plainly see that, you might say, "Look, what I think you're trying not to notice is that I'm in a bad place today." And if the occasion calls for you to say "I had some very bad news in my life this morning," then it may be important to say so. You're not disclosing for the purpose of helping yourself. You're rather saying, "You're not knowing how to deal with my being off today." Disclosures are not for the sake of your using him to make you feel better. But if it's plain that you're off, and he's trying to entertain you, and the only way you have of effectively drawing his attention to what's going on is to say, "You're having reactions because you can see I'm not here today in the way that I ordinarily am. I think the only thing you know how to do is to try to cheer me up. I'm wondering if maybe you'd be better off if you could be sad with me, and realize that such and such a thing happened to me. Or you might even be angry with me for not enjoying you as usual."

Male: So a disclosure for the purpose of speaking, of confronting a scenario, is different?

Larry: Absolutely. Because here, what you're trying to do is to say, "You're not dealing with my sadness. I believe you, and I believe we would feel more real as human beings if we shared a moment of sadness together. You can plainly see that I'm sad today. I believe you would feel more real if you could say, 'Elise, I'm sorry. I can tell that must really hurt, and that must be sad for you. I'm glad to see your eyes tearing up because you're letting me be real with you. My mother never would do that with me. Nobody could ever be sad or feel lonely in my family.'"

Elise: I look forward to getting to a place where that can occur.

Larry: The same interpretation must be made the other way around, in the reversal of roles, of course. But that'll be easier, because you'll be able to be more sensitive to him. It's easier to say, "I think you're laughing today because you feel like crying."

Elise: He's a playful baby. He is.

Larry: But playful babies also need to cry when the world hurts them or lets them down. The depressive position was not anything his mother was prepared to deal with, for whatever reason, with him. My guess is that when he was born, and maybe you'll get historical material on this, his mother was feeling depression more than she ordinarily did, maybe more than she did with any of her other children.

Male: Nobody ever cried on *Leave It To Beaver.*

Elise: No. So from a conceptual viewpoint, would you say that a therapeutic task in his treatment is to help integrate those split off parts, such that it's not that the depression is going to go away, it's that the depression is going to be acknowledged?

Larry: And felt as real.

Female: And felt as real and integrated into that other jovial part.

Larry: Yes. And that can only strengthen him. It can only make him feel better. Joy is great. We feel physically uplifted. But if we can't let down, if we can't lean on others for support when we need it, we end up shouldering the world, wearing ourselves out with strain. Knowing his depressive, depleted side can only give him more access to a total self. He doesn't believe that now.

Elise: No, he doesn't.

Larry: Winnicott (1975) suggests that babies are often used by their mothers as part of a defense against their own depression.

Elise: That would make sense.

Larry: He had to be jovial to be with Mother. He had to be happy in order to be a part of Mother's defense system. I think that for whatever reason, his mother was feeling a lot of depression that she was fending off when he was born, and the early months after. She managed to include this child as a part of her defense against her depression. The depressive position can't be established when he's in fact serving as a part of mother's defense. He can't realize the separateness, because he's not separate. Mother is including him as a part of her defense. So the depressive condition can't blossom fully at that level.

Male: How would a self psychologist view this case?

Larry: A self psychologist should be able to treat this man rather well by going after the twinship transference, with Mother at the affective level, and by going after the idealizing transference from Father. I think the Kohutian technique would probably be rather a good one for working with him. But I would be afraid that the deeper aspects of the scenario might not be soundly confronted. One of Kernberg's criticisms of self psychology is that aggression, and I'm adding depression, might not be interpreted by the self psychologist. The aggression might be soothed over and the depression covered up, rather than interpreted. I think that's an unfair criticism across the board. But I believe it could be a danger in a self psychology approach, if not carefully thought through.

I think that noticing the countertransference here is going to help you go to the deeper level. The main countertransference evolving is that you're not feeling quite real in this relationship. You tried, you gave him a hug at Christmas, but then he says, "You can't do that." You laugh, but then he says, "You can't do that." He's holding you in a place where you can't be real with him. I think the ultimate confrontation of the scenario is, "Why can't I be real? Why can't I enjoy you? Why can't I cry with you? Why can't you cry with me? Why can't we be real?" I believe a lot of depression and aggression have yet to emerge.

Elise: I wondered if his competitiveness is an extension of the aggression?

Larry: I think so.

Elise: I don't feel the aggression.

Larry: It's not there yet. I think it will be.

Male: What about keeping her in a certain place? The controlling of her?

Larry: That's aggressive.

Elise: Okay.

Larry: But it doesn't have a hostile bent.

Elise: No, it doesn't. At least not yet.

Larry: It's more an ambition and control.

Male: Is emergency room cutting aggression?

Larry: Yes, it's aggression. But it's sublimated. It's turned to something socially useful. I'm thinking that his aggression has turned into entertaining you, to holding you in such a way that it doesn't let you be alive—that's aggressive. Thank you very much, Elise.

Elise: Thank you all. I have a lot of new things to think about.

PART IV

THE ROYAL ROAD TO COUNTER-TRANSFERENCE

15

Countertransference Interpretation: Freud the Provocateur

Countertransference interpretation arises from emotional relatedness experiences of the analyst. Contemporary psychoanalytic research demonstrates that the greatest usefulness of countertransference interpretation lies in its power to point toward preverbal dyadic interactional experience with the mothering partner(s) in both its active and passive replications in the analytic relationship. These symbiotic or character scenarios arising from the unthought known (Bollas 1987) are remembered as affective responsiveness that is faithfully replicated in the subsequent relatedness modes and patterns of the analytic engagement. An other, a listener, an analyst must be actively present and engaged for the replicated transference to develop fully and clearly. In Freud's self-analysis there was no analyst. Though some transference feelings did develop toward his friend Wilhelm Fliess, Freud's analysis ended abruptly when he arrived at material from his own symbiotic period.

While it would be presumptuous to suppose that without

countertransference interpretation of the symbiotic replication
we could understand Freud's character in any full or valid way, as
an exercise in imagination I have found it illuminating to study
the dreams and letters that mark the close of his self-analysis and
to suppose that they represent resistance to the development of
deeper layers of analysis. What follows is my imaginative
reconstruction of what in Freud's symbiotic or character structure might have emerged through countertransference interpretation.

For reasons attributed to privacy and discretion, Freud
regularly omits aspects of his analysis of his own dreams in *The
Interpretation of Dreams* (1900). These omissions no doubt
constitute a crucial nexus that might lead one to a somewhat
different understanding of the dreams specifically, but also of
Freud's character. Is not the unexpurgated truth of the active
impulse life of one's soul, one's desire, and what it gives rise to,
after all, what one seeks to understand through psychoanalysis?
While Freud may dismiss his omissions as having a clearly sexual
meaning or probably as another aspect of revenge, he clearly
expects forgiveness for such motives, if not admiration for his
forthrightness and courage in admitting them. But what are the
motivating forces that Freud conceals—the ones that might not
be so forgivable, at least in his own eyes?

At the time Freud wrote his monograph, his thoughts were
preoccupied with infantile sexuality and various reactions to
impediments placed upon infantile wishes by the child's early
educators. He studied extensively, not only the oedipal incestual
wishes, but also the oedipal destructive wishes directed toward
those who would interfere with oedipal objectives and pleasures.
Perhaps partly because of his special interests and partly because
Freud was not writing from a position in history that would
enable him to grasp the primacy of early developmental issues
that occupy contemporary psychoanalytic studies, he failed to
elucidate the full nature of preoedipal interactions involved in
character formation, although he certainly understood their

importance. He failed to separate the so-called preoedipal bases for character from the sexualization and aggressivization of these same features in the later, superimposed, or more complex oedipal constellations called neurosis.

FREUD'S SYMBIOTIC DREAM AND HIS ASSOCIATIONS

Freud's dream, "Undressed, running upstairs" (Freud 1900), was one of a series of dreams he related to memories of the nurse in whose charge he had been left for much of his rearing until the age of two-and-a-half. The dream goes as follows:

> I was very incompletely dressed and was going upstairs from a flat on the ground floor to a higher story. I was going up three steps at a time and was delighted at my agility. Suddenly I saw a maid-servant coming down the stairs—coming towards me, that is. I felt ashamed and tried to hurry, and at this point the feeling of being inhibited set in: I was glued to the steps and unable to budge from the spot. [p. 272]

Freud explains that the day residue related to his previous evening's journey from the lower flat where he worked, through the connecting public staircase, to the upper flat where he lived. He says he was in "rather disordered dress, that is to say, I had taken off my collar and tie and cuffs" (p. 272). He explains that he always took three steps at a time, which he surmised related to the dream's wish-fulfillment—"the ease with which I achieved it reassured me as to the functioning of my heart" (p. 272). While associating to the dream, he recognizes the staircase and the identity of the maid-servant as that of an elderly lady whom he had continued to visit twice daily for a long time for the purpose of giving her an injection of morphine.

He dismisses the shame of the dream as "no doubt of a sexual nature" (p. 273). He explains that as a rule on his morning visits he was "seized with a desire to clear my throat as I went up the stairs and the product of my expectoration would fall on the staircase" (p. 273). He took the view that "the cleanliness of the stairs should not be maintained at my expense, but should be made possible by the provision of a spittoon" (p. 273). That is, he should be allowed to drop his body products where he pleases! The elderly, surly concierge of cleanly instincts saw things differently. "She would lie in wait for me to see whether I should again make free of the stairs" (p. 273). If she found that he had, she grumbled audibly and for several days would omit her usual greeting. Judging from Freud's account, the morning scene had turned into somewhat of a battleground. But the day before the dream, "the concierge's party had received a reinforcement" (p. 273) in the form of the maid-servant. After his visit, she stopped him and remarked, "You might have wiped your boots, Doctor, before you came into the room today. You've made the red carpet all dirty again with your feet" (p. 273). One association Freud makes between running up the stairs and spitting on the stairs is that "pharyngitis, as well as heart trouble, are both regarded as punishments for the vice of smoking" (p. 273). He further points out that he also had a reputation for untidiness with the authorities of his own house on account of that same habit! He draws the provisional conclusion that "a sensation of inhibited movement in dreams is produced whenever the particular context requires it" (p. 273), but carries the idea no further.

The following few pages in his work deal with nakedness in dreams as a revival of an intoxicating delight of early childhood. "They [young children] laugh and jump about and slap themselves, while their mother, or whoever else may be there, reproves them and says: 'Ugh! Shocking! You mustn't ever do that!'" (p. 277). This is the way Freud chooses to interpret the dream. "My own dream of running upstairs and of soon afterwards finding myself glued to the steps was equally a dream of exhibiting, since it bears the essential marks of being one" (p. 280).

This dream comes from a period of Freud's intense self-analysis. It has often been suggested that his physician friend, Wilhelm Fliess, in Berlin, served somewhat as Freud's analyst. Freud wrote to him frequently and developed an intense (some say homosexual) transference to him. In a letter written immediately after the dream (May 31, 1897) he writes to his friend, Fliess (Freud 1954) asking for secrecy and confides to him, "I am about to discover the source of morality" (p. 206). He begins by repeating a recent dream in which he was feeling over-affectionally toward his daughter, Mathilde, "but in the dream her name appeared in bold type as 'Hella'" (p. 206). In real life she regarded all Hellenes as heroes and had been weeping bitterly over the recent Greek defeats. The wish-fulfillment of this dream, Freud surmises, is the "wish to pin down a father as the originator of neurosis and put an end to my persistent doubts" (p. 206). This presumably refers to his consideration of the seduction hypothesis, the notion that hysterical neurosis was caused by father incest. A sketch of the dream in question (1954) hastily recorded before he left on summer holiday, immediately follows.

I was walking up a staircase with very few clothes on. I was walking very briskly as was emphasized in the dream (heart not affected!) when I suddenly noticed that a woman was coming up behind me, whereupon I found myself rooted to the spot, unable to move, overcome by that paralysis which is so common in dreams. The accompanying emotion was not anxiety, but erotic excitement. So you see how the feeling of paralysis peculiar to sleep can be used for the fulfillment of an exhibitionistic wish. Earlier that night I had really climbed the stairs from the flat below, at any rate, without a collar, and it had occurred to me that I might meet a neighbor. [pp. 206–207]

This alternate version of the dream contains some interesting variations of and associations to the dream themes, not the least of which is that the woman is approaching him from behind. At that moment, "I found myself rooted to the spot." The accompanying emotion was "not anxiety, but erotic excitement." The preceding paragraph on Hella and the defeat of the Greeks may relate to the variance of the woman coming up from *behind*, as well as Freud's sense of being caught and his further belief that he was about to discover the source of morality. None of his associations includes the common observation that all mammals are regularly "rooted to the spot" when frightened, startled, or caught unawares. In the monograph version of the dream (1900), the maid-servant was "coming down the stairs—coming towards me, that is. I felt ashamed and tried to hurry, and at this point, the feeling of being inhibited set in" (pp. 272–273). If, as Freud mentions elsewhere in his book, going upstairs in dreams is often associated with sexual arousal, then the dream suggests either being caught in masturbation or, if the maid is coming down on him, represents a seduction. The paralysis may allude to his persistent impotence.

It seems altogether too easy for Freud to admit publicly to exhibitionistic wishes and to acknowledge sexual shame, especially in light of the series of associations that emerge. But acknowledging incest wishes and impotence may have been too personal. The only other mention Freud makes of this dream is in two letters (Freud 1954, pp. 218–225) written to Fliess five months later. He indicates that at times he now had the impression that the self-analysis of his hysterical neurosis was coming to an end.

> I can only say that in my case, my father played no active role, though I certainly projected on to him an analogy of myself; that my "primary originator" (of neurosis) was an ugly elderly, but clever woman who told me a great deal about God and hell and gave me a high opinion of my own capacities. . . . [p. 219]

This formulation registers Freud's recognition that the oedipal themes involved in neurosis likely represent a thematic superimposition by analogy of more complex triadic modes over earlier dyadic relatedness modes along with whatever emotional issues may have been important for the child—here cleanliness, orderliness, stubbornness, and morality.

Freud then makes several allusions: to an overnight journey with his nurse when he was between the ages of 18 months and 2½, concluding that he must have seen her naked; to his infantile jealousy and guilt toward a one-year-younger brother who died in the first few months of life; and to his "companion in crime between the ages of one and two" (p. 219), a nephew a year older with whom some years later he behaved toward a year-younger niece in a way that he labeled "shockingly" (perhaps molest?). He continues, "I still have not got to the scenes which lie at the bottom of all of this. If they emerge and I succeed in resolving my hysteria, I shall have to thank the memory of the old woman who provided me at such an early age with the means for living and surviving. You see how the old liking breaks through again" (pp. 219–220). Freud concludes this letter with, "My recognition that difficulties of treatment derive from the fact that in the last resort one is laying bare the patient's evil inclinations, his will to remain ill, is growing stronger and clearer" (p. 220). In a postscript to this letter, dated the following day, Freud mentions a dream from the previous night in which his nurse reappears.

She was my instructress in sexual matters, and chided me for being clumsy and not being able to do anything (that is always the way with neurotic impotence: anxiety over incapacity at school gets its sexual reinforcement in this way. . . .) The whole dream was full of the most wounding references to my present uselessness as a therapist. Perhaps the origin of my tendency to believe in the incurability of hysteria should be sought here. Also, she washed me in reddish water in which she

previously washed herself (not very difficult to interpret; I find
nothing of the kind in my chain of memories, and so I take it for
genuine rediscovery); and she encouraged me to steal "Zehners"
[ten-Kreuzer pieces] to give to her. [p. 220]

Freud's follow-up dream suggests links between his hysterical impotency (and possible oedipal castration fears) and the
underlying humiliations of cleanliness education, which result
in incapacity at school, that is, a (sexualized) paralysis in
relation to the instructress. A further possibility is that the
meaning of Freud's insistent soiling of the old lady's red carpet
might relate to a symbolic replication involving red (menstrual)
bath water.

Several weeks later, Freud reports asking his mother if she
remembered his nurse. "Of course," she said, "an elderly woman,
very shrewd indeed. She was always taking you to church. When
you came home, you used to preach and tell us all about how
God conducted his affairs. At the time, I was in bed when Anna
was being born" (p. 221). His mother reported that shiny
Zehners and toys that had been given to the small Freud were
found among the maid's belongings. His brother, Phillip, got the
police and the nurse got ten months. Continuing his letter,
Freud refers to this last dream.

> Now I see how that confirms the conclusions from my dream
> interpretation. I have easily been able to explain the one possible
> mistake. I wrote to you that she (the nurse) got me to steal
> Zehners and give them to her. The dream really means that
> she stole herself. For the dream picture was a memory that I
> took money from a doctor's mother, . . . wrongfully. The real
> meaning is that the old woman stood for me, and that the
> doctor's mother was my mother. . . . If the woman disappeared
> so suddenly, I said to myself, some impression must have been
> left inside me. Where was it now? Then a scene occurred to me
> which for the last twenty-nine years has been turning up from
> time to time in my conscious memory without my understanding

it. I was crying my heart out because my mother was nowhere to be found. My brother Phillip (who was twenty years older than I) opened a cupboard (Kasten) for me, and when I found that mother was not there either, I cried still more, until she came through the door, looking slim and beautiful. [p. 222]

No longer pregnant? Freud surmises that when he could not find his mother, he must have begged his brother to open the cupboard because he feared his mother had vanished like his nurse not long before. He believes he must have heard that his beloved nurse was "boxed" or locked up (a play on the German word *eingekastelt*, the editor notes). A further possibility is that his awareness of reversals in the dream could be applied to his seducing the nursemaid, that is, stealing and getting her in trouble, and even possibly the fantasy of impregnating her or his mother. Did his impotence relate to guilt over the seduction of his nurse/mother?

Immediately following this passage in the letter, Freud speaks for the first time of the Oedipus complex and the success of the Greek myth in seizing on "a compulsion which everyone recognizes because he has felt traces of it in himself" (p. 223). In the next passage, he alludes to a similar underlying theme in *Hamlet*, quoting, "So conscience doth make cowards of us all." The letter ends with, "I have not yet set about trying to answer the question whether, instead of my hypothesis that repression always proceeds from the female side and is directed against the male, the converse may hold good, as you suggested" (p. 224). These passages in context make clear Freud's attempts to conceptualize the inhibitions of oedipal neuroses and their relation to father, conscience, and castration, while simultaneously, in his self-analysis, touching upon fears of preoedipal obstinacy, seduction, and abandonment in relation to mother. His discouragement that his self-analysis is coming to an end registers his growing awareness of an obstinate refusal to relinquish or be cured of the replications from his mother/nursemaid symbiosis and the accompanying symptoms of fear of travel, affect splitting, and sexual impotence. In another letter he states, "My nephew and my younger brother determined, not only the neurotic (hateful) side of all my friendships, but also their depth." In an explanatory footnote the editor quotes from Freud's *The Interpretation of Dreams* (1900, p. 483), "My emotional life has always insisted that I should have an intimate friend and a hated enemy."

INTROSPECTION AND INTERACTION AS PSYCHOANALYTIC MODES OF INQUIRY

There is a growing awareness in the psychoanalytic community that many preoedipal experiences and impressions may be optimally definable through *interactions* (or affective relational representations) with others. These preoedipal studies of dyadic interactions stand in a complementary relation to Freud's free-association method of interpretively studying, through verbal–symbolic interpretation, the formations of neurosis through the productions of introspection. Experience has suggested that preoedipal formations yield best to therapeutic study of transference replications through affective interaction in which countertransference serves as a key informer. The paradigmatic interpretation of neurotic transference is, "You hope for and/or fear the same loving and destructive treatment from me that formed the nexus of your early family life and you often do whatever you can to avoid or alternately inhibit whatever seems necessary in order to secure or maintain those feelings and attitudes with me as well as in your daily life." In contrast, the paradigmatic interpretation of preneurotic (symbiotic) replications is, "You feel that in order to be all right or to feel calm, you must obtain in our relationship the exact kinds of experiences that you once sought or shared with your primary caretakers.

You insist that I comply with your relatedness yearnings in order to replicate the experience in which you last knew the security of connection and the bond/bondage of love. Further, you become disappointed, enraged, and overcome with denial when you are confronted with the realization that my desire is not yours." Though Freud's neurosis may have yielded to some symbolic introspection and interpretation through his transference and correspondence with Fliess, he had no access to an analyst with whom to replicate his symbiosis and who, by interpreting the countertransference, might have helped him confront and relinquish his symbiotic scenario. Likewise, Kohut (1979) has said that Freud's narcissism was incompletely analyzed because he had no "self to selfobject resonance" with an analyst who could help him study it and work it through.

DREAM ANALYSIS

Returning to Freud's dream, it seems reasonable to conjecture that through his enactments with the concierge, the maid, and his family, Freud had indeed succeeded (as he suspected) in forming representations of his earlier symbiotic era—personal interactional pictures not governed by the social law of the oedipal superego but by the nature of the interpersonal exchange he enjoyed with exciting and frightening objects of his earliest (preoedipal) love. He cites naked children being chastised for their excitement and provocative naughtiness by mother and nursemaids. In representing wish and inhibition in the dream "Undressed running upstairs," (1900) Freud had indeed encountered the "source of morality," and simultaneously had arrived at a recognition that the difficulties of psychoanalysis "derive from the fact that in the last resort, one is laying bare the patient's evil inclinations, his wish to remain ill" (p. 220). Freud seems to be describing his own predicament, that is, his own "evil inclinations"—his will to remain ill—to maintain the symbiotically based provocative style. He reports this in the same brief letter in which he announces the impression that his analysis is coming to an end. One might ask if Freud's concept of the negative therapeutic reaction (Freud 1923), that is, a premature and violent breaking off of the analysis, didn't derive from the end of his self-analysis, in which he tapped his own moral masochism (Freud 1924) in the desire to retain symbiotic structure at the cost of symptom relief. In clinical studies in which individuals do manage to relinquish their symbiotic structure, we witness extraordinary mental anguish, psychotic regressions, and profound grieving since the foundational structure built on the first love is being lost.

THE DEVELOPMENTAL APPROACH IN PSYCHOANALYSIS

Stolorow and Atwood (1981), in perhaps the most brilliant single contribution to dreams since the Freud monograph, have expanded the Freudian doctrine that dreams represent the fulfillment of desire (wishes), into the broader proposition that dreams "always embody one or more of the dreamer's *personal purposes*" (p. 209). Their studies of "the representational world" (of self and others) have led them to propose that "the *need to maintain the organization of experience* is a central motive in the patterning of human actions" (p. 209) and that "the determination of the meaning of a dream is a matter of elucidating the ways in which the dream is embedded in the ongoing course of the dreamer's experiencing" (p. 208).

Stolorow and Atwood contrast two broad classes of dreams. The first incorporates Freud's approach to the dreamwork in which concrete symbols serve "to actualize a *particular* organization of experience in which specific configurations of self and object . . . are dramatized and affirmed" (p. 212). The second class of dreams occurs in a preoedipal context and serves "rather to maintain psychological organization per se" (p. 212). Freud's dream, "Undressed, running upstairs," along with the accompanying concrete behavioral enactments, might be considered such a dream. Its function would be to maintain the structural cohesion and temporal stability of the configurations of self and object representations established in his own early symbiosis and being lived out in his daily life, his forthcoming break with Fliess, and his later breaks with Jung and Ferenczi (his tendency toward affect splitting).

Another recent trend among psychoanalytic theorists toward use of developmental metaphors implies a more or less successive layering of self and other experiences from part-self and part-other organizing experiences, to the establishment of merger ties between self and others, to differentiated experiences of the other as an extension of or a part of the self, and finally, to the oedipal level of self and other constancy implied in neurosis. Widespread observation confirms that neurosis is seldom if ever encountered in its classical forms today. Many even question if there ever were such constellations in pure culture or if the classical ideas might be better thought of as the initial organizing abstractions of a new discipline. At any rate, the developmental view highlights the extent to which each possible layering of self and other experience has been attained and/or dominates and structures daily life and is likely to appear in dream representation.

A corollary of this use of developmental metaphors is that more advanced or complex layerings are built upon and to a great extent determined by qualities of previously achieved experience. This is the analogy concept introduced in the previously quoted letter (Freud 1954, p. 219) in which oedipal concerns arise out of and are superimposed on emotional constellations from earlier periods. The implication in Freud's early thoughts is that even people who have attained neurotic level structuring and beyond, with the waning of the Oedipus complex, have the foundation of their characters securely rooted in specific forms of preoedipal relatedness.

The task of the present chapter is that of identifying Freud's character scenario and of demonstrating that he had encountered it in relatedness interaction and dream and even recognized its importance and its extreme resistance to change. Freud expressed the hope that his own tendency toward holding a single person too closely and of either loving or hating that person too deeply, that is, affect splitting, as well as his own fears of traveling (separation?) and his sexual impotence would subside as he approached the "source of morality" in his self-analysis (Freud 1954, p. 219).

FREUD'S CHARACTER SCENARIO

In published passages already quoted, Freud would have us believe he is not at all concerned about his spitting on the stairs in an elderly lady's house or of tracking dirt in on the red rug—activities that constitute violations of boundaries in anybody's book. Wishing to be free of conventional restraints, he risks going into a public place (the stairway) in a state of undress, fearing that a neighbor may see him (catch him undressed, enjoying himself). From his associations in contiguous passages one is led to surmise that Freud wishes nothing more than to romp around naked, laughing and slapping himself like a toddler once again, but cannot because of the maidservants of the world who are devoted to cleanliness at all costs and who care to do nothing to lighten his life, such as to install a spittoon for him when he is seized by a desire to spit (when he is being punished for his oral vices). He wishes consciously that the desires in his dream were sexual or more specifically exhibitionistic (Freud 1954), for this would represent his expressing the best of what his nurse gave him—"a high opinion of my own capacities" (Freud 1954, p. 219).

Freud (1900) unconvincingly argues that "a sensation of inhibited movement in dreams is produced whenever the particular context requires it" (p. 273). He does not specify what the requirement might be; but he rules out any special modifications of his powers of movement, since only a moment earlier he was "running nimbly up the stairs." So the suddenly inhibited action is not gross muscular but sexual in nature. In his letter to Fliess (Freud 1954) he announces that "the accompanying emotion was not anxiety, but erotic excitement. So you can see how the feeling of paralysis peculiar to sleep can be used for the fulfillment of an exhibitionistic wish" (p. 207). This argument is also thin; even a simple explanation of fear of punishment for vice (heart problems and pharyngitis) would have been more convincing. Even better would be an admission that the erotic excitement was related to the game of being caught redhanded enjoying infantile play—nakedness—or to the excitement surrounding the give-and-take of dirtying, stubbornness, and oppositionality. The simple fact of the matter is that while the old lady (mother representation) is lying in bed upstairs (in childbirth) injected (drugged) by him, and/or impregnated, he has engaged the maid-servant in a battle for territorial rights. Some might characterize the exchange as a "battle of the bowels"—certainly the source of human morality. And how does Freud react? He refuses to be trained. (Is Hell[a] weeping bitterly over the Greeks losing?) He maintains it is his prerogative to intrude and deposit injections and body products in the mother/maid's territory. After all, didn't his nursemaid once believe it her prerogative to establish control over *his* territory, his (Greek) behind, as it were?

THE INTERACTIONAL ANALYST

Dipping deeply into early levels of characterological development in analysis requires another person to play or to reenact
various interactional roles, in this case the, "yes I will," "no you
won't," or "catch me if you can" games normally played out
during the terrible twos. In Freud's self-analysis, he had to find
someone with whom to do battle over his irresistible urge to soil.
Since he had no actual analyst, he challenged the concierge and
the maid-servant as well as the "authorities" in his own house
with the messing game. Analysts often see the symbiotic
transferences not only enacted in the analytic relationship but
outside the analysis in parallel transference. That Freud clearly
wanted things *his* way and made no bones about being belliger-
ent or "dirtying" the world with his shocking ideas is firmly
attested to by his own history in relation to the development of
the psychoanalytic movement. But how far was this preoedipal
(borderline or symbiotic) level of character scenario ever understood in Freud's self-analysis? Was his lifelong tendency toward
splitting of affects, which was recalled in connection with this
dream, ever softened? Were his difficulties in riding trains and
with impotence ever ameliorated? Or was it not here at the very
source of morality where Freud met his own final resistance to
cure, his moral masochism, and his own negative therapeutic
reaction? And if Freud had been cured of his invasive audacity,
would there be psychoanalysis today? The wish for a healthy
heart (moral as well as physical) in spite of the vice of continued
smoking, or even the wish to exhibit sexually are relatively easy
motivations to admit and to obtain forgiveness for. But the
social approbation that results from the erotized wish to be free
to push yourself into somebody else's territory, to intrude with
your personal creations if you feel like it, may result in being
startled when caught in the act (impotent?). If so, it is a
representation of a reversal, an active attempt to do to others

what he experienced his nurse doing to him—intruding bodily and dominating.

Surely someone will remind us that Freud was a cultivated gentleman and it would be unthinkable for him to be truly invasive, disgusting, or shocking in his motives. Perhaps, but how can his apparently blithe and innocent manner be maintained in the face of such invasive crimes? And how, with such cool published affirmation, can he assert that a spittoon should be installed so that whenever he feels like spitting (a reaction to being punished for pleasurable "vice"), he can? Nowhere did Freud attempt to justify his intrusive, soiling wishes. Nor, so far as we can tell, did he analyze his incestual wishes or his impotence.

The answer to Freud's apparent nonchalance (Freud 1954) may lie in the very dynamics he himself discovered in the related dream of, as he put it, his taking money wrongfully from a doctor's mother. Here he inferred a role reversal and surmised that it was his nurse who was the thief who took things that belonged to his mother. The facts were that she stole things from him. Studies of symbiotic scenarios regularly reveal to a greater or lesser extent the interchangeable identities and role reversals of the parties involved in the symbiotically structured interaction. The activities of symbiosis are often a two-way street due to the trauma of invasive caretakers giving rise to primary identifications with their interactive modes (Balint 1943). Whether Freud was afraid of abandonment due to his mother's pregnancy, his nurse's being locked up, or his own drive for independence, or whether he was simply terrified by the fear of God put into him by his nurse, his erotic dream was that of being caught in childish joyful abandon. But despite Freud's wanting to blame the nurse for stealing in the dream, it was he who stole (affection) from a doctor's mother, and she who was giving birth. He was immediately filled with shame and tried to escape but was paralyzed where he stood. Whatever else the dream may have represented to Freud, it stands as a monument to the seductions of childish obstinacy at its most glorious peak—desire sustained through endless reprimands and delight in naughty abandon, all of which is frozen in phobic impotence. The erotic attachment to primary love modes stubbornly persists until, through effective interpretive confrontation of the character scenario, as lived in the transference–countertransference exchange, it can be relinquished. But the relinquishing of the symbiotic scenario is tantamount to giving up the sexualized pleasures of mother love that form the very foundation of one's mind, one's reality, so it is not done easily. Clinical experience with giving up the scenario regularly produces excruciatingly painful fragmentation, psychotic episodes, and profound grief. Freud had no analyst with whom to work the countertransference feelings, and through them to analyze his symbiotic structures as transferred to the analytic affective relatedness exchange.

Freud's oppositional character scenario as revealed in his dream and the interactional associations, including his denial of impotence, reveal the heart of his desire—the wish, nay, the determination to remain an incurable and productive provocateur.

16

The Frontier of
Countertransference

Achieving analytic contact with the affective and interactional issues retained from early childhood is increasingly coming to be understood as a function of the analyst's capacity to sustain and to analyze intense countertransference stimulation. This is true not only for the wide range of personality organizations commonly referred to as borderline, but also for interactional issues in the analysis of people whose personalities are predominantly organized around more differentiated or focal selfother (narcissistic) or constant object (oedipal/neurotic) constellations. Human concerns characterized by these highly differentiated experiences of self and other, enmeshed in a spectrum of integrated positively and negatively colored affects, have evolved slowly out of an earlier or more basic matrix of relatedness concerns in which distinctions between self and other were not so clear or reliable, and in which affective colorations were more extreme, intense, or labile. The earliest or most basic human organizational strivings that are met or

contacted by an empathic human environment become transformed into various symbiotic styles of relating. The availability
of favorable opportunities for the replication and opposition of
established interactional styles determines in what areas and to
what degree experiences of separation and individuation from
primary bonding styles will become possible.

Analysts have tended to prefer a working stance that strives
to attain a measure of objectivity and to collect their observations and cast their interpretive formulations in an abstract
verbal-symbolic mode. But experience with interaction styles
derived from early symbiotic and separating patterns has consistently pointed away from empathy achieved in such abstract
modes, toward more archaic or concrete forms of empathic
attunement and interpretive responsiveness more in keeping
with the interactional nature of the experiences to be analyzed.

The unique achievement of human history relates to the
evolving capacity for transforming primary somatic sensations
and movements into complex secondary symbolic patterns of
meaning that can be acknowledged by others in shared forms
of communication. But in the analysis of specific, personal ways
of experiencing and organizing an individual's subjective world,
it has become clear that the path lies in quite the opposite
direction. From the beginning, psychoanalysis has sought to
define, and through the specificity of reflected definition, to
break down (analyze) personal configurations of (self and other)
relatedness in which idiosyncratic solutions retained from childhood experiences continue to hold sway over current relatedness
possibilities.

Freud's self-analysis, as set forth in his letters to his friend,
Wilhelm Fliess, shows how he came to emphasize the themes of
Oedipus Rex and *Hamlet*, not only because they were personally
relevant to Freud, but also because the test of time had
demonstrated their relevance to the lives of many others as well.
The careful study of oedipal themes in the psychoanalytic
situation has continued to demonstrate not only their relevance

as common if not universal narrative elements, but also the rich diversity of ways in which the Oedipus storyline can be applied to individually narrated life histories.

Freud's self-analysis included the emergence of certain selfother themes, notably in relation to disappointments in his idealized others (specifically Breuer and Fliess) and the lack of appreciation by others (specifically his university and medical colleagues) for his own grand visions and creative processes. The emergence of Freud's stubborn, dirtying, provocative qualities in his personal interactions and dreams as revealed in his letters to Fliess brought his analysis to an abrupt halt. Freud did, however, go so far as to suggest that perhaps the basic source of human suffering is not the problem of the oedipal father, but rather, more basic experiences with early mothering. His own personal memories and dreams had taken him back to troubling experiences with his nursemaid well before the age of 2.

Freud's resistance to emotionally experiencing and spelling out the exact nature of his persistent obstinacy, his proclivity for "dirtying" the world with personal products, the overclose seductive experiences of having his body washed by his nursemaid/sexual tutor in water tinted with menstrual blood, and the experience of having various personal possessions "robbed" from him, might well be worked through today if Freud's analyst were conversant enough with strong countertransference elements to be open to being reexperienced in such primitive and upsetting ways. Freud's train phobia, his migraine headaches, his impotence, and his relation to women might well have been considerably transformed by such resistance and replication analysis. But his symbiosis and provocative separation patterns were to remain unanalyzed. And, as a rich life of close friends and harsh rejections demonstrated, his symbiotic and separating themes continued to be lived out in a variety of ways.

Of course, there was no analyst trained in countertransference analysis to work with Freud. And Freud himself consistently taught that countertransference interferes with transference analysis of neurotic constellations—which it certainly does. Only now, after a century of psychoanalytic study, are we in a position to see that the attitudes and affects evoked in the early analysts by emotional interactions with their patients were as relevant to understanding personal issues as were the oedipal themes that could regularly be teased out in verbal-symbolic terms and cast into neurotic formulations. To what extent were the seduction experiences reported by Freud's early patients a result of internalization of oedipal involvements—screen memories or reconstructions of themes related to father—and to what extent were they derived from actual early symbiotic relatedness demands traumatically experienced much earlier in the nurturing environment and represented in later memory as father seductions? So far as we know, Freud's own seductions by his nursemaid and perhaps also by his mother were never analyzed. Nor was he in a position to study systematically the available countertransference responsiveness of his friend Breuer in relationship to the specimen case of *Anna O.*, or in himself or others, as replications achieved in the analytic ambience of early traumatic seductions.

We now have sufficient experience with analytic technique and developmental concepts to permit us to do better than Freud was able to do toward opening up countertransference for study. It is, however, difficult to muster up the courage of Freud in revealing relevant personal dimensions as he did in opening up his dreams and associations for public scrutiny. It is also difficult to match him on thoroughness, judiciousness, and systematic attention to detail so ingeniously displayed in his early case histories. But if Freud's self-analysis and self-disclosures provided the necessary breakthroughs to careful study of the transference–resistance dimension, may we not safely assume that our own courageousness and thoroughness can likewise lead to breakthroughs in systematizing yet earlier relatedness issues that are regularly activated in the replication/counterreplication dimension of analytic relatedness? And are we not just as likely as Freud to encounter severe resistances to the reactivation of earliest symbiotic and separating themes in ourselves and in relation to our work?

But we have a resource that Freud did not have—each other. We are now a community of individuals who regularly support one another through the emergence of dreaded oedipal desires and fears because we know that they are part of the human condition, and that our lives will be infinitely richer for understanding the ways in which these hidden themes influence our daily lives. Kohut has also taught us that retained narcissistic grandiosity, twinship demands, and idealizations that were once a part of our early differentiating experiences can be usefully revitalized, adding fresh possibilities to the ways in which we experience our most creative selves.

As a community, we now stand on the threshold of a bold realization that the specific and intense ways we experience attachments and separations and substitute various activities for those early interactions no longer need be considered threatening or shameful. Permitting ourselves to notice, live out, and spell out the ways in which we demand and renounce various forms of (symbiotic) love and connections may raise potentially threatening, seductive, and destructive themes. But developmental metaphors can light the way through these dark recesses of human life, just as Freud's original formulations heralded that the emergence of an oedipal wish or fear was not the end of the world. Likewise, Kohut's formulations have shown us that our narcissistic aggrandizements and mortifications can be assimilated skillfully and creatively into the ongoing meaning of our narrational life involvements.

There are attachment and separating themes still enshrouded with taboo and medical mysticism in our society. It remains a matter of social stigma for a person to use excessively or to refrain rigidly from enjoying various drug substances— clearly potential substitutes for a variety of longed-for experiences with oneself or with others. It has been a matter of public censorship to eat to the point of obesity or to refrain from eating to the point of anorexia or even to alternate eating patterns, as in bulimia—clearly possible expressions of various forms of relationship or yearned-for relationship to needed others. We imprison as sociopaths or character disorders those whose aggressiveness or intrusiveness impinges on others' rights while pitying those whose lack of assertiveness or repression of anger poses serious social or medical dilemmas for them. We label as perverse those who experiment with various sexual identifications and practices and yet laugh at "real men" for not daring to eat quiche or "traditional women" still looking for Peter Pan. The main somatic concerns of our times are cancer and heart disease—disorders now being consistently linked with stressful life experiences that produce a separating or individuating demand on the person's psychic life. There is the emergence into public awareness of those individuals displaying types of multiple personality. Such pictures are stigmatized by society as highly disturbed or even as evil, due to the frequent themes of sexual abuse, promiscuity, or mystical worship of the supernatural. Yet there is much disdain for anyone who adopts a rigidly consistent personality—a picture stigmatized as "red neck," barbaric, or religiously zealous or fundamental. These people are often viewed as dangerously ignorant, monolithic, and perhaps abusive. Whether a person displays multiple selves or a rigidly coherent single self, we tend to see these not as styles of relatedness, but rather stigmatize them as highly disturbed or narrow.

These various pictures once spoken of as character disorders, personality disorders, perversions, or borderline and psychotic states, can be viewed as variations on symbiotic, separating, and organizing themes, just as Freud came to view hysterical, phobic, and obsessive-compulsive pictures as variations of oedipal themes. Freud found the royal road to the repressed themes of neurosis to be symbolic analysis of dreams, slips, jokes, and sexuality, and later, the analysis of similar primary processes as they operated symbolically in transference and resistance. Kohut demonstrated that the royal road to narcissistic themes was through analysis of the vicissitudes of the self-to-selfother unit. Now the royal road opens for us upon new terrain—or is it actually so new? Perhaps it would be more accurate to say that our mappings are new—that we now have new understandings of Freud's and Breuer's early cases and of Kohut's notions of archaic forms of empathy and interpretation.

The royal road to understanding the human soul now leads into terrain labeled symbiosis and separation, and points in the direction of understanding various organizational strivings. The means of transport is now the countertransference or the merged dual unity of the replication/counter-replication emotional relatedness dimension.

SUMMARY

The systematic study of countertransference in relation to developmental concepts of empathy and interpretation remains a vast uncharted frontier of psychoanalysis. With the human relatedness dimension as a starting point for analytic inquiry, it has been possible to derive from a century of work a series of conceptual vantage points that have served as perspectives from which to listen—in the broadest sense—to the activities, interactions, and narrational collaborations that have come to characterize the psychoanalytic enterprise. The recent proliferation of developmental metaphors in psychoanalysis has opened the time-honored concepts of empathy and interpretation to new forms of scrutiny. A continuum of interpersonal responsiveness possibilities has been defined from (I) early organizational strivings through (II) symbiotic and separating scenarios and (III) self-to-selfother extensions toward (IV) the achievement of a variety of independent individual styles of appreciating and reacting to the human dilemma of psychic separateness.

At various points along this developmentally derived continuum, empathic contact and interpretation of personal meanings take on strikingly different characteristics. It follows that countertransference responsiveness, based as it is on empathic grasp of personal meanings, will function differently according to the particular issues to be presented for understanding at specific temporal junctures of analytic work.

Countertransference is likely to interfere with the understanding of differentiated oedipal issues that have become firmly embedded in a verbal-symbolic matrix. Countertransference is likely to facilitate empathic understanding of the ebb and flow of self-cohesion experience. Countertransference responsiveness constitutes the royal road for understanding issues of attachment and separation in which two souls must merge and mingle in oneness and separateness. Finally, intense countertransference responses in the presence of organizational (psychotic) strivings may serve to signal or to acknowledge the extreme frustrations involved in attempting to establish a bond with faulty, chaotic, and/or unorganized strivings and point toward moments in which human contact is a possibility and through which symbiotic bonding may be achievable.

Kohut's "deathbed" legacy contains not only his wisdom regarding the importance of archaic and concrete forms of empathy, but also his awareness that the community of practicing analysts has not been ready so far to turn its scholarly attentions to the more unsettling dimensions of preoedipal human relatedness.

CONCLUSION

Untamed or unintegrated rage, destructiveness, sexuality, and overconstricted life energies roam wildly in a myriad of affective and interactive forms in the forbidden territory of countertransference, where one cannot reliably know where one's own psychic representations end and the other's begin. However, once the land of idiosyncratic, symbiotic, and separating scenarios has been mapped out through the aid of the countertransference and understood by two, the analytic coup that requires the greatest ingenuity and skill is to find a way to help the person relinquish his or her silent addiction to personal stylized dyadic modes of relatedness. The analyst can now encourage the breaking of compulsive reliance on established patterns without reliance upon predetermined value systems or hidden moralities about health, cure, social adaptation, "the good life," or "analytic paradise." The analytic game is played simply in the name of establishing or creating, through narration and narrational interactions, more flexibility in relatedness possibilities than one already possesses. Analytic empathy and interpretation vary considerably, depending upon the developmental issues that are central to the organization of the individual personality or that come to be presented during different phases of the analysis.

I have hoped here to define the challenge I believe faces us at this juncture in the development of our discipline. We now possess an array of developmental concepts that can serve as working tools to help us in the systematic study of countertransference responsiveness. Furthermore, we now have a community of people engaged in the practice of analysis and analytically informed consultation that can serve as our support in teasing out as many variables and themes as possible from the rich, intriguing, but confusing terrain—the countertransference in relation to empathy and the interpretive process.

References

Bacal, H. (1983). Optimal responsiveness and the therapeutic process. In *Progress in Self Psychology*, vol. 1, ed. A. Goldberg, pp. 202–227. New York: The Guilford Press.

Balint, A. (1943). On identification. *International Journal of Psycho-Analysis* 24:97–107.

Bettelheim, B. (1983). *Freud and Man's Soul*. New York: Alfred Knopf.

Binswanger, L. (1956). *Sigmund Freud: Reminiscences of a Friendship*. Trans. N. Guterman. New York: Grune and Stratton.

Bion, W. R. (1962). *Learning from Experience*. New York: Basic Books.

——— (1963). *Elements of Psychoanalysis*. New York: Basic Books.

Blanck, G., and Blanck, R. (1979). *Ego Psychology II: Psychoanalytic Developmental Psychology*. New York: Columbia University Press.

Bollas, C. (1979). The transformational object. *International Journal of Psycho-Analysis* 59:97–107.

——— (1983). Expressive uses of the countertransference. In *Shadow of the Object: Psychoanalysis of the Unthought Known*, pp. 200–236. London: Free Association Press, 1987.

——— (1987). *Shadow of the Object: Psychoanalysis of the Unthought Known*. London: Free Association Books.

Breuer, J., and Freud, S. (1895). Studies on hysteria. *Standard Edition 2.*

Bridgman, P. W. (1927). *The Logic of Modern Physics.* New York: Macmillan.

Briggs, J., and Peat, F. D. (1984). *Looking Glass Universe: The Emerging Science of Wholeness.* New York: Simon and Schuster.

―――― (1989). *Turbulent Mirror: An Illustrated Guide to Chaos Theory and the Science of Wholeness.* New York: Harper and Row.

Campbell, J. (1982). *Grammatical Man.* New York: Simon and Schuster.

Capra, F. (1983). *The Tao of Physics.* New York: Bantam.

Crawford, C. (unpublished manuscript). *Disturbing Teenagers.*

Dyson, F. (1979). *Disturbing the Universe.* New York: Harper and Row.

―――― (1988). *Infinite in All Directions.* New York: Harper and Row.

Einstein, A. (1905). *Relativity: The Special and the General Theory.* Trans. R. W. Lawson. New York: Crown Publishers, 1961.

Eissler, K. (1953). The effect of the structure of the ego on psychoanalytic technique. *Journal of the American Psychoanalytic Association* 1:104–143.

Ekstein, R. (1984). *Prolegomena to the study of the languages of psychoanalysis and psychotherapy.* Paper presented at the Newport Center for Psychoanalytic Studies, Newport Beach, CA, October.

Ekstein, R., and Motto, R. (1966). *Children of Time and Space of Action and Impulse.* New York: Appleton Century Crofts.

Ferenczi, S. (1988). *The Clinical Diary of Sandor Ferenczi.* Cambridge, MA: Harvard University Press.

Freud, A. (1937). *The Ego and the Mechanisms of Defense.* New York: International Universities Press.

Freud, S. (1900). The interpretation of dreams. *Standard Edition* 4/5.

―――― (1901). The psychopathology of everyday life. *Standard Edition* 6.

———— (1905). Jokes and their relation to the unconscious. *Standard Edition* 8.

———— (1910). The future prospects of psycho-analytic therapy. *Standard Edition* 11:139–152.

———— (1912). The dynamics of transference. *Standard Edition* 12:97–108.

———— (1914). On narcissism. *Standard Edition* 14:69–104.

———— (1915a). Observations on transference-love. *Standard Edition* 12:156–173.

———— (1915b). Instincts and their vicissitudes. *Standard Edition* 14:111–140.

———— (1923). The ego and the id. *Standard Edition* 19:3–68.

———— (1924). The economic problem of masochism. *Standard Edition* 19:157–172.

———— (1925). Negation. *Standard Edition* 19:235–242.

———— (1926). The question of lay analysis. *Standard Edition* 20:179–260.

———— (1930). Civilization and its discontents. *Standard Edition* 21:59–148.

———— (1932). New introductory lectures on psycho-analysis. *Standard Edition* 22.

———— (1954). *The Origins of Psycho-Analysis*. New York: Basic Books.

Giovacchini, P. (1979). *Treatment of Primitive Mental States*. New York: Jason Aronson.

Gleick, J. (1987). *Chaos: Making a New Science*. New York: Penguin.

Glover, E. (1932). A psycho-analytical approach to the classification of mental disorders. In *On the Early Development of the Mind*, pp. 161–186. New York: International Universities Press.

Gregory, B. (1988). *Inventing Reality: Physics as Language*. New York: John Wiley and Sons.

Gribbin, J. (1983). *Spacewarps: A Book about Black Holes, White Holes, Quasars, and Our Violent Universe*. New York: Delta/Eleanor Friede.

———— (1984). *In Search of Schrodinger's Cat: Quantum Physics and Reality*. New York: Bantam.

———— (1986). *In Search of the Big Bang: Quantum Physics and Cosmology.* New York: Bantam.

———— (1988). *The Omega Point: The Search for the Missing Mass and the Ultimate Fate of the Universe.* New York: Bantam.

Guntrip, H. (1969). *Schizoid Phenomena, Object-Relations and the Self.* New York: International Universities Press.

Hartmann, H. (1950). Comments on the psychoanalytic theory of the ego. *Psychoanalytic Study of the Child* 5:74–96. New York: International Universities Press.

Hawthorne, N. (1967). "The Birthmark." In *Great Short Works of Hawthorne,* ed. F. C. Crews, pp. 300–317. New York: Harper and Row.

Hedges, L. E. (1983). *Listening Perspectives in Psychotherapy.* New York: Jason Aronson.

———— (1990). Videotape of *Interpreting the Countertransference.* Northvale, NJ: Jason Aronson.

Hedges, L. E., and Coverdale, C. (1985). *Countertransference and its relation to developmental concepts of empathy and interpretation.* Paper presented at the Newport Center for Psychoanalytic Studies, Newport Beach, CA.

———— (1985). Videotape of *Countertransference and Its Relation to Developmental Concepts of Empathy and Interpretation.* Distributed by Listening Perspectives Study Center, 1439 E. Chapman Ave., Orange, CA.

Heimann, P. (1950). On counter-transference. *International Journal of Psycho-Analysis* 31:81–84.

Heisenberg, W. (1958). *Physics and Beyond.* New York: Harper Torchbooks.

Herbert, N. (1985). *Quantum Reality: Beyond the New Physics.* New York: Doubleday.

Jacobson, E. (1954). The self and the object world: vicissitudes of their infantile cathexis and their influence on ideation and affective development. *Psychoanalytic Study of the Child* 9:75–127. New York: International Universities Press.

———— (1964). *The Self and the Object World.* New York: International Universities Press.

Jaynes, J. (1976). *The Origins of Consciousness in the Breakdown of the Bicameral Mind.* New York: Houghton Mifflin.

Kaplan, L. (1978). *Oneness and Separateness: From Infant to Individual*. New York: Simon and Schuster.

Kernberg, O. (1975). *Borderline Conditions and Pathological Narcissism*. New York: Jason Aronson.

———— (1976). *Object Relations Theory and Clinical Psychoanalysis*. New York: Jason Aronson.

———— (1984). "Cutting Edge Conference" sponsored by University of California, San Diego Medical School. Unpublished remarks.

Klein, M. (1946). Notes on some schizoid mechanisms. *International Journal of Psycho-Analysis* 24:97–107.

Kohut, H. (1959). Introspection, empathy and psychoanalysis: an examination of the relationship between mode of observation and theory. *Journal of the American Psychoanalytic Association* 7:459–483.

———— (1971). *The Analysis of the Self*. New York: International Universities Press.

———— (1972). Thoughts on narcissism and narcissistic rage. *Psychoanalytic Study of the Child* 27:360–401. New Haven: Yale University Press.

———— (1977). *The Restoration of the Self*. New York: International Universities Press.

———— (1979). Discussion at the UCLA Self Psychology Conference.

———— (1982). Introspection, empathy and the semi-circle of mental health. *International Journal of Psycho-Analysis* 63:395–407.

———— (1985). *How Does Analysis Cure?* Chicago: University of Chicago Press.

Kosinski, J. (1970). *Being There*. New York: Harcourt, Brace, Jovanovich.

Kuhn, T. (1962). *The Structure of Scientific Revolutions*. Chicago: University of Chicago Press.

Lacan, J. (1977). *Ecrits*. Trans. A. Sheridan. New York: W. W. Norton.

Lakoff, G., and Johnson, M. (1980). *Metaphors We Live By*. Chicago: University of Chicago Press.

Langs, R. (1982). *Psychotherapy: A Basic Text.* New York: Jason Aronson.

Little, M. (1981). *Transference Neurosis: Transference Psychosis.* New York: Jason Aronson.

—— (1985). Winnicott working in areas where psychotic anxieties predominate: a personal record. *Free Associations* 3. London: Free Association Books.

Llewellyn, K. N. (1989). *The Case Law System in America.* Ed. P. Gewirtz, trans. M. Ansaldi. Chicago: University of Chicago Press.

Lowen, A. (1971). *The Language of the Body.* New York: Collier Books.

—— (1988). *Love, Sex and Your Heart.* New York: Macmillan.

—— (1990a). *The Spirituality of the Body.* New York: Macmillan.

—— (1990b). Spring Conference of the Southern California Bioenergetics Society, San Diego, CA.

Mahler, M. (1968). *On Human Symbiosis and the Vicissitudes of Individuation: Infantile Psychosis.* New York: International Universities Press.

Mahler, M., Pine, F., and Bergman, A. (1975). *The Psychological Birth of the Human Infant: Symbiosis and Individuation.* New York: Basic Books.

Martin, J. (1983). Fictive personality development. In *Frontiers of Infant Psychiatry*, vol. 2, ed. J. Call, E. Galenson, and R. Tyson, pp. 113–120. New York: Basic Books.

Masterson, J. (1972). *Treatment of the Borderline Adolescent: A Developmental Approach.* New York: John Wiley and Sons.

Pagels, H. R. (1982). *The Cosmic Code.* New York: Bantam.

Peat, F. D. (1987). *Synchronicity: The Bridge between Matter and Mind.* New York: Bantam.

Reich, A. (1951). On counter-transference. *International Journal of Psycho-Analysis* 32:25–31.

Rose, G. (1980). *The Power of Form.* New York: International Universities Press.

Rossner, J. (1983). *August.* Boston: Houghton Mifflin.

Ryle, G. (1949). *The Concept of Mind.* New York: Barnes and Noble.

Sandler, J. (1960). On the concept of the superego. *Psychoan-*

alytic Study of the Child 15:128–162. New York: International Universities Press.

Sandler, J., and Rosenblatt, B. (1962). The concept of the representational world. *Psychoanalytic Study of the Child* 17:128–145. New York: International Universities Press.

Sartre, J. P. (1956). *Being and Nothingness.* Trans. H. E. Barnes. New York: Washington Square Press.

Schafer, R. (1976). *A New Language for Psychoanalysis.* New Haven: Yale University Press.

——— (1980). *On empathy and psychoanalysis.* Address presented to the Los Angeles Society for Psychoanalytic Psychology, March 7, 1980.

Schneiderman, S. (1980). *Returning to Freud: Clinical Psychoanalysis in the School of Lacan.* New Haven: Yale University Press.

——— (1983). *Jacques Lacan: The Death of an Intellectual Hero.* Cambridge, MA: Harvard University Press.

——— (1988). *An Angel Passes: How the Sexes Became Undivided.* New York: New York University Press.

Schwaber, E. (1981). Narcissism, self psychology and the listening perspective. *Annual of Psychoanalysis* 9:115–131.

——— (1983). Psychoanalytic listening and psychic reality. *International Journal of Psycho-Analysis* 10:379–391.

Searles, H. (1960). *The Nonhuman Environment.* New York: International Universities Press.

——— (1979). *Countertransference and Related Subjects: Selected Papers.* New York: International Universities Press.

Silver, A. S. (1989). *Psychoanalysis and Psychosis.* Madison, CT: International Universities Press.

Spence, D. (1982). *Historical Truth and Narrative Truth.* New York: Norton.

——— (1987). *The Freudian Metaphor.* New York: Norton.

Stanislavski, C. (1936). *An Actor Prepares.* New York: Theatre Arts Books/Methuen.

Stern, D. (1985). *The Interpersonal World of the Human Infant.* New York: Basic Books.

——— (1988). Comments at the UCLA Conference on Infant Research.

Stolorow, R., and Atwood, G. (1982). Psychoanalytic phenom-

enology of the dream. *Annual of Psychoanalysis* 10:205–220.
Stolorow, R., Brandchaft, B., and Atwood, G. (1987). *Psychoanalytic Treatment: An Intersubjective Approach.* Hillsdale, NJ: Analytic Press.
Stone, L. (1962). *The Psychoanalytic Situation.* New York: International Universities Press.
Tustin, F. (1972). *Autism and Childhood Psychosis.* London: Hogarth Press.
———— (1981). A modern pilgrim's progress: reminiscences of personal analysis with Dr. Bion. *Journal of Child Psychotherapy* 7:2, 175–179.
———— (1984). Autistic shapes. *International Review of Psycho-Analysis* 11:279–290.
Vygotsky, L. S. (1962). *Thought and Language.* Cambridge, MA: MIT Press.
———— (1978). *Mind in Society: The Development of Higher Psychological Processes.* Ed. M. Cole, V. John-Steiner, S. Scribner, and E. Souberman. Cambridge, MA: Harvard University Press.
Winnicott, D. (1947). Hate in the countertransference. In *Through Paediatrics to Psycho-Analysis*, pp. 194–203. New York: Basic Books, 1975.
———— (1948). Reparation in respect of mother's organized defence against depression. In *Through Paediatrics to Psychoanalysis*, pp. 91–96. New York: Basic Books, 1975.
———— (1949). Birth memories, birth trauma and anxiety. In *Through Paediatrics to Psychoanalysis*, pp. 174–193. New York: Basic Books, 1975.
———— (1960a). The use of an object and relating through identifications. In *Playing and Reality*, pp. 86–94. London: Tavistock, 1982.
———— (1960b). Ego distortion in terms of true and false self. In *The Maturational Processes and the Facilitating Environment*, pp. 140–152. Madison, CT: International Universities Press, 1965.
———— (1982). *Playing and Reality.* London: Tavistock.
Wittgenstein, L. (1953). *Philosophical Investigations.* New York: Macmillan.

Index